Strangers in a Familiar Land

American Society of Missiology Monograph Series

Series Editor, James R. Krabill

The ASM Monograph Series provides a forum for publishing quality dissertations and studies in the field of missiology. Collaborating with Pickwick Publications—a division of Wipf and Stock Publishers of Eugene, Oregon—the American Society of Missiology selects high quality dissertations and other monographic studies that offer research materials in mission studies for scholars, mission and church leaders, and the academic community at large. The ASM seeks scholarly work for publication in the series that throws light on issues confronting Christian world mission in its cultural, social, historical, biblical, and theological dimensions.

Missiology is an academic field that brings together scholars whose professional training ranges from doctoral-level preparation in areas such as Scripture, history and sociology of religions, anthropology, theology, international relations, interreligious interchange, mission history, inculturation, and church law. The American Society of Missiology, which sponsors this series, is an ecumenical body drawing members from Independent and Ecumenical Protestant, Catholic, Orthodox, and other traditions. Members of the ASM are united by their commitment to reflect on and do scholarly work relating to both mission history and the present-day mission of the church. The ASM Monograph Series aims to publish works of exceptional merit on specialized topics, with particular attention given to work by younger scholars, the dissemination and publication of which is difficult under the economic pressures of standard publishing models.

Persons seeking information about the ASM or the guidelines for having their dissertations considered for publication in the ASM Monograph Series should consult the Society's website—www.asmweb.org.

Members of the ASM Monograph Committee who approved this book are:

Sue Russell, Professor of Mission and Contextual Studies, Asbury Theological Seminary

Bonnie Sue Lewis, Professor of Mission and World Christianity, University of Dubuque Theological Seminary

RECENTLY PUBLISHED IN THE ASM MONOGRAPH SERIES

L. Lynn Thigpen, *Connected Learning: How Adults with Limited Formal Education Learn*

Craig S. Hendrickson, *Charismatic Leadership and Missional Change: Mission-Actional Ministry in a Multiethnic Church*

Strangers in a Familiar Land

A Phenomenological Study on Marginal Christian Identity

JAMES A. BLUMENSTOCK

American Society of Missiology Monograph
Series vol. 45

◈PICKWICK *Publications* · Eugene, Oregon

STRANGERS IN A FAMILIAR LAND
A Phenomenological Study on Marginal Christian Identity

American Society of Missiology Monograph Series 45

Copyright © 2020 James A. Blumenstock. All rights reserved. Except for brief quotations in critical publications or reviews, no part of this book may be reproduced in any manner without prior written permission from the publisher. Write: Permissions, Wipf and Stock Publishers, 199 W. 8th Ave., Suite 3, Eugene, OR 97401.

Pickwick Publications
An Imprint of Wipf and Stock Publishers
199 W. 8th Ave., Suite 3
Eugene, OR 97401

www.wipfandstock.com

PAPERBACK ISBN: 978-1-7252-5931-7
HARDCOVER ISBN: 978-1-7252-5932-4
EBOOK ISBN: 978-1-7252-5933-1

Cataloguing-in-Publication data:

Names: Blumenstock, James A., author.

Title: Strangers in a familiar land : a phenomenological study on marginal Christian identity / James A. Blumenstock.

Description: Eugene, OR: Pickwick Publications, 2020 | American Society of Missiology Monograph Series 46 | Includes bibliographical references.

Identifiers: ISBN 978-1-7252-5931-7 (paperback) | ISBN 978-1-7252-5932-4 (hardcover) | ISBN 978-1-7252-5933-1 (ebook)

Subjects: LCSH: Religion—Methodology | Identification (Religion)—Case studies. | Identity (Psychology)—Religious aspects—Christianity. | Christians—Thailand.

Classification: BR1195 B58 2020 (print) | BR1195 (ebook)

Composition/Song Title: Your Beloved

Writer Credits: Brent Helming

Copyright: © 1996 Mercy/Vineyard Publishing (ASCAP) Admin. in North America by Music Services o/b/o Vineyard Music USA

All scripture quotations, unless otherwise indicated, are taken from the New American Standard Bible® (NASB). Copyright © 1960, 1962, 1963, 1968, 1971, 1972, 1973,1975, 1977, 1995 by The Lockman Foundation. Used by permission. www.Lockman.org.

Manufactured in the U.S.A.   04/24/20

To my wife, Karen, for your unswerving loyalty and faith in me, your willingness to patiently listen to my, at times, esoteric phenomenological ramblings, and your kind and loving perseverance throughout this challenging journey.

To my daughter, Ella, for your understanding when daddy is in the office again, and for your unreserved expressions of love and kindness to help me get through the difficult days. I dedicate this book to the both of you.

Contents

Acknowledgements | ix
Introduction | xi

1. Identity Formation in Sociocultural Perspective | 1
2. Phenomenology of the Sacred Homeworld | 28
3. Negotiating Christian Identity | 55
4. Phenomenology as Method and Methodology | 75
5. Thai Buddhist Homeworld | 105
6. Verticality | 122
7. Emplacement | 150
8. Displacement | 175
9. Negotiation | 202

Conclusion: Retrospect and Prospect | 232

Appendix on Interview Questions | 241
Bibliography | 245

Acknowledgements

I would like to express my deepest gratitude to the many people who have come alongside me to provide assistance and encouragement throughout the years of this research:

To my supervisor, mentor, and friend Dr. Stuart Devenish for your rich wisdom, persistent encouragement, and wonderful ability to perpetually re-attune me to the "thing itself." Thank you for modeling the identity of a godly scholar and for believing that I could be one, too.

To my colleagues at Asia Biblical Theological Seminary for your patience, understanding, and prayers as I pursued this degree. A special thanks to Tim and Daron for the very helpful, if sometimes lengthy, discussions on matters of God, faith, and religious experience, and to Fawn and Aof for your assistance with translation and openness in sharing your own conversion narratives.

To the many churches and individuals who have financially contributed to my doctoral studies. This would not have been possible without you.

To several people and institutions who provided guidance, support, and insight at various stages throughout my research: Chaiyun Ukosakul, Justin Tan, Rowland Ward, Jeff Pugh, Darren Cronshaw, Joshua Iyadurai, Christo Lombaard, Stephen Spence, and the faculty and staff of Melbourne School of Theology.

To my parents, Richard and Helen Blumenstock, for your financial support, godly wisdom, and ceaseless encouragement. You are exemplars of what it means to love and be loved by God.

Introduction

"From the Gospel of Jesus Christ, people gain an entirely new vision of the world in which they live and to which they are tied with every fiber of their beings."[1] These words from the eminent, twentieth-century Dutch theologian and missiologist Johan Herman Bavinck remind us of the essentially transformative nature of religious conversion. More than merely the acquisition of new beliefs or the performance of new rituals, conversion encompasses nothing less than a thoroughgoing "transfer of worlds."[2] When converts meet with God, personal identities are re-shaped, perspectives of reality are revised, social attachments are reconfigured, and life values are re-aligned. One becomes a "new creature" (2 Cor 5:17) as it were, or, in the words of the Apostle Peter, one is "born again to a living hope" (1 Pet 1:3).

However, for many converts, this deeply transformative experience is also deeply disruptive. In portions of the world where religious, ethnic, kinship, and civic identities are intricately interwoven, and where Christians exist as a minority sub-group within a predominantly non-Christian religious environment, converts face the threat of social marginalization. By converting to what is perceived as a foreign religion, Christ-followers are often considered deviant, disrespectful, or even dangerous by the majority population. They have abandoned the community's religion, and, therefore, the argument goes, they have abandoned the community itself. Their new vision of the world, while personally transformative, puts them at odds with established and expected modes of being and behaving. Since they no longer

1. Bolt et al., *J. H. Bavinck Reader*, 291.
2. Berger and Luckmann, *Social Construction*, 157–60.

Introduction

inhabit the society's "normal" ethical patterns or social identities, they are considered not only different but also patently unacceptable. Within these environments, Christians are, in effect, strangers in a familiar land.

The country of Thailand is one such locale where Christian converts face the realities of a marginalized existence. It is commonly believed in Thailand that to be Thai is to be Buddhist. Unlike the West, where religion and culture are more or less hermetically sealed worlds, Thai society and culture remain thoroughly imbued with religious overtones. Folk Buddhism[3] governs kinship ties, rites of passage, worldview formation, intersubjectivity, self-understanding, and even civic policies and governance. This religio-cultural underpinning to Thai identity and society is compounded by the fact that approximately 94 percent of the population of Thailand adheres to some form of Buddhism.[4] Within this setting, therefore, religious conversion not only threatens one's place in the collective but also calls into question the very essence of one's "Thainess." How do converts navigate this reality of a marginalized existence? How do they understand themselves as both Thai and Christian? What is it like to be a stranger in the land of one's birth?

The purpose of this research is to answer these questions and others like it, not through established theories and formulations but rather from the perspective of the converts themselves. In this book, readers will be taken on a journey into the world of Thai Christians. They will discover the lived meanings implicit in meeting a loving and powerful God, joining an egalitarian and idealistic sacred community, experiencing misunderstandings, ostracism, and ridicule because of one's faith, and negotiating the delicate performance of one's altered religious identity while, at the same time, preserving pre-established kinship and friendship relations. The goal of this study, therefore, is not to explain but to understand, to attune our thoughts and emotions to the pre-reflective narratives of converts, and to co-experience with Thai believers the lived realities of being both Thai and Christian.

---

3. The phrase "Folk Buddhism" refers to the popular religion in Thailand which is an admixture of Therevada Buddhism and animism, especially the ancestral, spirit cult. See chapter 5 for a full discussion.

4. BDHRL, "International Religious Freedom Report."

Introduction

NATURE OF THE RESEARCH

The research question being explored in this book is, "What is the experience of in-marginality among late-convert Christians of Northern Thailand who have transferred from the Thai Buddhist lifeworld into the new sociocultural world of Christian belief and identity?" It is pertinent to begin with some definitions in order to clarify the meaning of this research question.

1. *Experience*: An immediate unit of meaning for an individual or community within the flow of time that may or may not have been an object of reflection.

2. *In-marginality*: The lived experience of exclusion from mainstream society and its activities and processes.[5] While recognizing that there exist variances of nuance among terms, I will be treating in-marginality, marginality, marginalization, social marginalization, and displacement as synonymous throughout this research.

3. *Late-convert*: Adult converts; that is, those who converted from Thai Folk Buddhism to Christianity subsequent to eighteen years of age.

4. *Christians of Northern Thailand*: Self-identifying Christians who are active church members in and surrounding the city of Chiang Mai, Thailand.

5. *Lifeworld*: The taken-for-granted and pre-reflective world, understood phenomenologically, that encompasses the natural attitude of everyday life.[6]

6. *Sociocultural world*: The unique system of construable signs of a particular community which serves to direct behavior and organize experience along with the intersubjective themes contributing to the formation of an individual's "thinking as usual" and personal identity.[7]

7. *Belief*: The cognitive and affective structuration and re-structuration, both as representing a tradition and one's personal meanings, appertaining to religious alternation.

---

5. Howat, "Marginality," 413. For more on what I mean by in-marginality, see the discussion in chapter 4.

6. Manen, *Researching Lived Experience*, 7; Schütz and Luckmann, *Structures 1*, 3–4.

7. Geertz, *Interpretation of Cultures*, 14, 49; Schütz, *On Phenomenology and Social Relations*, 79–82.

Introduction

8. *Identity*: One's subjective self-understanding that results from appropriating a society's objective reality (i.e., "world") as mediated by significant others.[8]

This research question will be explored utilizing the apparatus of interpretive or lifeworld phenomenology. As a philosophy that studies human experience and "the way things present themselves to us in and through such experience,"[9] phenomenology provides the methodological resources for adequately uncovering the lifeworld of Thai Christians from an emic perspective. Our reflections will proceed based on a series of in-depth interviews that were conducted with seven Thai Christians from Northern Thailand. The meanings disclosed during these interviews will be interpreted through three horizons or referential planes: (1) the social sciences, (2) philosophical phenomenology, and (3) the Christian religious tradition. Overall, this research represents an applied study within the field of the philosophy of religious experience.[10]

SIGNIFICANCE OF THE RESEARCH

As a theological educator and missionary who has worked in Thailand for over a decade, I have increasingly become aware of the unique challenges that face the Thai Church as a minority community within a predominantly Buddhist nation. As many scholars have observed, Thai converts encounter a variety of post-conversion, sociocultural adjustments as a result of world transfer, centering on issues of identity re-formation; namely, what it means to be both Thai and Christian.[11] As a result, the church in Thailand has historically struggled in their efforts toward conversion and discipleship within this context.[12] First, proselytization efforts have been hampered. According to a recent study, the top three obstacles to Christian conversion

---

8. Berger and Luckmann, *Social Construction*, 132–33.

9. Sokolowski, *Introduction*, 2.

10. According to Emmanuel Falque, the discipline of the philosophy of religious experience eschews an analysis of a religious "object" by means of logical and linguistic positivism, instead fully examining the subjective experience of the believer so as to attain the essence of religious phenomena. Falque and Shank, *Crossing the Rubicon*, LOC 2155–95.

11. See, especially, Johnson, "Exploring Social Barriers"; Bruijne, "Conversion"; Keyes, "Why the Thai Are Not Christians."

12. For more on the history of Christianity in Thailand, including the challenges faced by missionaries and local Christ-followers, see Smith, *Siamese Gold*.

Introduction

in Thailand relate to Thai identity. These include national-religious identity ("Thai people are supposed to be Buddhists"), kinship identity ("You cannot break the rules of the family"), and sociocultural identity ("You do not take part in rituals anymore").[13] Given the monopolistic nature of the social world in Thailand, that is, the fact that the entire society serves as the plausibility structure for a religious, namely Buddhist, world, Christianity is summarily dismissed as a foreign religion and conversion is perceived as a betrayal of one's family, nation, and culture. Second, Thai churches have experienced difficulties in member retention, largely due to social disruptions.[14] Religious alternation involves a process of inhabiting a new world while, at the same time, segregating from the potentially reality-disrupting influences of the old world. For many Thai converts, the pressures of the old world prove too great, leading to attrition and reversion if the Christian community fails to produce a sufficiently strong plausibility structure and alternate social reality.

These pressing challenges facing the Thai church pertain primarily to issues of social identity. In addressing the need for qualitative research into this phenomenon, missionary-scholar Alan Johnson writes,

> While in fact there may be some Thai Christians who do not "feel" very Thai I think it is wrong to assume that this applies across the board in the absence of some empirical data. This in fact would be a most interesting study, to talk with Thai Christians about how Thai they feel post-conversion and document how they come to understand themselves as a Thai and a Christian.[15]

This research intends to address this lacuna, not necessarily by presenting empirical data by which we may then generalize conclusions about how all Thai Christians "feel" but, instead, by describing and interpreting the experience of identity formation within the context of marginality as a lived experience. In other words, when tackling issues related to the formation of Christian identity in Thailand, it is necessary, I believe, first to understand the phenomenon, not through theory or quantification but from the privileged perspective of the believers themselves.

By unveiling and disclosing the lived experience of Thai Christians, this research will contribute to ongoing scholarship in several fields. First, a phenomenological description of in-marginality among Thai Christians

13. Bruijne, "Conversion."
14. Mejudhon, "Ritual of Reconciliation [2005]," 1.
15. Johnson, "Exploring Social Barriers," 142.

Introduction

will assist the fields of missiology and pastoral care by explicating the Thai Christian lifeworld, thus aiding missionary and pastoral efforts in evangelism and discipleship. Second, this research will inform the development of Thai local theologies, providing qualitative data that will reveal "present human experience"[16] as a valid source for theological expression.[17] Third, by utilizing the phenomenological apparatus, this book will contribute to broader discussions in the phenomenology of religion, especially related to Buddhist and Christian lifeworlds and the constitution of religious experience.[18] Finally, this study may be situated within the field of Southeast Asian religious studies as it pertains to understanding Christianity as a minority religion and assisting inter-religious relations in the region. Overall, my primary desire is that this book may aid efforts in the development of a local, theological anthropology that not only assists in new formulations of how "Thainess" and "Christianness" intersect, but also enhances contextualized understandings of Christian identity within any social environment where Christians exist as a marginalized sub-group. Now, let us begin our journey of exploration into the phenomenon of in-marginality as lived among Thai Christians.

---

16. Bevans, *Models*, 1–2.

17. Schreiter, *Constructing Local Theologies*.

18. For more on a phenomenology of Buddhist, religious experience, see Smart, *Buddhism and Christianity*; Laycock, *Mind as Mirror and the Mirroring of Mind*; Lusthaus, *Buddhist Phenomenology*; Park and Kopf, *Merleau-Ponty and Buddhism*; Varma, *Buddhist Phenomenology*.

1

Identity Formation in Sociocultural Perspective

INTRODUCTION

RELIGIOUS IDENTITY FORMATION IN contexts of marginalization is a fundamentally social phenomenon. Conversion, as we will see in this book, introduces two revised states of social existence: social segregation on the one hand, in that it displaces the convert from pre-existing religious and social identities, and social integration on the other, in that it immerses the convert in a new and transformative intersubjective community of saints. As we begin our study of this phenomenon, therefore, it is valuable for us first to survey the relevant theorizations within the social sciences to see how they might assist in our adumbration of the structure of marginalization within the Thai context. In this chapter, I will review literature in the disciplines of sociology, anthropology, and psychology to reveal the most relevant theorizations as they contribute to an understanding of the Thai Christian experience of in-marginality.

The chapter is structured into two primary sections: marginality and sociocultural identity formation. In the first section, I will cover marginality theory within three theoretical traditions: stranger as newcomer, "marginal man," and liminality. In the second section, I will survey both the social constructivist and social identity approaches to identity formation, both of which prioritize the essentially social nature of the self-concept.

MARGINALITY

Since the early twentieth century, due to an increase in social mobility, mass communication, and ethnic and political conflicts, sociologists and anthropologists have developed a heightened awareness of the role of the margin for understanding culture and society. Social structures are no longer perceived as stable and exhaustive definitions for all people in a given time and place. Instead, for each social structure, there exist those who live "on the hyphen": neither fully defined nor fully accepted according to the prevailing definitions and identifications of the dominant groups.[1] These individuals may be in a marginal position due to their race, ethnicity, religion, or simply because they are newcomers, but in all cases, they experience unique social and psychological effects. This section will delineate the sociocultural concept of marginality as expounded in three distinct, albeit related, theoretical traditions: the stranger, the "marginal man," and the liminal. I will trace each theory according to the works of its major contributors, highlighting similarities and differences among the traditions as well as key concepts relevant to the phenomenon under investigation.

The Stranger

Modern sociology's treatment of marginality arguably began with Georg Simmel's (1858–1918) concise but influential essay entitled "The Stranger."[2] The German philosopher pictured society as a web of interactions between people. The form of these interactions could be isolated from their content allowing the sociologist to study relationships that differ in substance but display the same formal properties. This approach, known as formal sociology, underpins Simmel's treatment of the stranger as an isolated social type or a "specific form of interaction"[3] that may appear in different societies at different times throughout history but displays similar behavioral patterns.[4]

For Simmel, the stranger is not a wanderer who comes and goes but the person who comes today and stays tomorrow. While being close in distance, the stranger is also remote. The stranger's position as a member of a society involves being both outside it and confronting it. Economically,

---

1. See Fine and Sirin, "Hyphenated Selves."
2. Simmel, "Stranger."
3. Simmel, "Stranger," 402.
4. "Simmel, Georg."

Identity Formation in Sociocultural Perspective

they are the outside merchants who settle down in the place of their industry while retaining a sense of mobility. Because they are not committed to the particular values of the group, they interact with the group objectively, openly, and with a high level of freedom. The nearness of the stranger allows the group to identify with them according to certain general characteristics such as national, social, or generally human qualities, but their farness is experienced in the lack of personal and particular relational features held in common.[5] The stranger *par excellence*, according to Simmel, were the European Jews who, despite being resident in European nations, have historically been categorized, in the first place, as inhabiting a particular social position as distinct from other citizens.[6] In other words, the Jew, like the stranger in general, "may be a member of a group in a *spatial* sense but still not be a member of the group in a *social* sense . . . *in* the group but not *of* it."[7]

Simmel's seminal essay initiated two major research traditions in sociology: the newcomer tradition and "marginal man" theory. These two traditions, while sharing significant theoretical commonalities, have produced divergent themes and angles of analysis.[8] In the following section, I will provide an extensive discussion of "marginal man" theory, but here I will briefly cover the newcomer tradition as developed by Schütz.[9]

Alfred Schütz[10] (1899–1959) played an enigmatic role in the history and development of modern sociology. While a phenomenological philosopher by trade and conviction, Schütz's forays into the social sciences have both shaped the direction of contemporary sociology[11] and instigated the consternation of fellow phenomenologists.[12] Indeed, classifying him as a phenomenologist or sociologist has proven difficult even in this research, requiring a dual treatment of his work. As a phenomenologist, Schütz's

5. Simmel, "Stranger," 402–7.
6. Simmel, "Stranger," 403, 408.
7. McLemore, "Simmel's 'Stranger,'" 86.
8. For an elaboration of this two-traditions thesis, see McLemore, "Simmel's 'Stranger.'"
9. Besides Schütz, Margaret Mary Wood had also produced a significant sociological study on the stranger. See Wood, *Stranger*.
10. Two Anglicized spellings of this German name—Schütz and Schuetz—are extant in the literature. I have chosen to utilize the former.
11. Most significantly as the professor and mentor of Thomas Luckmann and Peter Berger. See Berger and Luckmann, *Social Construction*.
12. Most notably and famously, Aron Gurwitsch. See Schütz et al., *Philosophers in Exile*; Natanson, "Alfred Schütz."

understanding of the constitutive nature of the lifeworld will be discussed in chapter 2. Here, however, I would like to survey his sociological contributions to the concept of the stranger as most fully expressed in his 1944 essay, "The Stranger: An Essay in Social Psychology."[13]

Schütz approached the type of the stranger from a social psychological and phenomenological perspective. To begin, Schütz described the stranger as "an adult individual of our times and civilization who tries to be permanently accepted or at least tolerated by the groups which he approaches."[14] The immigrant is the outstanding example, but a stranger may be anyone who enters a relatively closed social group of any size or form with the intention of remaining within that group. Essential to Schütz's thesis is his concept of the "cultural pattern of group life" or "thinking as usual." Society, he argues, provides for its members a "graduated knowledge of relevant elements."[15] This knowledge consists of a pre-theoretical set of "recipes" bequeathed by a culture "for interpreting the social world and for handling things and men in order to obtain the best results in every situation with a minimum of effort by avoiding undesirable consequences."[16] That is to say, cultures provide for its members "typical solutions for typical problems available for typical actors."[17] As long as social life is relatively stable, the knowledge handed down in the tradition is deemed reliable, and the recipes are accepted and applied by others in the group, members will follow the cultural pattern as a matter of course. However, the stranger, for whom the cultural pattern is foreign, must "place in question nearly everything that seems to be unquestionable to the members of the approached group."[18] Since they do not share in the history and traditions of the group, they must interpret group behavior based on their own cultural pattern. When they approach individuals, they are unable to treat them as mere performers of typical functions but only as individuals. This prevents them from developing a coherent picture of the group and a reliable set of expected responses. As a result of this dissonance between two divergent patterns of thinking as usual, the stranger becomes remote, hesitant, and distrustful. As Schütz explained, "The

---

13. Schütz, "Stranger." See also Schütz, *On Phenomenology and Social Relations*.
14. Schütz, "Stranger," 499.
15. Schütz, "Stranger," 500.
16. Schütz, *On Phenomenology and Social Relations*, 81.
17. Schütz, "Stranger," 505.
18. Schütz, "Stranger," 502.

cultural pattern of the approached group is to the stranger not a shelter but a field of adventure, not a matter of course but a questionable topic of investigation, not an instrument for disentangling problematic situations but a problematic situation itself and one hard to master."[19]

The "Marginal Man"

It was a student of Georg Simmel, Robert E. Park (1864–1944), who first coined the term "marginal man" to refer to a socio-psychological personality type who experiences the antagonistic clash of cultures at a personal level.[20] Park, a central figure in the Chicago school of sociology, adapted and expanded Simmel's treatment of the stranger in his 1928 article, "Human Migration and the Marginal Man."[21] In it, Park espoused a catastrophic theory of progress by which cultural differences arise and cultures advance through cooperative and competitive interactions such as migration and war.[22] Through migration especially, societies are secularized and individuals are emancipated as "primitive" cultures progress toward "civilization" through the cross-pollination of new cultures and the interbreeding of races.[23] While cities best represent the locale of racial assimilation and amalgamation, it is in the "marginal man" where cultures subjectively come into contact and collision.[24]

Following Simmel, Park's "marginal man" was a stranger, a wanderer who was not bound by local proprieties and conventions but was emancipated and enlightened. As a result,

> [He was] a new type of personality, namely, a cultural hybrid, a man living and sharing intimately in the cultural life and traditions of two distinct peoples; never quite willing to break, even if he were permitted to do so, with his past and his traditions, and not quite accepted, because of racial prejudice, in the new society in which he now sought to find a place. He was a man on the

---

19. Schütz, "Stranger," 506.

20. I recognize the gender exclusive nature of the term "marginal man" but will follow its usage as a specific sociological theory represented in the literature. Throughout this book, I will utilize quotation marks to signify this term as an established sociological label and not this author's own perspective on gender.

21. Park, "Human Migration."

22. Park, "Human Migration," 882–84; Goldberg, "Robert Park's Marginal Man," 200.

23. Park, "Human Migration," 887–88, 890.

24. Goldberg, "Robert Park's Marginal Man," 201.

margin of two cultures and two societies, which never completely interpenetrated and fused.[25]

For Park, as for Simmel before him, it was the European Jews who, due to their mobility and symbiotic relationship with the larger community, exemplified this personality most fully. They were the "first cosmopolite and citizen of the world" whose pre-eminence in trade, keen intellect, and idealistic sophistication made them a hallmark "city man."[26]

Internally, however, the mind of the "marginal man" harbors the conflict of the divided self: inner turmoil and intense self-consciousness produced by the internalization of the conflict of cultures. Far from transitory, this period of crisis and the concomitant psychological effects become relatively permanent features of the self, resulting in the formation of a personality type. Park believed this personality type, the "marginal man," is ordinarily a person of mixed blood who participates in two worlds. However, significant to this research, he also states, "The Christian convert in Asia or in Africa exhibits many if not most of the characteristics of the 'marginal man'—the same spiritual instability, intensified self-consciousness, restlessness, and malaise."[27] Whoever may appropriately fit within this category, it is in the mind of the "marginal man" where Park believed one may best study the processes of civilization and of progress.

Nearly a decade later, Park refined his understanding of the "marginal man," stressing that the emergence of this personality type results not only from cultural contact but cultural conflict. The "marginal man" is one who lives in two not merely different but antagonistic worlds. They arise at a time and place where new peoples and cultures are coming into existence, making them "the individual with the wider horizon, the keener intelligence, the more detached and rational viewpoint."[28]

Park's theoretical adjustments were expressed in his introduction to the 1937 book *The Marginal Man: A Study in Personality and Culture Conflict*,[29] written by one of his students at the University of Chicago, Everett V. Stonequist (1901–1979). Under Park's encouragement and counsel, Stonequist not only set out to analyze further the validity of the "marginal man" hypothesis but also to clarify and expand the theory through a systematization of the

25. Park, "Human Migration," 892.
26. Park, "Human Migration," 892.
27. Park, "Human Migration," 893.
28. Park, "Introduction," xvii.
29. Stonequist, *Marginal Man*. See also Stonequist, "Problem of the Marginal Man."

representative types, life phases, personality traits, and levels of adjustment. He began his study with an expanded definition:

> So the marginal man as conceived in this study is one who is poised in psychological uncertainty between two (or more) social worlds; reflecting in his soul the discords and harmonies, repulsions and attractions of these worlds, one of which is often 'dominant' over the other; within which membership is implicitly if not explicitly based upon birth or ancestry (race or nationality); and where exclusion removes the individual from a system of group relations.[30]

The social worlds in which the individual resides may include historic traditions, languages, political loyalties, moral codes, religions, or any combination of these, but these worlds must come into conflict and become internalized as acute personal difficulty or mental tension for the marginal personality type to appear.[31]

"Marginal men," as conceived by Stonequist, include two representative types: the racial hybrid and the cultural hybrid. The racial hybrid is the person of mixed racial ancestry whose biological origin places them between the two races. Their physical features set them apart from both parent races, presenting a difficulty for the community as it relates to social identification and role enactment. Examples include the Eurasians of India, "Cape Coloureds" of South Africa, and the "Mulattoes" of the United States.[32] Cultural hybrids, on the other hand, are those who, through migration or cultural diffusion, internalize the norms, mores, and patterns of two or more cultures. For Stonequist, the greatest examples of cultural hybrids include the previously colonized peoples of Asia and Africa, Jews, immigrants, and the "American Negro."[33] Following Park, Stonequist highlighted the Christian convert in non-Western cultures as an exemplary model of the cultural hybrid. He or she "is one who has been pulled out of the old order of things without necessarily becoming a part of the new order."[34] After abandoning their own customs and traditions, they fail to imbibe the missionary's

---

30. Stonequist, *Marginal Man*, 8.

31. Stonequist, *Marginal Man*, 3–4.

32. Stonequist, *Marginal Man*, 10–11. These terms for biracial categories, which may be considered insensitive or inappropriate, are Stonequist's and, thus, do not represent the position or opinions of this author.

33. Stonequist, *Marginal Man*, 54–119.

34. Stonequist, *Marginal Man*, 61.

Western traditions properly. As a result, they experience a break with their tribe, sometimes including severe social ostracism.

It is important to note, however, that in all cases of cultural hybridity, it is not the mere mixing of cultures that creates the "marginal man" but the experience of group conflict that flows from cultural differences.[35] When conflicting groups are in a relationship of inequality, members of the subordinate group will seek to adjust themselves to the dominant group that is believed to possess greater prestige and power. Marginal personalities emerge, therefore, as subordinate group members; after being partially assimilated and psychologically identified with the dominant group, they are never fully accepted by that group.[36]

Individuals in this marginal situation will experience at least three significant phases of personal development: (1) lack of awareness of the racial or national conflict, (2) crisis period during which the individual consciously experiences this conflict, and (3) period of adjustment or maladjustment to the situation.[37] Positively, the individual may adjust to the marginal situation by becoming a leader in the subordinate group (nationalist role) or by mediating between the clashing cultures (intermediary role). Indeed, the "marginal man's" insight into two cultures and their ability to analyze problems from more than one angle may instill in them a creative, international mindedness.[38] Negatively, however, the internal tension and continual restlessness caused by the marginal situation may lead to a breakdown in individual "life-organization" which may result in crime, delinquency, suicide, or psychosis.[39] The level of adjustment varies by individual and the degree of identification and subsequent repulsion by the dominant group, but it is ultimately a matter of psychological integration whereby the "marginal man" faces the realities of their social situation and attempts to cope through various means.[40]

Arguably Stonequist's greatest contribution to "marginal man" theory—and certainly the most controversial aspect of his work—was his categorization of the "marginal man's" personality traits. Consequent to the crisis experience in which the marginal individual experiences his or

---

35. Stonequist, *Marginal Man*, 88.
36. Stonequist, *Marginal Man*, 121.
37. Stonequist, *Marginal Man*, 121–23.
38. Stonequist, *Marginal Man*, 178–79.
39. Stonequist, *Marginal Man*, 159, 202.
40. Stonequist, *Marginal Man*, 208–9.

her world as disorganized and problematic are a number of psychological effects, both positive and negative. Fundamentally, the "marginal man" will develop a dual personality by which one imagines the self through two disparate looking-glasses, thus creating an internal mental conflict.[41] This internal conflict may lead, secondly, to an attitude of ambivalence or divided loyalty: the state of being torn between two courses of action leading to often-contradictory opinions and behavior.[42] Third, marginal situations may produce excessive self-consciousness and hypersensitivity. Perpetually conscious of their anomalous position, the "marginal man" may feel excessively deficient or inferior in light of the group's social definition. This hypersensitivity may result in withdrawal, excessive egocentrism, rationalization, or aggressiveness.[43] Not all personality traits are adverse, however. Stonequist identified two traits in particular that are weighted in the "marginal man's" favor. First, because of their in-between situation, the "marginal man" is an able critic of the dominant group and its culture. They are both an insider and an outsider, allowing them to note the contradictions and hypocrisies tacit in the dominant culture. Second, the "marginal man" is a skilled thinker. If, as Stonequist argues, perplexity and confusion provide the fertile ground for reflection, then the marginal person will likely experience more intense, creative, and objective mental activity.[44]

Given the complexity of the "marginal man's" psychological constitution, it is no wonder that Stonequist, like Park before him, identified the "marginal man" as the "key-personality in the contacts of culture" and the "crucible of cultural fusion."[45] Writing at a time and place where urbanization and modernization were rapidly bringing cultures into conflict, Stonequist's treatment of the mind of the "marginal man" was not only timely but also seminal for later sociological theorization. Indeed, the concept of marginality seems to touch upon not just the few who live on the hyphen, but upon the many who exist in an ever-shrinking world. For the

---

41. Stonequist, *Marginal Man*, 145. Stonequist alludes to W. E. B. DuBois's seminal work on the plight of African Americans in the early twentieth century and their experience of "double consciousness." The double conscious individual, DuBois writes, always feels his or her "two-ness . . . two souls, two thoughts, two unreconciled strivings; two warring ideals in one dark body, whose dogged strength alone keeps it from being torn asunder" (DuBois, *Souls of Black Folk*, 8).
42. Stonequist, *Marginal Man*, 146–47.
43. Stonequist, *Marginal Man*, 148–52.
44. Stonequist, *Marginal Man*, 155.
45. Stonequist, *Marginal Man*, 221.

purposes of this research, "marginal man" theory offers a useful horizon for adumbrating the constitutive structure of the Thai Christian religious experience of in-marginality.

The Liminal

The sociological conception of marginality, including both stranger and "marginal man" traditions, finds its anthropological counterpart in the concept of liminality. Although initially proposed by French anthropologist Arnold van Gennep (1873–1957) in his book *The Rites of Passage*,[46] liminality was most fully developed in the work of symbolic cultural anthropologist Victor Turner (1920–1983).[47] For both Gennep and Turner, liminality is the special state in a transition ritual wherein one is betwixt and between two fixed points in the social structure.[48] Gennep had identified three stages of rites of passage: separation, margin (or limen), and re-aggregation. Separation removes the ritual subject from his or her position in society while re-aggregation returns him or her to a new status within that society, although inwardly transformed and outwardly changed. Between these stages of social structure[49] is a period of anti-structure when the initiand is neither here nor there; suspended, as it were, in a marginal state outside of society's roles, statuses, and norms. It is in this inter-structural sphere, Turner believed, where the basic building blocks of culture are exposed and great myths, philosophical systems, and works of art are generated.[50]

Turner developed his understanding of liminality by observing the ritual practices of the Ndembu people of Zambia. Passage rituals, particularly initiation rites, he observed, involve a process of transitioning initiands from one status in society to another. The in-between or liminal phase, however, places the transitional-beings or "liminars"[51] in a state of

46. Gennep, *Rites of Passage*.

47. Turner, *Ritual Process*; *Dramas, Fields, and Metaphors*; "Variations"; "Betwixt and Between."

48. Pentikainen, "Liminality."

49. Defined as the "more or less distinctive arrangement of mutually dependent institutions and the institutional organization of social positions and/or actors which they imply" (Turner, *Dramas, Fields, and Metaphors*, 272).

50. Turner, *Ritual Process*, 128; "Betwixt and Between," 55.

51. Turner utilizes numerous designations for those in the liminal phase: transitional-beings, liminal *personae*, liminaries, liminars, among others. For the sake of consistency, I have chosen to use the term "liminar" to refer to a person in the liminal state and

structural limbo. They become invisible or even structurally "dead" to their society. They are "neither here nor there; they are betwixt and between the positions assigned and arrayed by law, custom, convention, and ceremonial."[52] This removal of status may be symbolized through stripping the initiands naked, sending them away to secluded areas, and even treating them as corpses by forcing them to lie motionless in the posture of customary burial.[53] Their condition is one of ambiguity and paradox. They no longer fit in structural categories, and, as a result, are considered unclean, undifferentiated, and poor. The former life is stripped away so that a process of "growth, transformation, and reformulation of old elements in new patterns" may emerge.[54] Consequently, the liminal phase becomes a stage for reflection, creativity, and religious experience.[55]

During the liminal period, initiands enter a very simple social structure of complete submission to the instructor and complete equality with one another. Spontaneous, immediate, and concrete social bonds, falling under the principle, "each for all, and all for each," form among liminars.[56] Turner labels this sense of comradeship "communitas." Relying heavily on Martin Buber, Turner describes communitas as an existential and spontaneous "I and Thou" relationship wherein individuals confront one another directly and without the constraints implicit in structural differentiation.[57] As initiands are leveled and stripped of all social rank and status, a sentiment of humankindness emerges whereby participants experience a sense of "we're in this together." These bonds often last a lifetime, even after the ritual is over, and the initiands return to their respective statuses in society.

For Turner, liminality and communitas are not limited to the ritual processes of traditional cultures. The betwixt and between period, along with its concomitant sense of comradeship, can be identified in religious movements such as the early Franciscans,[58] religious social processes such as pilgrimages,[59] and modern social movements such as the hippies of the

---

"initiand" to refer to the individual as he or she experiences all phases of a given ritual.

52. Turner, *Ritual Process*, 95.
53. Turner, "Betwixt and Between," 48; *Ritual Process*, 95.
54. Turner, "Betwixt and Between," 49.
55. Turner, "Betwixt and Between," 53.
56. Turner, "Betwixt and Between," 50.
57. Turner, *Dramas, Fields, and Metaphors*, 47.
58. Turner, *Ritual Process*, 140–50.
59. Turner, *Dramas, Fields, and Metaphors*, 166–210.

1960s.⁶⁰ The sheer variety of liminal experiences in both traditional and modern cultures led Turner to distinguish between liminal and liminoid phenomena. Liminal phenomena, he argues, reside largely in the tribal genres. They are tied to natural breaks in the flow of sociocultural processes (such as calendrical or biological rhythms), centrally integrated into the total social process of a given community, and tend to have a common meaning for the community's members. In contrast, liminoid phenomena appear in industrialized genres. They are tied to the leisure sphere of individual life, develop outside or on the margins of central economic and political processes, are largely plural, fragmentary, and experimental, and tend to be more idiosyncratic and quirky.⁶¹ Whereas in a liminal ritual the liminar looks forward to returning to a stable, integrated social order, "in the liminoid there is no returning to where the world was before, only movement into a future that continually undermines both the prevailing order and the nature of the sacred within the society."⁶²

Several other implications of Turner's theory of liminality are also pertinent. First, liminality may become a permanent feature of an individual's or group's lived experience. In traditional rites of passage, liminars are removed from society only to be eventually re-aggregated. There is always the expectation of return. However, for some the liminal period becomes a permanent condition. The Christian, for instance, is one whose entire religious life is marked by passage: "A stranger to the world, a pilgrim, a traveler, with no place to rest his head."⁶³ He or she has an expectation of returning "home," but that home is beyond earthly existence. Therefore, his or her lived experience on earth is that of liminality. Jaclyn Colona and Guillermo Grenier claim that Cuban exiles in America present another example of permanent, albeit structured, liminality.⁶⁴ As exiles, Cuban Americans do not seek integration with American society but continually long for re-aggregation into the Cuban national and geographical social structure. However, in this indefinite time of betwixt and between, the exilic community's identity becomes that of liminality. They coalesce into enclaves, forming a density and diversity of structural relationships, all the while regarding "their ancestral homeland as their real and ideal home

---

60. Turner, *Ritual Process*, 112–13.
61. Turner, "Variations," 43–45.
62. Roxburgh, *Missionary Congregation, Leadership, and Liminality*, 48.
63. Turner, *Ritual Process*, 107.
64. Colona, "Structuring Liminality."

Identity Formation in Sociocultural Perspective

to which they should return" and considering themselves "the 'other' in the hostland; not fully accepted—culturally, economically, politically, and socially."[65] As Bahar Rumelili argues, not only small communities but also entire nations may experience permanent liminality due to their particular geographical, political, and/or cultural positions.[66] Such cases prompted Iver B. Neumann to conclude that "there are no stable societies from which to be taken away and be returned to. With everything in flux, Gennep's scheme of a pre-liminal, luminal *(sic)*, and post-liminal phase collapses, and the possibility of perpetual liminality opens up before us."[67]

A second implication is that the liminal space is one of vast potential and creativity. It creates conditions for reflection and imagination as initiands are stripped of most, if not all, social and cultural constraints and "forced to think about their society, their cosmos, and the powers that generate and sustain them."[68] Because it transgresses the norms that govern structure, liminality is a seedbed for not only artistic and philosophical expression but also deep religious experience. Visions and powerful religious encounters often accompany these transitional phases of life. "The margins, therefore, become the place most characterized by the sacred."[69]

Third, liminal periods are intimately associated with identity formation, re-formation, and trans-formation. While Turner alludes to this fact, numerous scholars have since highlighted and expounded upon the nature of this association. Colona and Grenier explain that the liminality of exile creates a social identity rooted not in integration but in a communal "vision of return." With the enduring hope of a return home, exiles maintain the homeland and its traditions as lived experience while remaining geographically within the hostland.[70] Roxburgh, in discussing the implications of liminality for the Western Church, asserts that while liminality may initially cause confusion and difficulty for a group, it also holds great potential for "transformation and new configurations of identity."[71]

---

65. Colona, "Structuring Liminality," 47.

66. Rumelili, "Liminal Identities." Rumelili provides the example of Turkey as a country liminally suspended between Europe and the Muslim world.

67. Neumann, "Introduction," 478.

68. Turner, "Betwixt and Between," 53.

69. Roxburgh, *Missionary Congregation, Leadership, and Liminality*, 31.

70. Colona, "Structuring Liminality," 47. For another study on the relationship between liminality and identity, see Beech, "Liminality."

71. Roxburgh, *Missionary Congregation, Leadership, and Liminality*, 29, 43.

Based on this research, it is apparent that liminality and communitas are powerful forces in identity formation as individuals and societies undergo periods of significant transition.

Finally, it is apposite to conclude this section with a brief comparison between marginality and liminality theories. In *Dramas, Fields, and Metaphors*, Turner differentiates liminality from both outsiderhood and marginality. For him, outsiderhood refers either to the condition of being permanently and by ascription set outside a society or to being temporarily and voluntarily set apart from society in order to play a particular role. "Such outsiders," he explains, "would include, in various cultures, shamans, diviners, mediums, priests, those in monastic seclusion, hippies, hoboes, and gypsies."[72] Marginals, on the other hand, are "simultaneously members . . . of two or more groups whose social definitions and cultural norms are distinct from, and often even opposed to, one another."[73] They may include second-generation immigrants, persons of mixed ethnic origin, or those who are moving from one social class to another. Marginals often look to the subordinate group for communitas and to the dominant group for structural reference. They, like liminars, are also betwixt and between; but, unlike them, they do not have assurance of a final stable resolution of their ambiguity.[74] Liminars, by contrast, are members of a single group, are typically not suspended in a permanent state of transition,[75] and look forward to eventual re-integration into a particular social structure.

SOCIOCULTURAL IDENTITY (TRANS-)FORMATION

Identity theories are varied and prolific, originating from within such disciplines as philosophy, anthropology, sociology, theology, and psychology, but applied to nearly every field imaginable, including organizational management, political theory, education, ethnic relations, and even children's literature, to name just a few.[76] For the purposes of this research, two theoretical

---

72. Turner, *Dramas, Fields, and Metaphors*, 233.

73. Turner, *Dramas, Fields, and Metaphors*, 233.

74. For further discussion on Turner's distinction, see Holmes, "Liminality and Liturgy," 389; Colona, "Structuring Liminality," 45.

75. Although, as we have seen, many scholars have argued that liminality may be experienced in modern society as a perpetual state.

76. To cite just a few examples: Otubanjo, "Embedding Theory in Corporate Identity"; Pavlović, "Literature, Social Poetics, and Identity Construction"; Hourigan, "Invisible Student"; Nagel, "Constructing Ethnicity"; Coats, "Identity."

traditions are perceived as pertinent horizons for revealing the constitutive nature of the phenomenon under investigation. These include, first, Peter Berger and Thomas Luckmann's sociology of knowledge, particularly the social construction of identity and alternation theory; and, second, what is known as the social identity approach as initially proposed by Henri Tajfel and John Turner. These two theoretical traditions will be the focus of the following sections, with input from other theorists and disciplines as they contribute to the overall clarity of the conceptualizations.

Social Construction of Identity

Peter Berger (1929–2017), along with his colleague, Thomas Luckmann (1927–2016), produced one of the most influential books on sociology in the mid-twentieth century, *The Social Construction of Reality: A Treatise in the Sociology of Knowledge*.[77] Berger and Luckmann's thesis, as the title of the book suggests, is that objective social reality, as it is perceived, internalized, and indwelt by a given society, is essentially an historical and sociological construction of its inhabitants that is created and maintained through an ongoing and dialectical process of externalization and internalization. As an objective reality, society emerges from the very nature of humans as being both open to the world and malleable. Unlike animals, humans are instinctually underdeveloped; that is, they are produced not as much through biological constitution as through interrelation with their environment, both natural and social. This self-production does not occur in isolation but always in an intersubjective relation of externalization. As humans respond to one another in habitual[78] and typical ways, a social order is formed that serves to control human activity through the establishment of predefined patterns of conduct. Eventually, as this social order is handed down to subsequent generations, it "thickens" into an objective world, perceived in consciousness as both massively real and unalterable.[79] Through language, this world gains a certain logic that integrates the society's institutions and forms the everyday, pre-theoretical knowledge necessary for institutionalized conduct.[80]

---

77. Berger and Luckmann, *Social Construction*.

78. Nelson Goodman states: "Reality in a world, like realism in a picture, is largely a matter of habit" (Goodman, *Ways of Worldmaking*, 20).

79. Berger and Luckmann, *Social Construction*, 59.

80. Clifford Geertz calls this knowledge "common sense," which, he explains, comprises a culture's down to earth, colloquial wisdom that is historically constructed,

As socially constructed realities, social worlds require a process of legitimation to explain and justify the salient elements of the institutional order—that is, its plausibility—to subsequent generations. It does this by ascribing cognitive validity to its objectivated meanings.[81] Berger and Luckmann identify four levels of legitimation: incipient legitimation, which is implicit in a culture's vocabulary; rudimentary theoretical legitimation, which are highly pragmatic explanatory schemes such as proverbs, maxims, and folk tales; explicit theoretical legitimation, which provide fairly comprehensive frames of reference for an institutional sector as produced by specialized personnel; and symbolic universe legitimation, which comprise the largest "bodies of theoretical tradition that integrate different provinces of meaning and encompass the institutional order in a symbolic totality."[82]

Symbolic universes, the authors explain, order and legitimate everyday roles and priorities by placing them in the context of the most general frame of reference conceivable. Indeed, this is the level of legitimation where "a whole world is created."[83] Symbolic universes are *Weltanschauungen*, or worldviews,[84] most commonly but not exclusively expressed in religion.[85] Conceived of as implicit in the very structure of the cosmos, perhaps even divinely sanctioned, this world or universe provides a "canopy" under which inhabitants find protection from existential chaos, anomy, and terror. As a result of this protective function, other universes are perceived as threats, especially in monopolistic situations that presuppose a high degree of social-structural stability. Berger and Luckmann explain,

> As long as competing definitions of reality can be conceptually and socially segregated as appropriate to strangers, and *ipso facto* as irrelevant to oneself, it is possible to have fairly friendly relations with these strangers. The trouble begins whenever the "strangeness" is broken through and the deviant universe appears

---

followed as a matter of course, practical for everyday life, and largely ad hoc and inconsistent. See Geertz, *Local Knowledge*, 76, 84–91. Similar concepts would include Pierre Bourdieu's "habitus" and Victor Turner's "root paradigms." See Bourdieu, *Logic of Practice*, 52–65; Turner, *Dramas, Fields, and Metaphors*, 64.

81. Berger and Luckmann, *Social Construction*, 93.
82. Berger and Luckmann, *Social Construction*, 94–95.
83. Berger and Luckmann, *Social Construction*, 96.
84. Berger et al., *Homeless Mind*, 99.
85. See Geertz, *Interpretation of Cultures*, 102–8.

as a possible habitat for one's own people. At this point, the traditional experts are likely to call for the fire and the sword.[86]

Universe-maintenance of this sort occurs through a dual process of therapy, tools for curing potential deviants, and nihilation, the conceptual liquidation of whatever does not fit within one's universe.[87] The end goal of these processes is the solidification of a world that, while socially constructed, becomes an objective, even reified, home in which inhabits find integrated meaning and existential protection.[88]

A final component of the externalization and objectivation of social reality, and as a segue to our discussion on internalization, is the objectivation of identity through typifications and roles. For Berger and Luckmann, implicit in the production of an institutional order is the typification of one's own and others' performances. Specific types of actions are ascribed to certain types of actors, becoming taken-for-granted episodes in the routine of everyday life. As the actor reflects on their own actions, a segment of their self is objectified as the performer of those socially available typifications. They become the "nephew-thrasher," "sister-supporter," "initiate-warrior," "rain-dance virtuoso," etc.[89] "In sum, the actor identifies with the socially objectivated typifications of conduct *in actu*, but reestablishes distance from them as he reflects about his conduct afterward. . . . In this way both acting self and acting others are apprehended not as unique individuals, but as *types*."[90] When these typifications occur in the context of an objectified body of knowledge within a social order, they become roles. "By playing roles, the individual participates in a social world. By internalizing these roles, the same world becomes subjectively real to him."[91] Roles represent the institutional order; that is, institutions manifest themselves through the actual performance of roles. Roles become reified as they are apprehended as an inevitable fate whereby one believes, "I have no choice in the matter, I have to act this way because of my position."[92] As a result, identity itself is reified as the individual totally identifies with his or her socially assigned typifications.

---

86. Berger and Luckmann, *Social Construction*, 122.
87. Berger and Luckmann, *Social Construction*, 113–16.
88. See also Steinbock, *Home and Beyond*.
89. Berger and Luckmann, *Social Construction*, 73.
90. Berger and Luckmann, *Social Construction*, 73.
91. Berger and Luckmann, *Social Construction*, 74.
92. Berger and Luckmann, *Social Construction*, 91.

These reified identities are most comprehensively legitimated through symbolic universes. By anchoring the self in a cosmic reality that protects one from the contingencies and anomic threats of social existence, symbolic universes tell the self who one really is. Indeed, the fact that this real self is divinely known allows the individual to "live in society with some assurance that he really is what he considers himself to be as he plays his routine social roles."[93] In this sense, identity is protected under a sacred canopy in which the world is legitimated as a microcosm of the divine structure of the cosmos.[94] The individual transcends his or her own individuality and uniqueness and loses themselves in the all-embracing fabric of meanings provided by the religious nomos.[95]

Subjectively, one internalizes a society's reality and understands one's fellowmen through a process of socialization, both primary and secondary. In primary socialization, children, without any choice in the matter, imbibe a social world by emotionally identifying with significant others. Through this identification, children acquire a "subjectively coherent and plausible identity"[96] that essentially creates and maintains the self by reflecting the attitudes, expressed mainly through language, of significant others.[97] Berger and Luckmann explain, "To be given an identity involves being assigned a specific place in the world. As this identity is subjectively appropriated by the child ('I *am* John Smith'), so is the world to which this identity points."[98] In this way, what was real outside becomes what is real within. And this reality, this internalized world, is not one of many possible worlds, but *the* world, "the only existent and only conceivable world," that becomes firmly entrenched as the child's "home world."[99]

Secondary socialization, however, is always subsequent to primary socialization and, as a result, is necessarily less rooted in consciousness and more susceptible to displacement. Secondary socialization involves the internalization of sub-worlds, institutions composed of role-specific

---

93. Berger and Luckmann, *Social Construction*, 101.
94. Berger, *Sacred Canopy*, 34.
95. Berger, *Sacred Canopy*, 54–55.
96. Berger and Luckmann, *Social Construction*, 132.
97. This entails that the self is both individual and social. Jenkins, *Social Identity*, 50. See also Beech's discussion of centripetal (internalizing) and centrifugal (externalizing) orientations of the self. Beech, "Liminality," 288.
98. Berger and Luckmann, *Social Construction*, 132.
99. Berger and Luckmann, *Social Construction*, 134, 136.

Identity Formation in Sociocultural Perspective

knowledge. Since these sub-worlds are communicated through teachers (not parents), are more voluntary in nature, and often lack a strong emotional charge, they are never truly home. They always carry a veneer of artificiality. In fact, sub-worlds, since they are most often interpreted through the perspective of one's objectivated home world, necessitate continual legitimation and reinforcement to maintain their plausibility.[100] This ongoing maintenance of subjective reality, whether home worlds or sub-worlds, requires a specific social base, or a "plausibility structure," in which conversations take place that continually strengthen the plausibility of one's reality and identity. Indeed, an internalized world can only be maintained as long as one retains one's significant relationships with that world's community.[101] The firmer the plausibility structure is, the firmer will be the world that is based upon it. Likewise, the less firm the plausibility structure is, the "more acute will be the need for world-maintaining legitimations."[102]

Despite the primacy of a home world and the fragility of sub-words, it is possible for an individual to shift or transfer from one world to another, transforming one's subjective reality. The reason for this is that the construction of social reality is essentially a dialectical process; that is, one not only receives a reality through primary socialization but also contributes to the production of reality through externalization. Individuals and entire societies are in a continuous process of externalizing and internalizing worlds and modifying subjective realities.[103] Because of this, the transformation of subjective reality, or switching worlds, becomes a viable possibility. Berger and Luckmann call this phenomenon "alternation." Alternation is the process of re-socialization that comes about through near-total transformation of subjective reality. Cases of alternation require at least three social conditions: the availability of an effective plausibility structure that is mediated to the individual by means of significant others, the displacing of previous worlds by means of the new plausibility structure (geographically, ideally, but mentally at minimum), and the forming of a legitimating apparatus that reinterprets the old reality.[104] In alternation, an individual disaffiliates themselves from their previous community and enters a new

---

100. Berger and Luckmann, *Social Construction*, 144–45.

101. Berger and Luckmann, *Social Construction*, 155.

102. Berger, *Sacred Canopy*, 47–50.

103. The same is true of identity, precluding any essentialist notions of the self. See Ybema et al., "Articulating Identities," 306.

104. Berger and Luckmann, *Social Construction*, 157–60.

community mediating a new reality. Alternated individuals, i.e., converts, thus experience a reversal of emplacement and displacement, alien and familiar, abnormal and normal.[105] In cases where re-socialization is only minimally effective, "cool alternation" may result whereby individuals internalize the new reality, but only for specific purposes, performances, and roles.[106] Since identity is essentially a product of socialization, full alternation will necessitate identity transformation while cool alternation may not.

Berger and Luckmann's social constructivist epistemology, as is apparent in this brief survey, grounds identity in humanly constructed and processual realities. World-building is the collective enterprise whereby one not only produces a world but also produces oneself.[107] As a result, identity is essentially understood as one's location in a social world.[108] This theoretical supposition underpins not only Berger and Luckmann's sociology of knowledge but also social psychology's theorization of the self as developed in the social identity approach. To this theory we now turn.

Social Identity

Social psychology, as the scientific study of human social behavior, has largely conceptualized issues of self and identity from within the domain of interpersonal interaction.[109] Concern with the personal self rather than the collective self[110] has dominated theoretical and empirical accounts of identity, even when group processes and intergroup relations are the objects of investigation.[111] In contrast, the social identity approach, as initially developed by Henri Tajfel (1919–1982) and John C. Turner (1947–2011), sets out

---

105. See also Steinbock, *Home and Beyond*; Bouma-Prediger and Walsh, *Beyond Homelessness*; Casey, *Getting Back into Place*.

106. Berger and Luckmann, *Social Construction*, 172.

107. Berger, *Sacred Canopy*, 6.

108. Berger et al., *Homeless Mind*, 73.

109. Hogg and Abrams, *Social Identifications*, 8.

110. Marilynn Brewer and Wendy Gardner identify two basic categories of the self: the personal self ("those aspects of the self-concept that differentiate the self from all others") and the social self ("those aspects of the self-concept that reflect assimilation to others or significant social groups"). Within the social self are interpersonal (or relational) identities which are formed through personalized bonds of attachment with specific others and collective identities which are derived from "membership in larger, more impersonal collectives or social categories." The social identity approach is concerned primarily with collective identities. Brewer and Gardner, "Who Is This 'We'?," 83.

111. Ellemers et al., "Self and Social Identity," 162.

Identity Formation in Sociocultural Perspective

to explain "how people's conception of who they are (their self-concept) is associated with their membership of social groups and categories, and with group and intergroup behaviors."[112] Underlying social identity research is an "anti-individualistic metatheory," operating on the fundamental hypothesis that "individuals define themselves in terms of their social group memberships and that group-defined self-perception produces psychologically distinctive effects in social behavior."[113] In other words, this approach places the emphasis in research not on the *individual in the group* but rather on the *group in the individual*.[114] This section will discuss what is commonly known as the "social identity approach" or "social identity perspective," comprising two primary theories: social identity theory and self-categorization theory. After surveying both theories, highlighting the role of collective processes on individual identity formation, we will conclude with an application of social identity theory for interdependent cultural contexts and ethnic identity.

Social identity theory was initially developed to explicate intergroup discrimination and its application to real-life social conflict and change. As opposed to traditional theories that focused on patterns of individual prejudice and discrimination, Tajfel and Turner looked to group categorization and group membership as key determinants in understanding cases of intergroup conflict. They began by suggesting that human interaction ranges on a spectrum between two extremes of social behavior. At one extreme is interpersonal behavior in which the interaction between individuals is fully determined by their interpersonal relationships and individual characteristics. At the other extreme is intergroup behavior in which interactions are fully determined by their memberships in social groups or categories.[115] The more intense is an intergroup conflict, the more likely it is that members of the opposing groups will behave toward each other according to their respective group memberships.[116]

---

112. Hogg, "Social Identity Theory," 749.
113. Turner, "Foreword," vii–viii.
114. Hogg and Abrams, *Social Identifications*, 3.
115. Social groups are "two or more individuals who share a common social identification of themselves or, which is nearly the same thing, perceive themselves to be members of the same social category" (John C. Turner quoted in Hogg and Abrams, *Social Identifications*, 7). Social categories refer to the division of people on the basis of race, class, religion, nationality, etc. that define an individual's place in society and exist in contrast with another category. Hogg and Abrams, *Social Identifications*, 13.
116. Tajfel and Turner, "Integrated Theory," 34.

A key component of intergroup behavior is social competition. Based on experimental research known as the "minimal group paradigm," Tajfel and Turner found that competitive group behavior arises under the most minimal of conditions. In one study, simply telling participants that one was a member of a group, even on the arbitrary basis of a flip of a coin, was enough for them to form an in-group bias while maximizing out-group differentiation.[117] These findings indicate that by making salient "us and them" distinctions, people naturally enhance similarities within the group and differences among groups. The reason for this, the authors believe, lies in the individual's desire to maintain or enhance self-esteem. In order to have a positive self-concept, people are motivated to think of their groups as good groups that are positively distinct from and superior to relevant out-groups.[118] In cases where social identity is unsatisfactory due to relative group inferiority, members may leave the group, redefine elements of the comparative situation, or directly compete with the out-group in an attempt to bolster positive social identity.[119] These processes, Tajfel and Turner conclude, not only underlie cases of intergroup conflict but also form the basis for ethnocentric behavior.[120]

While social identity theory is primarily a conceptualization of intergroup behavior, self-categorization theory targets the cognitive processes inherent in intragroup behavior. Building on the distinction between personal identity (*me* versus *not me* categorizations) and social identity (*us* versus *them* categorizations), self-categorization theory argues that at certain times the self is categorized and defined in terms of a social class of people outside the individual person doing the experiencing.[121] Identities, the theory argues, are context-dependent and, therefore, fluid; that is, the relevant social context determines which categorizations are most suitable to guide behavior within that context.[122] The salience of social categorizations is guided by fit. "Fit refers to the extent to which the social categories are perceived to reflect social reality; that is, the extent to which they are seen to be diagnostic of real-world differences."[123] A high level of fit ensues when category distinctions maximize

117. Tajfel and Turner, "Integrated Theory," 38–39.
118. Hornsey, "Social Identity Theory," 206–7.
119. Tajfel and Turner, "Integrated Theory," 43–44.
120. Tajfel and Turner, "Integrated Theory," 45; Turner, "Social Identity."
121. Turner et al., "Self and Collective," 454.
122. Ellemers et al., "Self and Social Identity," 165.
123. Hornsey, "Social Identity Theory," 208.

Identity Formation in Sociocultural Perspective

perceived intergroup differences and minimize intragroup differences, either at the level of general comparison (comparative fit) or group-determined, normative beliefs (normative fit). For example, while one may prioritize one's "Frenchness" when compared to Americans, he or she may prioritize his or her "Catholicness" when compared to Protestants.[124] The context, therefore, determines the relative fit of a given social categorization based on perceived differences or similarities.

A key behavioral consequence of this process of self-categorization is depersonalization or stereotyping whereby people are "perceived as, are reacted to, and act as embodiments of the relevant in-group prototype rather than as unique individuals."[125] As social categories become salient, there is a tendency to perceive both the in-group and the relevant out-group in homogenous terms. *They* (e.g., the French) always believe and behave according to certain predictable patterns while *we* (e.g., Americans) believe and behave differently. This process of stereotyping functions to enhance group cohesion and cooperation and forms the basis for "social attraction," positive feelings toward members of the in-group that are governed by prototypicality rather than by personal preferences or friendships.[126] It is important to remember, however, that, like categorization salience, the content of a prototype varies with context. As in-group/out-group comparisons change within a particular setting, so, too, does the relevant stereotypical features.[127] In sum, self-categorization theory argues that social identity emerges as people in a given context self-categorize according to certain prototypical features that are shared by the in-group and distinguished from the out-group, thus making the self "the expression of a dynamic process of social judgment" that is variable according to social context.[128]

Two applications of social identity and self-categorization theories are pertinent to this research. First, this approach to social identity comports

---

124. Brewer and Gardner argue that not only do changes in levels of self-categorization reflect differences in views of the self, but also differences in worldviews. As self-definition adjusts according to the categorization salient in a given context, so, too, does one's salient "values, beliefs, and cognitive representations of the social world" (Brewer and Gardner, "Who Is This 'We'?," 91–92).

125. Hogg et al., "Tale of Two Theories," 261.

126. Hogg, "Social Identity Theory," 750.

127. Turner et al., "Self and Collective," 457–58.

128. Turner et al., "Self and Collective," 458; Onorato and Turner, "Fluidity in the Self-Concept," 275–76.

well with recent psychological research on non-Western construals of the self. In their highly influential article "Culture and the Self: Implications for Cognition, Emotion, and Motivation,"[129] Hazel Rose Markus and Shinobu Kitayama argue for a two-fold categorization of self-construals based on cultural difference: the independent view of the self predominant in Western societies versus the interdependent view of the self exemplified in non-Western societies.[130] The independent construal of the self arises from "a faith in the inherent separateness of distinct persons."[131] The independent self organizes behavior according to a belief in the unique configuration of internal attributes and the consequent need for self-actualization. Others are important as standards of reflected appraisal that serve to verify and affirm the inner core of the self. By contrast, interdependent construals of the self view the self "as interdependent with the surrounding context, and it is the 'other' or the 'self-in-relation-to-other' that is focal in individual experience."[132] Behavior is guided not by the inner self, but by the thoughts, feelings, and actions of others in the relationship, particularly of the in-group. Markus and Kitayama argue that the "self-system"[133] of interdependent selves results in certain cognitive, emotive, and motivational consequences as distinct from independent selves. The authors provide the table below to summarize these consequences:

Feature compared	Independent	Interdependent
Definition	Separate from social context	Connected with social context
Structure	Bounded, unitary, stable	Flexible, variable
Important features	Internal, private (abilities, thoughts, feelings)	External, public (statuses, roles, relationships)

129. Markus and Kitayama, "Culture and the Self."

130. University of Michigan social psychologist Richard E. Nisbett presents a similar case for the fundamental difference in cognitive processes between Westerners and East Asians. See Nisbett, *Geography of Thought*.

131. Markus and Kitayama, "Culture and the Self," 226.

132. Markus and Kitayama, "Culture and the Self," 225.

133. Defined as the assortment of self-relevant schemata that evaluate, organize, and regulate one's experience and action.

Identity Formation in Sociocultural Perspective

Feature compared	Independent	Interdependent
Tasks	Be unique	Belong, fit-in
	Express self	Occupy one's proper place
	Realize internal attributes	Engage in appropriate action
	Promote own goals	Promote others' goals
	Be direct; "say what's on your mind"	Be indirect; "read other's minds"
Role of others	Self-evaluation: others important for social comparison, reflected appraisal	Self-definition: relationships with others in specific contexts define the self
Basis of self-esteem	Ability to express self, validate internal attributes	Ability to adjust, restrain self, maintain harmony with social context

Table 1: Summary of Key Differences Between an
Independent and Interdependent Construal of Self[134]

Their findings demonstrate that the psychological processes of non-Western individuals tend to be more directed by the social self, whether interpersonal or collective, than by the personal self. They conclude,

> The most significant difference between these two construals is in the role that is assigned to the other in self-definition. Others and the surrounding social context are important in both construals, but for the interdependent self, others are included within the boundaries of the self because relations with others in specific contexts are the defining features of the self. In the words of Lebra (1976), the individual is in some respects "a fraction" and becomes whole when fitting into or occupying one's proper place in a social unit.[135]

A final point of application as it relates to social identity and the phenomenon under investigation regards the nature and expression of ethnic identity. Ethnic identity, according to the social identity approach, is essentially a social categorization that may become salient in certain contexts, resulting in stereotypical in-group/out-group ethnic comparisons. The content of these comparisons is not static and well defined but fluid, according

---

134. Markus and Kitayama, "Culture and the Self," 230.
135. Markus and Kitayama, "Culture and the Self," 245–46.

to what an individual or group regards as significant for a particular context. In other words, ethnic identities are processual and socially constructed, generated in interaction at boundaries, and variable according to the relevant out-group.[136] However, these identities are not arbitrary but rather stem from what Clifford Geertz calls "primordial attachments," such as assumed blood ties, race, language, geographical region, religion, or custom.[137] The relevance of these attachments varies according to a process of ethnic identity negotiation, involving both internal definition (i.e., self-identification) and external definition (i.e., categorization).[138] As a result of this negotiation, one may experience either "ethnic thickness," a strong identification with and connection to one's group, or "ethnic thinness," a weak identification with and connection to one's group.[139]

Social identity theorization highlights the cognitive processes underlying group identity dynamics, concluding that identity formation is not simply a matter of personal or interpersonal processes. It is essentially an "anti-individualistic metatheory" that has far-reaching implications for understanding identity formation, including ethnic identity, in non-Western societies. As a result, the social identity approach provides a germane horizon for a phenomenological investigation of Christian religious experience in Thailand.

CONCLUSION

In this chapter, we have surveyed pertinent theorizations within the disciplines of sociology, anthropology, and psychology as they relate to the experience of marginality and the formation of identity. We have noted important distinctions inherent in marginality theory, including the difference between strangers as newcomers, "marginal men" as dual-culture or dual-race, and liminars as undergoing a period of marginality within a single culture. We have also approached issues of identity formation and transformation from a social constructivist and social psychology standpoint. In both traditions, identity formation is a fluid and social enterprise, encompassing an internal/external dialectic that is both personal and collective. Understanding identity construction for marginal individuals, then, requires careful attunement to the self-in-community, especially as it relates

---

136. Jenkins, *Social Identity*, 102–3. See also Jenkins, *Rethinking Ethnicity*.

137. Geertz, *Interpretation of Cultures*, 259–63.

138. Jenkins, *Rethinking Ethnicity*, 49.

139. Gushiken, "Is a Christian Identity Compatible with an Ethnic Identity?," 35.

to in-group/out-group cognitive and relational processes. These theorizations, therefore, will aid our interpretation of the interview data, allowing us to reveal the intersubjective components inherent in the phenomenon of in-marginality. Before we move to that interpretation, however, we must first review the nature of religious identity formation as an experiential and intersubjective transfer of sacred worlds. To do that we will now turn to the diverse yet fertile discipline of philosophical phenomenology.

2

Phenomenology of the Sacred Homeworld

INTRODUCTION

As occurring in the field of the philosophy of religious experience, this research is pursuing a phenomenological account of the Thai Christian experience of in-marginality that emerges from religious alternation. As a methodology, phenomenology will provide access to the lived world of Thai Christians, allowing for an emic analysis based on in-depth interviews. However, as a philosophy, the phenomenological tradition, rooted in the influential works of Edmund Husserl and Martin Heidegger, presents a horizon that has much to contribute toward adumbrating the essential themes under investigation. So far, we have reviewed theorizations within the human sciences that pertain to issues of conversion within contexts of marginalization. In this chapter, we will survey contributions in philosophical phenomenology as they relate to the concepts of world, intersubjectivity, home, and the sacred. Overall, I will suggest that fundamental to any religious experience is a pre-cognitive, sacred lifeworld that orients the religious person platially,[1] bodily, and intersubjectively.

PHENOMENOLOGY OF WORLD

In everyday parlance, the concept of "world" is readily understood, albeit under numerous guises. While we speak of historical, cultural, social, planetary, or even personal worlds with familiar acuity, the concept itself, as it

---

1. The adverbial form of the word "place," which carries significant phenomenological meaning as distinct from "space." See discussion below.

Phenomenology of the Sacred Homeworld

spans these various senses, is rarely clarified systematically. What is a world and how do humans inhabit a world? As a philosophy of appearances, phenomenology, beginning with Husserl, has been naturally preoccupied with the world problematic. German philosopher Klaus Held goes so far as to suggest, "The world is the actual subject matter of phenomenology."[2] In this section, we will survey the world-concept as investigated phenomenologically, particularly in the writings of Edmund Husserl and Martin Heidegger. For purposes of clarity and to highlight specific themes directly related to the phenomenon under investigation, the primordial intersubjective nature of the world-concept will be discussed in a later section.

The Moravian philosopher Edmund Husserl (1859–1938) is widely regarded as the founder of the phenomenological movement. Initially trained as a mathematician, in 1884 Husserl engaged in philosophical studies under Franz Brentano, having been stimulated by Brentano's descriptive psychology and his conception of intentionality.[3] Early in his career, Husserl pursued a philosophical analysis of the methods and unproven presuppositions of mathematics, an inquiry which inspired his later attempts to reform philosophy into a neo-Cartesian "science grounded on an absolute foundation" that reduces appearances to their "pure Essence" (*eidos*).[4] In pursuit of this transcendental philosophy, Husserl understood the concept of world as the universal horizon wherein all appearances have their place.[5] Husserl's early works approached this universal horizon from the standpoint of a transcendental phenomenology of world-constitution, while the later Husserl applied a genetic and generative phenomenology of the lifeworld.[6] Both standpoints will be considered.

---

2. Held, "Finitude of the World," 187.

3. Moran, *Introduction*, 23. Intentionality is understood as the directedness of the cogito; that is, every act of consciousness is a consciousness *of* something. Meaning is not found only in the object or in the subject, but in the intentional relationship between subject and object. See Husserl, *Ideas*, 108.

4. Husserl, *Cartesian Meditations*, 1; *Ideas*, 40; Buckley, "Edmund Husserl," 326.

5. Held, "World, Emptiness, Nothingness," 154.

6. While we may see a change of priority from Husserl's earlier writings to his later writings, there are no fixed, clear-cut stages. As Anthony Steinbock argues, there are "strains of thought or methodological motivations running throughout his work that are often interwoven with other strains or motivations" (Steinbock, "Homeworld/Alienworld," 70).

Strangers in a Familiar Land

In the natural attitude,[7] all human subjects have an awareness of a spatio-temporal world[8] that they experience immediately and intuitively and in which objects are given to them in a manifold of profiles or adumbrations.[9] This world offers a background or horizon of possible experiences. As an object is genuinely perceived by consciousness, it is also, at the same time, potentially perceived spatially and temporally in its "field of perception" and is given as situated in a sense-referential context of potentially perceived objects.[10] This involves a sense of "I can" wherein references implicit in a horizon may be given to consciousness as explicit themes.[11] These possibilities open up further experiences within new horizons which, taken together, represent a single nexus of infinite possibilities for all conceivable horizons—i.e., the world as universal horizon.[12] As Husserl explains, "All actual experiences refers (*sic*) beyond itself to possible experiences, which themselves again point to new possible experiences, and so *in infinitum*.... Every hypothetical construction of practical life and of empirical science is related to this shifting but ever-present horizon through which the world-thesis receives its essential meaning."[13]

However, for Husserl, the world-horizon as assumed in the natural attitude presents a barrier to uncovering pure essence as constituted in the absolute existence of consciousness. This is because consciousness itself is not part of the world but is the reason why a world exists for us in the first place. The world is a "phenomenon of being" such that, whether it objectively exists or not,[14] is still mine.[15] It is constituted—that is, opened up or made meaningful—by consciousness. In sum, without consciousness, there is no world.[16] Thus, for Husserl, philosophy is

---

7. The natural attitude or standpoint is the naïve, unreflective, and everyday experiencing of the "fact-world" that is always there as a taken-for-granted reality, antecedent to any theorization. Husserl, *Ideas*, 96, 140. See also Moran, *Introduction*, 142.

8. Husserl calls this world a surrounding world or world-about-me (*Umwelt*). Husserl, *Ideas*, 93.

9. Husserl, *Logical Investigations*, 155–57.

10. Husserl, *Ideas*, 91–93; *Cartesian Meditations*, 44–45.

11. Husserl, *Cartesian Meditations*, 45.

12. Held, "Finitude of the World," 188, 190; Landgrebe, "World as a Phenomenological Problem," 39.

13. Husserl, *Ideas*, 135.

14. For Husserl's thought experiment on world nullification, see Husserl, *Ideas*, 137.

15. Husserl, *Cartesian Meditations*, 18–23; *Ideas*, 139.

16. Moran, *Introduction*, 144.

Phenomenology of the Sacred Homeworld

grounded in "transcendental subjectivity" whereby one turns not to the world, but "to the *ego cogito* as the ultimate and apodictically certain basis for judgments."[17] This turn necessitates a bracketing or putting out of play[18] of anything belonging to the world, even the world itself according to the natural attitude, so that one may apprehend the pure ego via the transcendental-phenomenological reduction.[19] In this way, the world as universal horizon, or as ground for the natural attitude, becomes itself a phenomenon or object for pure and absolute consciousness.

Later in his life, Husserl began to see the shortcomings inherent in his "Cartesian way," that is, the transcendental method of bracketing the world in order to probe pure consciousness. "While it leads to the transcendental ego in one leap," Husserl admitted, "it brings this ego into view as apparently empty of content, since there can be no preparatory explanation; so one is at a loss, at first, to know what has been gained by it."[20] As a supplement, Husserl proposed a new regressive approach that begins with the structures of the lifeworld (*Lebenswelt*),[21] or the prescientific "ground of human world-life," and moves toward an eidetic and eventually transcendental description of the constitutive conditions of world-experience.[22] In our mundane, pre-philosophical understanding, we may apprehend world as composed of a particular set of categories, customs, values, and rules of conduct for a particular sociocultural group in a particular period of time. This is not just *a* world, but *the* world that is always already there for those people, having arisen through historical, embodied, and intersubjective processes.[23] However, this sense of world, even though it is the sense most commonly utilized in the sociological and anthropological sciences, is merely incidental. These mundane and diverse sociocultural worlds do not, in themselves, effectively describe the essential structures of the lifeworld as both ground and horizon, but they

---

17. Husserl, *Cartesian Meditations*, 18.

18. Husserl called this bracketing the *epoché* (ἐποχή), a term from early Greek philosophy meaning abstention.

19. Husserl, *Cartesian Meditations*, 20–21; *Ideas*, 99–100, 140.

20. Husserl, *Crisis*, 155.

21. Lifeworld (*Lebenswelt*) may be taken as equivalent to Husserl's earlier notions of surrounding world (*Umwelt*). See Oliveira, "Husserl, Heidegger," 134. For a detailed typology of Husserl's notion of lifeworld, see Steinbock, *Home and Beyond*, 87–88.

22. Husserl, *Crisis*, 154–55. Steinbock, *Home and Beyond*, 84.

23. Husserl, *Crisis*, 280–81, 317; Landgrebe, "World as a Phenomenological Problem," 52–53.

do provide "leading clues" for doing so.[24] By starting with the lifeworld as always already there,[25] phenomenology can then investigate both the temporal genesis and socio-historical generation of meaning in order to reveal the essential constitution of the world.[26] Therefore, Husserl's later thought allowed for a phenomenology that takes the world as a possible starting point, not in its modes of givenness but its cultural, historical, normative, and intersubjective modes of pregivenness.[27]

Husserl's student and eventual successor at the University of Freiburg, Martin Heidegger (1889–1976), had a complex personal and professional relationship with his mentor.[28] While always remaining a self-proclaimed phenomenologist, Heidegger moved beyond Husserl's transcendental phenomenology with its priority on the absolute and worldless ego, arguing, instead, for a "fundamental ontology"[29] that seeks to provide an "anti-Cartesian, anti-subjectivist, anti-dualist, and anti-intellectualist" exploration of humans as bound up in a world through "concernful" dealing.[30] In other words, rather than pursuing an analysis of *how* the world is constituted for consciousness, Heidegger aligned with a phenomenology of the world that is closer to Husserl's lifeworld-concept; that is, revealing *Dasein*[31] in its average everydayness as always already absorbed in a world.[32]

The basic or essential state of *Dasein*, for Heidegger, is "being-in-the-world."[33] One does not first have an internal essence by which he or she then occasionally takes up a relationship with the world as something

---

24. Steinbock, "Husserl's Static and Genetic Phenomenology."

25. Or, as Husserl avers, "To live is always to live-in-certainty-of-the-world" (Husserl, *Crisis*, 142).

26. Or, as Husserl labels them, the genetic and generative analyses of meaning. Husserl, *Crisis*, 253–55, 280–83, 321.

27. Steinbock, "Homeworld/Alienworld," 71–72.

28. For a summary of this complex relationship, see Kisiel, "Husserl and Heidegger"; Oliveira, "Husserl, Heidegger,"; Moran, *Introduction*; Held, "Finitude of the World."

29. Heidegger's fundamental ontology, or "existential analytic of *Dasein*," understands *Dasein* (humans) as essentially concerned about being, particularly being in a world. Therefore, phenomenology must first answer the question of the meaning of being in order to adequately attend to the "things themselves" (Heidegger, *Being and Time*, 33–34). See also Nenon, "Martin Heidegger," 300.

30. Moran, *Introduction*, 193.

31. *Dasein*, literally "being-there," is Heidegger's way of referring to persons as the kind of being for whom its being is an issue for it. Heidegger, *Being and Time*, 27, 32.

32. Heidegger, *Being and Time*, 36–38.

33. Heidegger, *Being and Time*, 78.

Phenomenology of the Sacred Homeworld

out there or "present-at-hand." Instead, *Dasein* is what it is because it inhabits a world. "It is always 'outside' alongside entities which it encounters and which belong to a world already discovered."[34] Stated differently, "The world is 'in' one's own existence and existence is 'in' the world, in the sense that the world is human and humans are worldly."[35] As Heidegger insists, "a bare subject without a world never 'is' proximally, nor is it ever given"; therefore, it is impossible to understand the pure ego through a Husserlian bracketing of the world. Instead, we approach *Dasein* in its practical, historical, and non-cognitive bodily comportment with things in its surrounding world (*Umwelt*).[36]

To clarify this conception of being-in-the-world, Heidegger performed an ontology of the "worldhood of the world."[37] *Dasein*, in its everydayness, operates in the world through practical dealings. I do not encounter things as they are in themselves in objective space (present-at-hand) but as "equipment" (ready-to-hand) or objects in my proximal environment that are there for my practical, bodily engagement. For example, the hammer typically shows itself as ready-for-hammering, not as an object made of wood and steel with certain spatial dimensions and weight. Heidegger states,

> In dealings such as this, where something is put to use, our concern subordinates itself to the "in-order-to" which is constitutive for the equipment we are employing at the time; the less we just stare at the hammer-Thing, and the more we seize hold of it and use it, the more primordial does our relationship to it become, and the more unveiledly is it encountered as that which it is—as equipment.[38]

Further, equipment is always encountered within a referential totality, or context, of equipment. Through "circumspection," we encounter the equipment non-thematically in a surrounding environment of equipment wherein everything has its place.[39] Therefore, *Dasein* does not engage the world, primordially, through cognitive acts of meaning-giving whereby objects in the world become thematic, but through "absorbed coping," or the inconspicuous familiarity we have beforehand with the world.[40]

---

34. Heidegger, *Being and Time*, 89.
35. Dahlberg et al., *Reflective Lifeworld Research*, 79.
36. Heidegger, *Being and Time*, 94; Moran, *Introduction*, 228–33.
37. Heidegger, *Being and Time*, 91–95.
38. Heidegger, *Being and Time*, 98.
39. Heidegger, *Being and Time*, 107, 116.
40. Heidegger, *Being and Time*, 137; Dreyfus, "Overcoming the Myth of the Mental,"

While only mentioned briefly, Heidegger understood *Dasein's* "circumspective concern" within its environment as occurring bodily, centering it in a spatial region of what is proximally ready-to-hand.[41] In a like manner, Husserl alluded to the "lived body" (as opposed to the objective physical body), which he described as that in which one "holds sway" kinesthetically and sensationally as the "nullpoint of orientation" in the world.[42] However, it was French phenomenologist Maurice Merleau-Ponty (1908–1961) who went the furthest in developing a phenomenology of the body as the means of one's comportment in the world. Like Heidegger, Merleau-Ponty understood humanity as primordially being-in-the-world; that is, as already in a world constituted for us prior to acts of cognition.[43] However, he also insisted that we always inhabit this world bodily. "The body is our general medium for having a world" in the sense that our body knows, acts, and elicits meaning prior to any act of thought as the work of a pure "I."[44] The unique configuration of our bodies combined with their motor functions within a physical, temporal, and spatial environment results in "matrices of habitual action" whereby the world is given to us in pre-predicative experience.[45] This is an "embodied view of meaning" that "looks for the origins and structures of meaning in the organic activities of embodied creatures in interaction with their changing environments."[46] As a result, the body is our means of communication with the world "as the horizon latent in all our experience and itself ever-present and anterior to every determining thought."[47]

Not only is our being-in-the-world bodily in nature, it is also spatial/platial.[48] Equipment, for Heidegger, never occurs in some random spa-

---

48.

41. Heidegger, *Being and Time*, 82, 135–42.

42. Husserl, *Ideas*, 114–15; *Crisis*, 106–8, 161–64, 215–19. See also Behnke, "Body."

43. Merleau-Ponty, *Phenomenology of Perception*, ix–xvii, 137–41, 369–456; Merleau-Ponty, *Structure of Behavior*, 125–26, 168–69.

44. Merleau-Ponty, *Phenomenology of Perception*, 139–47.

45. Moran, *Introduction*, 419.

46. Johnson, *Meaning of the Body*, 11.

47. Merleau-Ponty, *Phenomenology of Perception*, 92.

48. Jeff Malpas understands space as implying openness or expansiveness and tending toward the "homogenous, the regular, and the uniform." Space is quantifiable and measurable. Place, on the other hand, is bounded or limited, heterogeneous, and is the locus of "meaning, memory and identity." Place has a content and character that belongs to it and, as such, is more qualitative and relational. Malpas, "Thinking Topographically,"

tial position but always has its place for *Dasein* as "to-hand" within the referential totality.[49] Furthermore, as circumspective being-in-the-world, *Dasein* has spatiality by "de-severing" or bringing-close and through directionality, such as right and left.[50] Therefore, *Dasein* is always "there"; that is, in an "existential spatiality" of nearness and farness, familiarity and unfamiliarity, by which it has its world.[51] In fact, it is difficult to think of *Dasein's* being-in-the-world at all without the concreteness of being-in-place. As Edward Casey avers, "To be in the world, to be situated at all, is to be in place."[52] Place is the limit and condition of all that exists. It creates a sense of home, anchoring and orienting us "somewhere in particular," thereby situating our identities geographically, culturally, historically, and socially.[53] Indeed, as Jeff Malpas argues, our entire autobiography, including our memories and even our very identities, are tied to a particular, embodied habitation in the place-world.[54] Therefore, places for us are not arbitrary locations in homogenous, mathematical space, but "sites of interaction and identity; potentials for shaping and being shaped; worlds that provide taken-for-granted environmental and spatial order as that order can offer moments of pleasure and freedom."[55]

This brief survey of the world-concept in phenomenology has revealed what we may call the primordial and embodied situatedness of humans in their place-world. Prior to acts of cognition, and, indeed, as the very ground for those acts, humans are always already absorbed in a historically and culturally sedimented lifeworld that we inhabit bodily as the environment for practical, lived experience.[56] As Husserl's student,

---

3–4. See also O. F. Bollnow, who refers to this distinction as mathematical space vs. lived-space in Bollnow, "Lived-Space."

49. Heidegger calls this a region. Heidegger, *Being and Time*, 136.

50. Heidegger, *Being and Time*, 138–44.

51. Heidegger, *Being and Time*, 171; Blattner, *Heidegger's Being and Time*, 75. See also Heidegger, "Building, Dwelling, Thinking."

52. Casey, *Getting Back into Place*, xv. See also Malpas, *Heidegger and the Thinking of Place*, 113–35.

53. Casey, *Getting Back into Place*, 15, 23, 31.

54. Malpas, *Place and Experience*, 175–93.

55. Seamon, "Place, Place Identity, and Phenomenology," 18.

56. Therefore, a phenomenology of world that highlights the non-cognitive, embodied, and pre-predicative nature of being-in-the-world is not only different from, but also more fundamental than the concept of worldview as understood as a basic system of beliefs about God, the cosmos, and humanity. For a further discussion, see Smith, *Desiring*

Ludwig Landgrebe, rightly observed, "It is essentially impossible to find men in any 'pre-worldly' state, because to be human, to be aware of oneself as a man and to exist as a human self, is precisely to live on the basis of a world.... The world has always been there already, as a presupposition for the possibility of particular experiences in it, a presupposition for anyone anywhere finding himself as a human being."[57] This world-presupposition, however, is never that of a private world of the single individual, but always an intersubjective "with-world" that is formed in and governed by social relationship. To this topic we now turn.

THE INTERSUBJECTIVE LIFEWORLD

As with world, intersubjectivity has occupied a central position for phenomenology.[58] The reason for this seems to have arisen from the intimate and essential interconnection between world and intersubjectivity; that is, every world is always a world with others. In this section, we will briefly introduce Husserl's and Heidegger's respective approaches to intersubjectivity, highlighting their unique phenomenological perspectives on the social world. More time, however, will be dedicated to Alfred Schütz's social phenomenology, particularly his marriage of Husserl's lifeworld-concept with the human sciences as found primarily in his work *The Structures of the Lifeworld*. It is believed that Schütz's treatment of the social structures of the lifeworld presents a useful horizon for adumbrating the essential themes of the phenomenon under investigation.

Intersubjectivity presented a significant problematic for Husserl,[59] given his philosophical preoccupation with the transcendental ego as the "ultimate and apodictically certain basis for judgments."[60] While in the natural attitude we understand that the world about us is there for us all, the transcendental-phenomenological reduction restricted Husserl to the stream of pure consciousness.[61] Therefore, the problem for him was not as much how I understand the other but rather how the other is constituted

---

the Kingdom, 63–71; Smart, *Worldviews*, 11–15; 48–54.

57. Landgrebe, "World as a Phenomenological Problem," 53.

58. Iso Kern suggests that, because it intersects various thematic spheres, intersubjectivity "encompasses the whole of phenomenology" (Kern, "Intersubjectivity," 356).

59. For thorough treatments of Husserl's phenomenology of intersubjectivity, see Haney, *Intersubjectivity Revisited*; Hart, *Person and the Common Life*.

60. Husserl, *Cartesian Meditations*, 18.

61. Husserl, *Ideas*, 95; *Cartesian Meditations*, 89.

Phenomenology of the Sacred Homeworld

for me as an "alter ego."[62] In his famous Fifth Cartesian Meditation, Husserl dealt with this topic by arguing that we do not grasp the other originally and fully, but rather as an "appresentation." As we encounter the body of the other, we immediately apprehend it as an animate organism with a set of "psychic determinations" analogous to my own.[63] Husserl argued that our ability to "pair" with others in this way is through empathy or, as Bruce Bradfield explains, the "intuitive reliving of the experience of the other, whilst acknowledging that the experience 'belongs' to the other."[64] Therefore, Husserl's transcendental phenomenology of the other was grounded in a self-understanding by which the world is constituted as an "objective world, as a world that is identical for everyone."[65]

As could be expected, Martin Heidegger approached the problem of the other from a significantly different angle. Rather than grounding intersubjectivity in the transcendental ego by which one constitutes others through pairing, he argued that we always already encounter others through our circumspective absorption in the world as a "with-world" (*Mitwelt*).[66] "Being-with," like being-in-the-world, is essential or primordial to *Dasein*. As we "concernfully" deal in a proximal environment of what is ready-to-hand, we are always, at the same time, encountering others who share this world as *Daseins* themselves.[67] Therefore, others are not constituted by subjective consciousness, but belong to the very being of *Dasein* itself. "As Being-with, *Dasein* 'is' essentially for the sake of Others."[68] Furthermore, in everyday concern, Heidegger argued, others

---

62. Husserl, *Cartesian Meditations*, 90.

63. Husserl, *Cartesian Meditations*, 109, 112–14. Of course, Husserl's treatment of intersubjectivity is much more complex and diverse than can be treated in this brief survey. For an introductory analysis of this diversity, see Duranti, "Husserl"; Kern, "Intersubjectivity."

64. Bradfield, "Examining the Lived World," 5–6; Husserl, *Ideas*, 387; *Cartesian Meditations*, 120; *Crisis*, 231, 255.

65. Edmund Husserl quoted in Moran, *Introduction*, 178–79. Emmanuel Levinas directly attacked Husserl's account of the other, contending that the other is not encountered as another me, but always as a transcendental "face," leading to a primordial ethic whereby the other has priority over the self. Levinas, *Totality and Infinity*.

66. Heidegger, *Being and Time*, 155.

67. Heidegger, *Being and Time*, 156.

68. Heidegger, *Being and Time*, 160. Along these lines, Heidegger argued that empathy, therefore, is not the basis for constituting intersubjectivity (a la Husserl), but is itself only possible because *Dasein* is the kind of being who has "being-with." Heidegger, *Being and Time*, 162.

are given to us as the "they" (*das Man*).⁶⁹ The "they" is the shared social horizon that determines what is normative for a given society. It is the way one does things such that it is understood as normal or average for all members of society.⁷⁰ In its everydayness, then, *Dasein* "draws its pre-ontological way of interpreting its Being" from the "they," thereby leading to what Heidegger called "inauthenticity."⁷¹

Alfred Schütz, while heavily influenced by the writings of Husserl, sought to produce an original, systematic phenomenology and sociology of the lifeworld that was on the frontier between philosophy and social science.⁷² To accomplish this, Schütz focused his attention on the everyday life or paramount reality of the natural attitude. The everyday world, Schütz argued, is not just a world of individual consciousness and other objects, but is, from the outset, "an intersubjective world, common to all of us, in which we have not a theoretical but an eminently practical interest."⁷³ Unlike Husserl's attempt to solve the problem of intersubjectivity through transcendental subjectivity, Schütz believed that this intersubjective world must be approached as the fundamental precondition for all human experience that is unquestionably accepted by members of a society.⁷⁴ Two key features of Schütz's social phenomenology, the "we-relationship" and the "social stock of knowledge," are of particular significance.

If the intersubjective world functions as the everyday, presupposed condition for all human experience, how exactly do we enter into relations with the other? Schütz answered this question through a careful categorization of the diverse structures of social relations. He began in a similar way as Husserl, claiming, "All experience of social reality is founded on the fundamental axiom positing the existence of other beings, 'like me.'"⁷⁵ With a resemblance to pairing and empathy, Schütz argued that relations with the other are founded upon a "reciprocity of perspectives," meaning that we relate to the other through our ability to interchange standpoints

---

69. Heidegger, *Being and Time*, 164. This term has also been translated as "the one" (Hubert Dreyfus) or "the anyone" (William Blattner).

70. Blattner, *Heidegger's Being and Time*, 69–70.

71. Inauthenticity refers to the kind of being-in-the-world that is "completely fascinated by the 'world' and by the *Dasein*-with of Others in the 'they'" (Heidegger, *Being and Time*, 166–68, 220).

72. Luckmann, "Preface," xiii; Kersten, "Alfred Schütz," 636–39.

73. Schütz, *On Phenomenology and Social Relations*, 73.

74. Wagner, "Introduction," 31.

75. Schütz and Luckmann, *Structures 1*, 61.

Phenomenology of the Sacred Homeworld

and align with them regarding what is relevant for acting in a shared world.[76] At its most intimate, we perform this reciprocity of perspectives within the "we-relationship." Through face-to-face encounters with the other, we enter one another's stream of consciousness in the vivid present, what Schütz called, "growing old together," forming a common environment in which we are aware of and sympathetically participate in the lives of others.[77] These encounters treat the other as a "Thou," as a person like me, developing and confirming the intersubjectivity of the lifeworld as a world of common experience.[78] However, we do not encounter everyone in this proximal and immediate manner. We have mediate and impersonal relations with certain others from the perspective of a "they-orientation." The most pervasive example of this orientation is our relation with contemporaries, or those with whom one shares the same present span of world time, whom we encounter anonymously by means of "derived typifications" (such as postal employee, police officer, etc.).[79] Finally, besides the we-relationship and the they-orientation, Schütz classified the unique nature of our relationships with both predecessors, whom we encounter passively as already past and fixed, and successors, whom we encounter as completely indeterminable and highly anonymous.[80] Taken together, these diverse relationships, as founded upon the reciprocity of perspectives, form the constitutive relational structures of the lifeworld.

As we experience the social world in all its diversity of relational structures, we experience it as a pre-constituted and pre-organized world of ready-made cultural patterns that are accepted unquestionably as a matter of fact. These patterns are handed down by a society as "trustworthy recipes for interpreting the social world and for handling things and men in order to obtain the best results in every situation with a minimum of effort by avoiding undesirable consequences."[81] Schütz called these patterns "thinking as usual," or the "of-course" assumptions of a particular social group that forms,

---

76. Schütz and Luckmann, *Structures 1*, 60. Schütz also argued, in line with Husserl, that we grasp the psychological life of the other through appresentation. Schütz, *On Phenomenology and Social Relations*, 164.

77. Schütz, *On Phenomenology and Social Relations*, 184–87.

78. Schütz and Luckmann, *Structures 1*, 62–68.

79. Schütz and Luckmann, *Structures 1*, 69, 74–77.

80. Schütz, *On Phenomenology and Social Relations*, 231–35; Schütz and Luckmann, *Structures 1*, 87–92.

81. Schütz, *On Phenomenology and Social Relations*, 81.

through a process of historical sedimentation, the social stock of knowledge.[82] As biographically situated entities, humans depend on this stock of knowledge as a scheme of interpretation and a set of typical solutions for everyday, practical existence.[83] It allows for habitual and routine action, eliminates troublesome inquiries, governs social behavior, and defines what is thematically relevant.[84] While the recipes contained in this stock of knowledge are normally proven through practical success and social guarantees, they may, at times, come into consciousness as inadequate for confronting certain everyday problems. In these cases, one may tend toward theoretical thinking in an attempt to form "a new explication of the current experience and of the horizons surrounding it that have now become questionable, or of the schemata which have up until now been regarded as sufficient."[85] These cases are relatively rare, however, as the existence of a common system of typifications, relevances, roles, and positions allow individuals to feel subjectively at home as members of the in-group.[86]

What our brief survey of the intersubjective lifeworld as the locus of our embodied and emplaced situatedness has revealed is that the self, as being-in-the-world, is always a cultural self. As Romin Tafarodi argues, "The only *I* that we can experience and talk about with meaning is embodied and sociohistorically specific, not transcendentally universal."[87] Therefore, while phenomenology is not in the business of describing the factual-empirical structures explicit and implicit in a given culture (this would be the task of the human sciences), there is an appropriate basis for a "cultural phenomenology" that takes culture seriously in the pursuit of adumbrating the existential meaning structures of phenomena.[88] Perhaps

82. Schütz, *On Phenomenology and Social Relations*, 80–82; Schütz and Luckmann, *Structures 1*, 7–8.

83. Schütz's concepts of thinking as usual and the social stock of knowledge bear a resemblance to Charles Taylor's theorization on the social imaginary. For Taylor, the social imaginary consists "of the ways people imagine their social existence, how they fit together with others, how things go on between them and their fellows, the expectations that are normally met, and the deeper normative notions and images that underlie these expectations." This largely unstructured and inarticulate understanding of our situation forms the background "within which particular features of our world show up for us in the sense they have" (Taylor, *Modern Social Imaginaries*, 23–25).

84. Schütz and Luckmann, *Structures 1*, 108, 125, 204.

85. Schütz and Luckmann, *Structures 1*, 14.

86. Schütz, *On Phenomenology and Social Relations*, 82–83.

87. Tafarodi, "Toward a Cultural Phenomenology of Personal Identity," 30.

88. For more on cultural phenomenology, see Csordas, "Embodiment"; Tafarodi,

the best means of pursuing this cultural phenomenology, particularly as it relates to intersubjectivity, is by applying Husserl's generative phenomenology of homeworld/alienworld. In the next section, therefore, I will present a synopsis of this approach, particularly what it may mean for a phenomenology of home.

A PHENOMENOLOGY OF HOME

Up to this point, we have seen that a world, phenomenologically speaking, is, as Merleau-Ponty quipped, "not what I think, but what I live through."[89] It is the assumed, pre-given, and pre-constituted environment or background for all lived experience, which we primordially inhabit bodily, intersubjectively, and platially. As such, one's world is never just *a* world, it is always *the* world in which one is immersed; that is, it is home. In this section, we will review the phenomenological conception of home as the locus of the intersubjective lifeworld. After a discussion on the lived experience of home, we will proceed to outline Husserl's generative constitution of home as expanded by American phenomenologist Anthony Steinbock.

In his description of the nature of lived space, Max van Manen comments, "Home is where we can *be* what *we are*."[90] We experience home as a place of permanence and familiarity where stories are told, identities are formed, and inhabitants are trusted.[91] Because of this, home is a place of comfort, security, and protection where we can be ourselves. "It is in 'home' where the significance of individual lives is most concentrated, where people feel they belong, where love of place is strongest."[92] However, home can mean different things to different people. It may mean speaking one's mother-tongue, being around certain loved ones, enjoying favorite foods, using familiar objects, living according to personal habits, entering known places, or being immersed in a beloved landscape.[93] Certainly, the concept of home is emotionally evocative and, as a result, difficult to describe, but it is also that which is most cherished and familiar. It is where we live according to an organized pattern of routine with others who follow the same

---

"Toward a Cultural Phenomenology of Personal Identity"; Groark, "Toward a Cultural Phenomenology of Intersubjectivity."

89. Merleau-Ponty, *Phenomenology of Perception*, xvi–xvii.
90. Manen, *Researching Lived Experience*, 102.
91. Bouma-Prediger and Walsh, *Beyond Homelessness*, 56–60.
92. Relph, "Place in Geography," 11449.
93. Schütz, *On Phenomenology and Social Relations*, 296.

predictable system of relevances within a common, proximal space-time environment.[94] In this sense, home is primal to having a world; in fact, it *is* the world we inhabit such that it forms our identities and shapes our existential being-in-the-world.

Where do we find home? Alfred Schütz, in his essay entitled, "The Homecomer," claimed, "The home is the starting-point as well as terminus. It is the null-point of the system of coordinates which we ascribe to the world in order to find our bearings in it."[95] Most commonly, we identify this null-point with a particular physical structure we call a house. While we may say that the earth or a nation or a town is our home, it is one's house that serves as the "reference point from which he builds his spatial world."[96] As the epicenter of our dwelling,[97] the house stands in a "membered spatial surrounding" of concentric regions of familiarity. When we leave the house, we enter a protected neighborhood of trusted relationships, familiar surroundings, and meaningful places. However, as we move further away from the house, we are increasingly overcome by breadth, strangeness, and distance.[98] Eventually, we leave the protective and secure region of home and enter a strange and foreign world where the self becomes threatened by both anomie and atopia.[99] However, while our sense of home is most often tied to a geographical location, it is not necessarily so. It is possible, through our customs, speech, or eating habits, to take home with us as we travel.[100] Conversely, and more related to this research, it is also possible to feel like a stranger within one's own geographical place of birth and residence. To understand why this is so, it is important for us to consider how "home-worlds" are constituted generatively.

Besides the transcendental subjectivity of his "Cartesian way," another strain of Husserl's phenomenology invoked the generative framework of homeworld and alienworld.[101] Husserl had proposed an approach to the

---

94. Schütz, *On Phenomenology and Social Relations*, 297–300.

95. Schütz, *On Phenomenology and Social Relations*, 296. Similarly, Bouma-Prediger and Walsh claim, "Home is the axis of the world, the point of orientation, around which all else makes sense" (Bouma-Prediger and Walsh, *Beyond Homelessness*, 63).

96. Bollnow, "Lived-Space," 32.

97. Heidegger, "Building, Dwelling, Thinking."

98. Bollnow, "Lived-Space," 33–35.

99. Anomie may be defined as the lack of social norms or values while atopia is the estrangement one feels from being displaced. See Casey, *Getting Back into Place*, x–xi.

100. Steinbock, *Home and Beyond*, 234.

101. Husserl, *Cartesian Meditations*, 142; *Crisis*, 253, 281, 321–31. While these

intersubjective lifeworld that moves beyond the world as horizon for immediately experienced modes of givenness to a world that is in the process of becoming, intersubjectively, geologically, and historically, over the generations.[102] Known as generative phenomenology, this approach seeks to uncover the historical character of lifeworlds as co-constituted in the interaction between home and alien.

Generative phenomenology is interested in disclosing the historical generation of homeworlds, which serve as the "normal" environment or milieu for lived experience. Human beings are born into an already-existing, normatively significant lifeworld that is pre-reflectively and affectively familiar.[103] This social and cultural world serves as the territory, both ground and horizon, for sense-constitution and typical, habitual action. It guides our comportment in the world by providing contextual norms that are considered necessary for optimal living in a given community.[104] This is our "homeworld." It is our "first sphere of normality" such that, "an individual is normal only in and by virtue of the normal historical community . . . that is, the 'subject' is always the subject *of* a normal cultural world."[105]

How do homeworlds come into being? They are not simply the product of individual biographies or contemporary, communal lived experience. Instead, they arise "geo-historically" and intersubjectively through the sedimentation of a historical tradition via encounters between home and alien.[106] Neither home nor alien is, by itself, an original sphere. Instead, as Anthony Steinbock argues, they are co-generative in that there is a "co-constitution of the alien through appropriative experience of the home," and a "co-constitution of the home through the transgressive experience of the alien."[107] What this means is that a homeworld, as the "normal" lifeworld for an individual person or society, arises historically over generations of

---

concepts originated with Husserl, this section will primarily review Anthony Steinbock's non-foundational account of Husserl's generative phenomenology. Steinbock, *Home and Beyond*.

102. Steinbock, *Home and Beyond*, 3, 172.

103. Steinbock, *Home and Beyond*, 151–53.

104. Steinbock, *Home and Beyond*, 156–69.

105. Steinbock, "Homeworld/Alienworld," 74.

106. Steinbock, *Home and Beyond*, 171–72. Alien is not to be understood as equivalent to "other." As Steinbock explains, "other" simply means second while "alien" entails foreignness or strangeness. Steinbock, "Homeworld/Alienworld," 73–74. See also Steinbock, *Home and Beyond*, 59.

107. Steinbock, *Home and Beyond*, 190–93.

repeated "liminal"[108] encounters with alienworlds or the "abnormal" lifeworlds of the stranger.[109] While we encounter this alien in the mode of inaccessibility (that is, as having a homeworld themselves with a generatively deep tradition that is irreducible to my homeworld), the alienness of the alien always permeates home experience.[110] Who *we* are arises in distinction to who *they* are. Through repeated encounters with the alien, limits are established but they are also transgressed, allowing the alien to influence the formation of the home and vice versa.[111]

Home, therefore, contains a "generative density," or a tradition, by which sense is handed down through the generations, forming the unique values, norms, and styles of homelife. This is not simply a biophysical process related to blood and race, however. Instead, generative connections arise psychically and transcendentally "by participating in a community or in a tradition; it concerns various styles of homelife, taking up or rejecting the values of a homeworld, repeating or criticizing life and culture through past and future generations."[112] Therefore, it is possible for an outsider to enter into and participate in the generative continuity of an already-existing homeworld by appropriating the tradition of the community. "Because we appropriate a tradition," Steinbock argues, "the sense that was not our 'own,' so to speak, transforms our own being-sense, *we become other through others.*"[113]

How does this appropriation of home take place? First, Steinbock argues that narratives serve to constitute and reconstitute homeworlds, allowing for repeated appropriation over generations. Narratives are effective because they (1) make the history of the homeworld concordant, (2) connect past and present with the future, (3) make sense of competing narratives, (4) allow for renewal of the tradition for each generation, (5) integrate members of a community into the generative structure of life and thought, and (6) provide a mythical orientation that gives meaning to the

---

108. By liminal, Steinbock means, "not merely that home and alien are formed by positing limits, but that they are *mutually delimited* as home and as alien, as normal and as abnormal" (Steinbock, *Home and Beyond*, 179).

109. Steinbock, *Home and Beyond*, 178.

110. Steinbock, *Home and Beyond*, 243–45.

111. Waldenfels, "Boundaries of Orders," 75.

112. Steinbock, *Home and Beyond*, 193.

113. Steinbock, *Home and Beyond*, 196.

Phenomenology of the Sacred Homeworld

past in a way that is concordant with the present.[114] Second, appropriation occurs at varying levels within an intersubjective environment of "home-comrades." In community, homeworlds are constituted and identities are formed. Steinbock states, "The identity of the individual, then, is revealed as a homecomrade in communal and historical interaction. Who we are is *how* we are as home."[115] One need not be acquainted with these homecomrades, however, to share the same homeworld. Instead, "By sharing in the same rituals and customs . . . by bringing to expression our particular generative historicity, we can already participate with others intimately as homecomrades without having to know exactly who each other is."[116] Further, not everyone participates as a homecomrade in the same way. There are varying levels of appropriation and disappropriation, normal and abnormal. The alien may impose itself on some more than others due to age, negligence, revolt, or unique biographical experience. The essence of appropriating a homeworld, therefore, is not simply a matter of co-existing in the same area as others or being born in a certain community but involves inhabiting a community's tradition and participating in its generativity.[117]

This generativity of homeworlds, including the process of appropriation and disappropriation, leads to two important implications. First, homeworlds are not isolated but intersect and overlap with one another. The alien is not necessarily in another country but may exist in the same town or even the same neighborhood, thereby imposing their alienness in close proximity. Second, homeworlds may reside in the past and be preserved through collective memory or narrative. For example, one may move to a foreign country but never feel "at home" in that new land. This may lead to a "homesickness" for one's "primordial homestead," the tradition of which is carried on in memory, imagination, daily customs, etc. A good example of this may be the Jewish Diaspora, which, through the continuation of relatively stable and coherent traditions, maintains its homeworld within foreign lands. In a like manner, Steinbock argues that a homeworld may also reside in the future: a "promised land" that transcends both the geographical and temporal dimensions of current existence.[118]

---

114. Steinbock, *Home and Beyond*, 214–19.
115. Steinbock, *Home and Beyond*, 223.
116. Steinbock, *Home and Beyond*, 224.
117. Steinbock, *Home and Beyond*, 224–30.
118. Steinbock, *Home and Beyond*, 234.

In sum, homeworlds carry within them not only a generative density, but also a "generative momentum."[119] While deeply rooted in geography, community, and specific time periods, homeworlds extend far beyond these particulars. They structure our lived, bodily experience as our "near world" even when we are far away from our home location. Steinbock explains, "Just because I stop actively thinking about a thought that I have been working on for days does not mean that 'I' stop thinking about it; I continue to work on it even when I do not want to, even in my sleep. In the same way the generative momentum of a homeworld works through us even when we ostensibly leave it."[120] Therefore, home is not an automatic given, solely determined by geography, birth, and culture. Instead, as an intersubjectively appropriated tradition, home is a complex entity: always in process, tied to specific communities and traditions, intersecting numerous alienworlds, and, as we will see in the next section, even transcending time and place.

THE SACRED HOMEWORLD

Peter Berger asserts, "Viewed historically, most of man's worlds have been sacred worlds."[121] While the largely desacralized West has exerted a disproportionate influence in forming modern conceptions of the world, often relegating religion to an anthropological projection (Feuerbach) or a psychological neurosis (Freud), the majority of cultures, both geographically and historically, have lived in worlds thoroughly imbued with the transcendent. The human person, as *Homo religiosus*, has pursued the enterprise of world-construction from a distinctly religious perspective, founding homeworlds on hierophanic experiences that serve to orient communities around a sacred fixed point or center. Indeed, as Mircea Eliade (1907–1986) argues, for most humans, "the very fact of living in the world has a religious value."[122]

Despite the pervasiveness of religious experience in forming humanity's being-in-the-world, phenomenology has historically struggled with how to attend to matters of the numinous. If phenomenology is the systematic discussion of what appears, how is it to understand the nature of

---

119. Steinbock, *Home and Beyond*, 234.
120. Steinbock, *Home and Beyond*, 234.
121. Berger, *Sacred Canopy*, 27.
122. Eliade, "World, the City, the House," 191; Petrus and Bogopa, "Natural and Supernatural," 2.

Phenomenology of the Sacred Homeworld

revelation as that which is, by definition, elusive, hidden, or invisible?[123] As a philosophy clearly dominated by presentation as a mode of givenness, how is phenomenology to clarify modes of givenness that transcend the presentation of objects and point to a vertical experience of mystery and reverence?[124] These tensions have given rise to numerous attempts to understand religious experience and the sacred lifeworld under the rubric of the phenomenology of religion.

After summarizing Husserl's and Heidegger's treatment of God, George Kovacs concludes,

> The question of God is not an immediate concern of phenomenology because phenomenology analyzes primarily man's understanding of himself and of the world. Some phenomenologists consider it irrelevant to the scope of phenomenology and thus they try to ignore it. Does this mean, then, that phenomenological thinking has nothing to contribute to this issue? Does phenomenology, indeed, remain entirely neutral and indifferent toward this problem? Phenomenology has much to say about the question of God.[125]

What exactly does phenomenology have to say about the question of God? The discipline of the phenomenology of religion has pursued this concern, albeit from a variety of methodological perspectives. According to Archana Barua, phenomenology of religion is "a 'reflection' on religious 'appearances' . . . a methodological approach to the study of religious phenomena" so as to develop "insight into the essential structures and meanings of religious experience."[126] Its task is not so much to prove or disprove the existence of God but to investigate lived, religious experience from an insider's perspective. Stuart Devenish explains, "For the phenomenology of religion, it is not God who stands at center-stage (because God is not a phenomenon available for scientific study); but is it is the religious believer or community in his [their] presentational actions, thoughts, rituals and sacred dramas which provides the phenomenal material upon which the

---

123. Leeuw, *Religion*, 683; Pearl, "World Restructuring," 13–14. Louis Dupré states the question this way, "How could a phenomenological analysis ever result in an 'essential intuition' (*Wesensschau*) of an object that lies beyond experience?" (Dupré, *Religious Mystery*, 5).

124. Steinbock, *Phenomenology and Mysticism*, 7–13. See also Dupré, *Dubious Heritage*.

125. Kovacs, *Question of God*, 33–34.

126. Barua, *Phenomenology of Religion*, 47.

phenomenology of religion feeds."[127] More will be said about the methodological values and constraints of the phenomenology of religion in chapter 4, but here we will survey the discipline's contributions toward unveiling the lifeworld of *Homo religiosus*.

Based on the assumption that experience is a "reliable medium of disclosure through which the real world is made manifest and comes to be apprehended by us,"[128] early phenomenologists of religion sought to understand the religious world through the primordial experience of transcendence. Rudolf Otto's (1869–1937) classic work *The Idea of the Holy* pioneered the systematic study of this experience by investigating what he called the "non-rational" or "supra-rational" elements of religion.[129] For Otto, that which grounds religious expression is a primordial, numinous experience of the Holy as both *mysterium tremendum* and *fascinans*. On the one hand, the numinous is encountered as "wholly other,"[130] producing intense feelings of awe, dread, and unapproachability. The mysterious and awful majesty of the numinous fills "the mind with blank wonder and astonishment," what Otto called a "stupor," resulting in religious humility and a sense of creaturehood.[131] On the other hand, that which is "wholly other" presents itself at the same time as uniquely attractive and fascinating. Deity entrances the creature, conveys mercy, love, and grace and arouses feelings of yearning and desire. "These two qualities, the daunting and the fascinating," Otto writes, "now combine in a strange harmony of contrasts, and the resultant dual character of the numinous consciousness, to which the entire religious development bears witness . . . is at once the strangest and most noteworthy phenomenon in the whole history of religion."[132] Otto concluded his study by arguing that this dual-nature experience of the Holy, along with its concomitant rational components,

---

127. Devenish, "Dancing Sharma."

128. Smith, "Experience of the Holy," 239.

129. As opposed to the rational elements of religion that involve conceptual attributions of God such as is found in theological discourse. Otto believed that the non-rational and rational elements of religious consciousness interpenetrate to create a single fabric, but religious experience always, by nature, exceeds the rational. Otto, *Idea of the Holy*, 1–4, 44–47.

130. By using this term, Otto is not suggesting that the Holy is beyond experiential awareness for the believer, but simply that the Holy is not to be confused with the subject. See Ryba, "Idea of the Sacred," 27.

131. Otto, *Idea of the Holy*, 26.

132. Otto, *Idea of the Holy*, 31.

Phenomenology of the Sacred Homeworld

is an *a priori* cognition that is qualitatively different from any natural sense perception and attests to its own certitude. "They are themselves not perceptions at all, but peculiar interpretations and valuations, at first of perceptual data, and then—at a higher level—of posited objects and entities, which themselves no longer belong to the perceptual world, but are thought of as supplementing and transcending it."[133] While everyone is capable of having this *a priori* cognition, only those who are "awakened" and given a special "endowment," Otto believed, are genuinely able to recognize the Holy in its appearances and manifestations.[134]

In Otto's wake arose numerous phenomenologists concerned with further uncovering the *eidos* of religious experience. Among them, Gerardus Van der Leeuw (1890-1950) arguably exerted the most influence. In his groundbreaking work *Religion in Essence and Manifestation*, Leeuw presented a wide-ranging typology of religious phenomena rooted in the manifestation of Power. Power is that experience of "Something Other" that may be understood as personal or impersonal, particular or universal, and that causes both fear and attraction. Power establishes boundaries between that which is its own, the sacred, and that which is powerless, the profane.[135] Humans, not content with "mere life," must seek the sacred, "to be replete with Power," leading to certain outward and inward religious actions.[136] In a similar vein, Eliade investigated the experience of the sacred as manifested to man in hierophanies.[137] Eliade, like Leeuw before him, sought an essential typology of the sacred world of the religious person, claiming that the sacred is a particular, existential mode of being-in-the-world.[138] To disclose further the nature of the sacred homeworld, and in light of our previous discussions on the intersubjective lifeworld, we will highlight four components of Leeuw's and Eliade's theses that are of particular importance to this research: sacred place, sacred time, sacred body, and sacred community.[139]

---

133. Otto, *Idea of the Holy*, 113.

134. Otto, *Idea of the Holy*, 144, 177.

135. Leeuw, *Religion*, 23-28, 47.

136. Leeuw, *Religion*, 195.

137. Hierophany he defines simply as "the act of manifestation of the sacred" (Eliade, *Sacred and the Profane*, 11).

138. Eliade, *Sacred and the Profane*, 14.

139. By highlighting the works of Leeuw and Eliade, I am not suggesting that their phenomenological reflections are without fault. As Dupré points out, both phenomenologists, as they pursued their comparative analyses of religious phenomena, "totally

Strangers in a Familiar Land

As we have seen, essential to humanity's having a world is to be situated somewhere in particular. The human subject does not live in homogenous, mathematical space, where all points have equal value, but in a world oriented according to particular places that carry a strong emotive and valuative force. For the religious person, this orientation occurs in relation to the sacred. Leeuw argued that the sacred "must possess a form: it must be 'localizable,' spatially, temporally, visibly or audibly." In other words, the sacred must "take place."[140] Spatially, this occurs through the creation of "positions" in which power and the effects of power are repeated.[141] These sacred spaces are places of worship and may include natural locations, temples, houses, or even entire villages or towns. Whatever the specific location, this space evokes awe due to the manifestation of power, often resulting in it becoming a locus for the practice of religious rituals.[142] For Eliade, the creation of sacred space ontologically founds a world. The breaking of space into that which is sacred and that which is profane "allows the world to be constituted, because it reveals the fixed point, the central axis for all future orientation."[143] This activity, grounded in an hierophanic irruption of the sacred, orients the religious person in the "chaos of homogeneity," allowing them to take up their abode "in a real and effective world."[144] Most fully exemplified in the temple, sacred space opens communication between heaven and earth, effectively "re-sanctifying" the world.[145] Therefore, for Eliade, the formation of sacred space is cosmogenic in nature; it situates the religious person, including their country, city, village, and house, in the "center of the world."[146] As a result, Eliade concludes, "The world becomes apprehensible as world, as cosmos, in the measure in which it reveals itself as a sacred world."[147]

---

sidestepped the ontological problems in an area where those problems were most pressing." A true phenomenology of religion must exceed description and classification by retracing the act of faith from within as centered on a passively-given, "transcendent moment" (Dupré, *Religious Mystery*, 3–8).

140. Leeuw, *Religion*, 447.
141. Leeuw, *Religion*, 393; Chidester, "Poetics and Politics," 214.
142. Leeuw, *Religion*, 394–402.
143. Eliade, *Sacred and the Profane*, 21.
144. Eliade, *Sacred and the Profane*, 26–28; "World, the City, the House," 192.
145. Eliade, *Sacred and the Profane*, 59, 63.
146. Eliade, *Sacred and the Profane*, 43–44.
147. Eliade, *Sacred and the Profane*, 64.

Phenomenology of the Sacred Homeworld

The sacred lifeworld also includes a temporal rhythm that oscillates between intervals of sacred and profane time. Time, like space, is not homogenous. Time is always some definite time within the flowing stream of duration. As the religious person encounters Power, they must halt. "He then makes a section, a *tempus*; and he celebrates a 'sacred time,' a festival."[148] Eventually, Leeuw argued, a liturgical calendar is created that indicates which moments of time possess value and power.[149] Sacred time, since it re-actualizes a sacred event that took place in the mythical past, is indefinitely repeatable.[150] As the religious community celebrates its festival, it does so in continuity with generations that have gone before all the way back to the primordial beginning. As a result, sacred time elevates the religious self above the present, everyday reality of the profane, into the realm of the eternal and the transhuman. It recovers the sacred dimension of life as participants once again "experience the sanctity of human existence as a divine creation."[151] The participation in sacred time and sacred history, therefore, carries salvific significance. As Eliade explains, "For religious man, reactualization of the same mythical events constitutes his greatest hope; for with each reactualization he again has the opportunity to transfigure his existence, to make it like its divine model."[152]

While mentioned only briefly, and certainly not at the depth or originality of Husserl's concept of the lived body, both Leeuw and Eliade referenced the unique embodiment of the sacred self.[153] Much of Leeuw's discussion on the body occurred within his comparative analysis of religious conceptions of the soul; however, he did hint at a more originary sense of sacred embodiment in his chapter on the sacraments. He states,

> Life consists not in man controlling things just as he himself pleases, but in his mobilizing the powerfulness of what appear as things. Actually, in other words, there are no "things": there are only conduits and containers, which under given conditions can retain power within themselves. Thus the "things," with which man comes into contact, are either receptacles which he must fill with power or wheels that he must set in motion . . . they are

---

148. Leeuw, *Religion*, 385.
149. Leeuw, *Religion*, 386–87.
150. Eliade, *Sacred and the Profane*, 69.
151. Eliade, *Sacred and the Profane*, 89.
152. Eliade, *Sacred and the Profane*, 1–6, 107.
153. See also Csordas, *Sacred Self*.

connected with God directly and immediately, and God can at any moment breathe into them new life and grant them fresh potency; He makes instruments of His Power out of "things," He creates and renews them. Thus a deed, a word, a person can at any moment become "powerful," either because of the fullness of power that is in man and that forces power into them, or because of the fullness of Power in God the Creator.[154]

"Things," as much as they are endowed with power, Van der Leew called "sacramentals." This sacralization of the ordinary occurs at a very physical level: food, money, birth, death, sex, etc. That is to say, the sacred self's embodied comportment in the world, from everyday functions to liturgical rituals, emanates from a primordial mobilization and manifestation of Power. Consequently, as Eliade asserts, "life is lived on a twofold plane; it takes its course as human existence and, at the same time, shares in a transhuman life, that of the cosmos or the gods."[155] All of a person's vital experiences may carry spiritual significance, but, even more, their body may be understood as a microcosm of the sacred cosmos, the center of communication with the transcendent.[156]

Finally, the sacred world of *Homo religiosus* is essentially an intersubjective world, formed within the context of a sacred community. Leeuw recognized this vital component of the sacred lifeworld when he said, "In its relationship to Power, then, human life is first of all not the life of the individual, but that of the *Community*."[157] Solitude, he believed, excites dread in humans: it breeds insecurity by bringing us face-to-face with the powerfulness and uncertainty of existence itself. While dread leads to God, "in solitude there is nothing whatever."[158] Thus, community provides protection in the face of crisis. Since, in religion, humanity is continually confronted by new crises of existence, religion is inherently communal. "Thus whoever is severed from the community cannot live; homesickness gnaws at his soul."[159] For the sacred self, this community is one: the sacred community in which resides the "powerful life." While Leeuw's treatment of sacred intersubjectivity is relatively brief, Eliade, despite the fact that

---

154. Leeuw, *Religion*, 361–62.
155. Eliade, *Sacred and the Profane*, 167.
156. Eliade, *Sacred and the Profane*, 171–77.
157. Leeuw, *Religion*, 191.
158. Leeuw, *Religion*, 242.
159. Leeuw, *Religion*, 243–44.

he investigated the meaning and nature of the communal practices of religious life, failed to discuss it at all. Therefore, for further help in uncovering this vital dimension to religious existence, we will briefly appeal to the work of Edward Farley.

Farley, in his book *Ecclesial Man*, is attempting what he calls a "phenomenological theology"; that is, an "inquiry within theological prolegomenon which attempts to expose the situation in which realities are apprehended by faith."[160] His task is to uncover the pre-theoretical and pre-conscious structures of faith where most of faith's apprehensions take place. The everyday faith-world of religious people, particularly Christians, is a determinate world involving activities such as attending church, taking communion, praying, seeking forgiveness, etc. However, these everyday religious activities, while occupying the foreground, are founded upon a background matrix, a pre-conscious stratum, that mediates faith's apprehensions through "the distinctive sociality of the community of faith."[161] Farley calls this community of faith, "*ecclesia*." Constitutive of *ecclesia* is an imagery that is redemptive in orientation and communal in its intentional structure. To put it another way, members of the *ecclesia* co-intend each other in modes of redemption, with a noematic content involving pre-theoretical stories and images that condition the apprehensions of faith. These stories and images are fundamental, forming the necessary sub-stratum for any second-order ecclesiastical or theological reflections.[162] "Participation in *ecclesia* means, therefore, a modification of human existence toward redemption."[163] The primordial intersubjectivity of *ecclesia*, then, as founded on the redemptive presence of the Transcendent, mediates a social reality and shapes the consciousness of the participant in an originary and immediate manner.[164] As a result, faith does not just change perspectives but essentially modifies human make up and alters one's perception of the surrounding world.[165]

---

160. Farley, *Ecclesial Man*, 19.
161. Farley, *Ecclesial Man*, 76–77, 86.
162. Farley, *Ecclesial Man*, 106–26.
163. Farley, *Ecclesial Man*, 128.
164. Farley, *Ecclesial Man*, 166, 212.
165. Farley, *Ecclesial Man*, 213–14.

CONCLUSION

As we have seen in this chapter, humans not only have a world, they are "thrown" into a world. Prior to any reflective act, and as the necessary ground to such an act, humans comport themselves bodily in an intersubjective place-world that functions as the primal background for all practical engagement with their surrounding environment. This world is not just *a* world, it is *the* world; it is home. For the religious person, however, this homeworld is a sacred world founded on a mysterious and fascinating experience of the transcendent. "Faith has a 'world of its own,'"[166] complete with its own language, community, field of intended realities, and unity.[167] In other words, the unique intersubjective lifeworld of *Homo religiosus* is a generatively-deep homeworld: the null-point of orientation, the communal background for being-in-the-world, and the primal home in which one finds existential meaning and belonging.

As we will see in this research, religious alternation in Thailand is experientially complex, encompassing nothing less than a thoroughgoing transfer of socio-religious homeworlds. Therefore, it is precisely this homeworld as embodied, platial, intersubjective, and hierophanic, that forms the theoretical substratum for investigating the Thai Christian experience of in-marginality. This homeworld is not a generic world but one that carries a generative density rooted in the historical teachings and actions of Jesus and the Christian Church. We will now investigate this topic of identity formation as occurring in the Christian tradition.

---

166. Farley, *Ecclesial Man*, 101. Similarly, French phenomenologist Henry Duméry, avers, "When they are open, the eyes of faith cause a world to come into being" (Duméry and Dupre, *Faith and Reflection*, 11).

167. Farley, *Ecclesial Man*, 101–4.

3

Negotiating Christian Identity

INTRODUCTION

THE PHENOMENON OF IN-MARGINALITY is not unique to Thai Christians. Since the inauguration of the church in the first century, Christ-followers throughout the world and at various times throughout history have had to negotiate carefully their religious identities as members of a subordinate subgroup within dominant, non-Christian social environments. In this chapter, we will review some of the most significant examples of Christian identity negotiation within contexts of marginalization. We will begin by reviewing the literature pertaining to the early church to observe how the first few generations of Christians understood themselves in the face of Roman persecution. Finally, our study will take us to contemporary issues of Christian identity in the majority world, with our focus being on qualitative works on conversion and Christian identity in Asia as well as Christian identity formation in Thailand.

SOCIAL IDENTITY IN THE EARLY CHURCH

The historical life, teaching, and events of Jesus of Nazareth, particularly his crucifixion and resurrection, not only initiated a new religious movement which was eventually termed, "Christianity,"[1] but also established for his fol-

---

1. Recent scholarship has extensively debated the proper use of religious designations for first-century religious movements. While I recognize the importance of this debate, especially for disciplinary studies within the field of late antiquity, for the sake of simplicity and familiarity, I will continue to use the terms "Christian," "Christianity," "Jew," and "Judaism" throughout this section to refer to these early groups and movements.

lowers an epicenter and foundation for the formation of a new and distinct identity. While deeply rooted in the narratives and self-understandings of the people of Israel, and emerging within the context of Second Temple Judaism, this new identity in Christ challenged established religious and ethnic boundaries, radically re-evaluated existing identities, and upset prevailing social conventions. Thus, early Christians experienced significant and escalating marginalization as they sought to understand and live out their contested identities.[2] In this section, we will review contemporary scholarship related to the formation of Christian identity within the early church (death of Christ to the rise of Constantine in 313 AD). We will begin by assessing the level and nature of marginalization as experienced by these early Christians and then discuss how the apostles, martyrs, and early Christian writers acted as "entrepreneurs of identity"[3] in forming and maintaining early Christian self-understanding.

The early church existed as a marginalized sub-group in Roman culture and society. Legally, even though the New Testament church found protection under the Jewish synagogues (since many Roman officials considered them a sect of Second Temple Judaism), their presence as a unique and potentially subversive group was becoming increasingly recognized. The label "Christian" seems to suggest as much. As a Latinism, *Christianus* denoted the followers, supporters, or adherents of Christ.[4] It was initially coined by outsiders, either the Roman administration or general population in Antioch,[5] to refer to those who "belong to Christ"; however, the term was not innocuous. Similar designations of the time (such as *Brutianus, Augustianus, Caesarianus*, etc.) had distinctly political overtones, suggesting that the term "Christian" was intended to be mildly contemptuous, perhaps even derogatory, as it was used to designate Christians as a

---

However, by using these terms I do not mean to suggest that these group identities were fixed and clearly defined during this time period. For further discussion, see Boyarin, *Border Lines*; Esler, *Conflict and Identity*; Hegedus, "Naming Christians."

2. Dunn, *Neither Jew nor Greek*.

3. Esler, *Conflict and Identity*, 109.

4. Horrell, *Becoming Christian*, 165–66; Trebilco, *Self-Designations and Group Identity*, 289–91; Hegedus, "Naming Christians," 176–77.

5. Acts 11:26. Horrell and Trebilco argue that the term was initially coined by the Roman administration, while Hegedus suggests that the evidence points to the general population. For discussion, see Hegedus, "Naming Christians," 177; Horrell, *Becoming Christian*, 168–69; Trebilco, *Self-Designations and Group Identity*, 278.

potentially subversive group, socio-politically.⁶ Further, the first-century Christ-followers, especially those from Gentile backgrounds, faced varying degrees of suspicion and hostility from their neighbors due to the exclusivity of Christian allegiance and the enactment of an alternative ethic.⁷ The letters of 1 Peter and Hebrews were written to address these problems directly.⁸ In 1 Peter, the author wrote to the "diaspora" (1:1) in Asia minor who lived as "aliens and strangers"⁹ (2:11) among the resident population. While some scholars, such as John Elliott and Karen Jobes, argue that these terms represent the literal, sociological situation of the addressees, most recognize that Peter was using them metaphorically to indicate both the reality of Christian marginalization within society and the necessity to remain distinct ethically.¹⁰ According to David Horrell, "These are not, then, people for whom the wider culture is alien and strange, but people whose conversion to Christianity has *created* an alienation, the consequences of which need to be worked out."¹¹ It is unlikely that these early Christ-followers encountered severe physical abuse or martyrdom, something which would come in the second and third centuries, but they certainly experienced slander, reproach, and shame which took their toll on internal solidarity and feelings of group self-worth.¹²

The book of Hebrews was written for a similar audience who, as a minority group, were enduring social ridicule from the dominant group.¹³

---

6. Trebilco, *Self-Designations and Group Identity*, 290; Hegedus, "Naming Christians," 177.

7. Elliott, *Home for the Homeless*, 72–74, 79–105.

8. For the sake of time and space, I am highlighting 1 Peter and Hebrews as examples of the sociocultural issues facing the early, New Testament church. Of course, other New Testament books could be added to this list.

9. Greek: παροίκους καὶ παρεπιδήμους.

10. See Elliot and Jobes for a literal interpretation, and Horrell, Seland, and Bechtler for arguments in favor of a metaphorical interpretation. Elliott, *Home for the Homeless*, 21–58, 131–32; Jobes, *1 Peter*, 24–41; Horrell, *Becoming Christian*, 100–132; Seland, "Proselyte Characterizations in 1 Peter?"; Bechtler, *Following in His Steps*, 64–83.

11. Horrell, *Becoming Christian*, 216; Bechtler, *Following in His Steps*, 83–84.

12. Elliott, *Home for the Homeless*, 79–83, 101–5; Bechtler, *Following in His Steps*, 87–94.

13. While the traditional view holds that the addresses of the book of Hebrews were Jewish Christians, Marohl suggests that the entire debate is founded on a faulty conceptual framework that utilizes problematic conceptions of the nature of the groups in the first century and then applies those categories to the mind of the author of Hebrews. A better approach, he suggests, is not to ask whether the addresses were Jews or Gentiles,

However, unlike the addressees of 1 Peter, it appears that members of this particular group were in danger of apostasy.[14] Living in a collectivist culture, which was essentially comparative and competitive, early Christians would have created and maintained their sense of identity through social comparison with out-groups.[15] This would have entailed a pursuit of honor, a commodity which was deemed a limited good at the time, for the in-group through social competition with the relevant out-groups.[16] However, as David deSilva has convincingly argued, the Christian addressees of the book of Hebrews were not able to preserve the group's honor, but, instead, were feeling shame and receiving disapproval before the public court of opinion.[17] They were encountering "a great contest in the face of suffering," sometimes being "publicly exposed to insult and persecution," even the confiscation of property (Heb 10:32–34, NIV).

In the second and third centuries, persecution of Christians intensified. While commonly known as "the age of the martyrs," in point of fact, persecution during this time period was sporadic and regional, more focused on disrupting the social unity of the Church than on prohibiting private, intellectual convictions or cleansing the empire of the Christian "race."[18] Indeed, it was not until the time of Decius (250 AD), and especially during the Great Persecution under Diocletian and Galerius (303–313), that the Church experienced systematic, empire-wide attacks, resulting in substantial losses of life.[19]

Even more significant than the extent of the persecutions, at least for our purposes, were the motivations behind them. While early on many wondered about the mysterious activities in which Christians engaged

---

but to perceive the letter through the lens of intergroup comparison; namely, the "faithful" versus the "unfaithful." Marohl, *Faithfulness and the Purpose of Hebrews*.

14. Heb 2:1–4; 3:12; 6:4–8; 10:26–31; 12:5–9.

15. Collectivist cultures are allocentric; that is, they place the interests, expectations, and norms of the group above those of the individual. In this context, apostasy is not as much disbelief as disaffiliation from the group, the exchange of loyalty from one collective to another. Crook, "Agents of Apostasy."

16. In social identity theory this is called "intergroup comparison." For an application of social identity theory to the book of Hebrews, see Marohl, *Faithfulness and the Purpose of Hebrews*.

17. deSilva, *Despising Shame*; "Despising Shame." For a more general treatment of honor and shame in the New Testament, see deSilva, *Honor, Patronage, Kinship, and Purity*.

18. Bushur, "Ignatius of Antioch's Letter," 13; Chadwick, *Early Church*, 29–31.

19. Wright, "Testimony of Blood," 397.

behind closed doors, with cannibalism and licentiousness topping the list of accusations, most persecutions were sparked by the Imperial desire for political order, social stability, and religious conformity throughout a diverse and extensive empire.[20] The point of conflict often centered around the practice of sacrifice, whether it be to the Roman gods or to Caesar. In antiquity, religious observance was inextricably intertwined with political security, civic loyalty, and social acceptance. Any attempt to dislodge religion and society, such as in the modern notion of the separation of church and state, was simply non-existent. Within this setting, the ritual of sacrifice was considered the preeminent gesture of piety that both represented one's loyalty to the empire and maintained one's network of relationships.[21] "Therefore," Elizabeth Castelli explains, "a refusal to participate in this sacrificial order—for whatever reason—would have been viewed by the vast majority of the empire's population as a rejection of all manner of socially ordering elements—kinship, gender identities, and so on—and therefore as utterly nonsensical, irrational, foolhardy, impudent, sacrilegious, and antisocial."[22]

For Christians, whose worldview was founded on the exclusivity of allegiance to Christ's Lordship, sacrifice to the Roman gods or to the emperor was tantamount to idolatry, if not apostasy. Their refusal to participate in these religio-political rituals, therefore, resulted in charges of obstinacy, atheism, and sedition.[23] Christians, it was believed, dangerously and foolishly upset the equilibrium between humans and the gods, thus inviting natural catastrophes and threatening to disrupt the coveted *pax romana*.[24] This is why Tertullian (160–220 AD) could famously complain, "They think the Christians the cause of every public disaster, of every affliction with which the people are visited. If the Tiber rises as high as the city walls, if the Nile does not send its waters up over the fields, if the heavens give no rain, if there is an earthquake, if there is famine or pestilence, straightway the cry is, 'Away with the Christians to the lion!'"[25]

20. Castelli, *Martyrdom and Memory*, 37–38.

21. Middleton, "Enemies of the (Church and) State," 167–68; Castelli, *Martyrdom and Memory*, 37–38, 50–51.

22. Castelli, *Martyrdom and Memory*, 50.

23. Gonzalez, *Story of Christianity*, 39–48; Schaff, *History of the Christian Church*, 42–44. Pliny the Younger's letter to Trajan around 113 AD indicates that the profession of Christianity was, in itself, a punishable offense. Pliny, *Letters* 96.

24. Middleton, "Enemies of the (Church and) State," 167.

25. Tertullian, *Apology* 40 (ANF 3:47).

Strangers in a Familiar Land

How, then, did the apostles and early Christian writers act as "entrepreneurs of identity" for these early, marginalized Christ-followers? To answer this question, several scholars have looked to social psychology, particularly social identity theory, for assistance.[26] Essential to this theory is the supposition that one's identity, especially in collectivistic cultures, is defined largely in terms of the groups to which one belongs. Groups differentiate themselves from other groups, i.e., create boundaries, in ways that will enhance their self-esteem, thus inculcating in each member a sense of belonging and a positive self-concept. To apply this to New Testament studies, Esler suggests that Paul, and perhaps other New Testament authors, constituted the in-group of Christ-followers vis-à-vis two symbolic out-groups: Jews and Gentiles.[27] These out-groups functioned as negative stereotypes when Paul and others wished to maintain an impermeable boundary between the in-group and the out-groups (for example, to prevent Gentile Christians from becoming Jews or to prevent apostasy).[28] However, when internal unity was the priority, a common and overarching in-group identity, such as "in Christ," was highlighted, relativizing ethnic differences in order to reduce intragroup conflict.[29] In either case, essential to maintaining a positive group identity were the utilizations of self-designations and self-understandings that would serve to enhance self-esteem in the face of increasing marginalization.

One example of how early Christians upheld a positive social identity is by implementing what social identity theorists term "social creativity." This strategy has to do with altering or redefining the elements of the comparative situation in order to enhance the positive distinctiveness of the in-group.[30] Horrell argues that this strategy was used in 1 Peter 4 to reverse a negative label that might cause shame, *Christianus*, into a designation of honor. While

---

26. See chapter 1 for an overview of the social identity approach. This discussion will assume that the reader has a working knowledge of the relevant concepts.

27. Esler, "Family Imagery," 92–95. These groups are considered symbolic since they do not necessarily represent the self-understandings of the people they are meant to represent. Marohl, *Faithfulness and the Purpose of Hebrews*, 66–67.

28. Esler, "Family Imagery," 95–96. For example, the Gentiles/Greeks/pagans are portrayed as sinners (Gal 2:15), evil idolaters, (1 Pet 4:3) and foolish (1 Cor 1:23), while the Jews are portrayed as stumbling over Christ (1 Cor 1:23), equally sinful (Rom 2:17–29), and under a curse for relying on the law (Gal 3:10).

29. Theissen, "Letter to the Romans and Paul's Plural Identity," 301–4; Esler, *Conflict and Identity*, 26; Campbell, "Gentile Identity."

30. Horrell, *Becoming Christian*, 207–8.

claiming the name would likely result in degradation and humiliation from outside society, Peter exhorted his readers to bear the name as a badge of honor and pride, as a way to bring glory to God.[31] Similarly, in 1 Peter 2, the author called the addressees "aliens and strangers," reminding them of their lived experience of social marginalization. However, Peter was using these terms as positive self-designations, in line with the identity of God's people throughout the Hebrew Scriptures, to highlight their distinctiveness from pagan society.[32] The author of Hebrews followed a similar tack. As his readers faced significant negative evaluations from and loss of status within the dominant group, possibly leading to apostasy, the need to remain faithful to the in-group became a priority. To encourage faithfulness, the author reversed society's estimation of honor and shame, arguing that the only court of opinion that truly matters is God's. The great heroes of the faith in chapter 11 demonstrated the significance of this honor reversal, but it was Jesus who exemplified true honor best. Through his shameful death on the cross, Jesus "despised the shame," rejecting the world's evaluation and any regard for his own reputation, and, as result, became the "author and perfecter of our faith" who is now seated at the right hand of God. The recipients are encouraged, therefore, to "not grow weary and lose heart" as they face their own difficult realities of social marginalization.[33]

In the second and third centuries, martyrdom assumed a much greater role in the formation of Christian identity. In his book *Dying for God: Martyrdom and the Making of Christianity and Judaism*, Daniel Boyarin avers, "Being killed is an event. Martyrdom is a literary form, a genre."[34] While many people have been executed for crimes against the state throughout history, not every criminal may be considered a martyr. That is because martyrdom is a "'discourse' . . . a practice of dying for God and of talking about it."[35]

> Martyrdom is not simply an action. Martyrdom requires audience (whether real or fictive), retelling, interpretation, and world- and

---

31. Horrell, *Becoming Christian*, 207–9.

32. Elliott, *Home for the Homeless*, 42–45; Bechtler, *Following in His Steps*, 135–38. Incidentally, Peter does not exhort his readers to withdraw from society but rather to be model citizens so that outsiders have no reason for accusation. 1 Pet 2:12–3:17. Seland, "Resident Aliens in Mission," 576.

33. Heb 12:1–3; deSilva, *Despising Shame*, 145–90.

34. Boyarin, *Dying for God*, 116.

35. Boyarin, *Dying for God*, 94. See also Matthews, *Perfect Martyr*, 4.

meaning-making activity. Suffering violence in and of itself is not enough. In order for martyrdom to emerge, both the violence and its suffering must be infused with particular meanings.[36]

This infusion of meanings into suffering, Elizabeth Castelli continues, produces a "collective memory": the corporate interpretation of the past that provides ideological meaning and self-understanding for the present.[37] In this way, martyr narratives served to shape individual identities by reconceiving the apparent disgrace of the victims in a way that drew readers into the symbolic world of the community.[38] For early Christians, whose lived experience of persecution threatened their very existence, the collective memories formed through martyrdom discourse provided the essential framework for turning this chaos of violence into a privileged and idealized system of meaning.[39]

Early Christian martyrological literature was extensive. Known as the *Acts of the Martyrs*,[40] these texts were widely read among Christians throughout the Roman empire, giving impetus and shape to what would eventually grow into a cult of the martyrs. The authors of these texts adopted multiple rhetorical strategies that were effective for shaping corporate identity and inspiring a culture of resistance within the context of persecution. Many of these strategies can be found in the most famous of the martyr narratives, the *Martyrdom of Polycarp*, a text which quickly became the template for this burgeoning genre.[41] Polycarp was the Bishop of Smyrna in the early- to mid-second century, famous for having been a disciple of the Apostle John. In the account of his martyrdom, Polycarp is presented analogously to Jesus, mimetically reflecting the biblical passion

---

36. Castelli, *Martyrdom and Memory*, 33.

37. Castelli, *Martyrdom and Memory*, 10–13.

38. Castelli, *Martyrdom and Memory*, 9–32; Lieu, *Christian Identity*, 253; Leemans, "Martyrdom of Sabas the Goth," 209.

39. Castelli, *Martyrdom and Memory*, 34.

40. The *Acts of the Martyrs* is the name often given to an extensive compilation of martyrdom accounts, ranging from court proceedings to highly fabricated legends, that occurred during the first few centuries AD. Many of these works were widely distributed and highly influential among early Church communities. Costelloe, "Acts of the Martyrs," 90–94.

41. Leemans, "Martyrdom of Sabas the Goth," 209–10. It is believed that Polycarp was martyred in Asia Minor between 155–168 AD, but the date for the writing of this text is a topic of much debate among scholars. For discussion, see Moss, "On the Dating of Polycarp."

narratives.[42] Polycarp, facing the accusation of atheism and the demand to sacrifice and swear by the genius of the emperor, astounds the raging crowds and officials with his firm resolution and eloquence, climactically affirms his identity as a Christian, and then willfully accepts his execution as a sacrifice, an "acceptable burnt-offering unto God."[43]

Of the numerous rhetorical strategies found in this short narrative, one that is of special significance for the genre as a whole—and to this research in particular—was the climactic declaration, *Christiana sum*: "I am a Christian."[44] Found consistently throughout the martyrological literature, this simple and forthright identifying statement was the central action of the martyr; "a ritualized and performative speech act associated with a statement of pure essence."[45] Rather than being merely descriptive, the statement itself, literally speaking, constituted the speaker as a Christian. Judith Lieu explains: "For it is when confronted with the choice of confession or denial that the true commitment for or against identity is made, and so, implicitly, until that moment there is only potential. Those who 'fail' have miscarried or failed to attain their birth, whereas others only here achieve their true identity."[46] The confession, *Christiana sum*, therefore, is the ultimate insider designation.[47] It represents the giving of one's self to the providence of God, the redefinition and reordering of familial, social, and civic identities, and the readiness to publicly and courageously identify with Christ in his sufferings.[48] As such, this declaration—and the inevitable death that followed—contributed to the valorization of the martyrs, making them into heroes or "super-Christians," thereby providing for this young and beleaguered Church exemplars for the formation of a common social identity.[49]

---

42. Castelli, *Martyrdom and Memory*, 61; Wright, "Testimony of Blood," 388.

43. *Martyrdom of Polycarp*, 12–14 (ANF 1:41–42).

44. Or Greek, χριστιανός εἰμι.

45. Boyarin, *Dying for God*, 95.

46. Lieu, *Neither Jew nor Greek?*, 225.

47. Judith Lieu writes, "'Christian' has thus become not merely a statement of allegiance, comparable to other patterns of allegiance, and possibly even compatible with some; it does not function as one among a number of, or even within a hierarchy of, identities, in the way that we have come to think of most experience and construction of identity. 'Christian' serves as a total and ultimate, an exclusive act of definition and so of redefinition; it affirms a new, all-encompassing, non-negotiable, and even non-communicable identity" (Lieu, *Neither Jew nor Greek?*, 226–27).

48. Jensen, *Martyrdom and Identity*, 2; Lieu, *Christian Identity*, 254.

49. Wright, "Testimony of Blood," 387–88; Huebner, "Between Victory and

Strangers in a Familiar Land

To conclude this section, we will survey one additional rhetorical strategy frequently utilized during this time period to affirm and shape Christian identity: ethnoracial discourse. In the *Martyrdom of Polycarp*, as Polycarp stands trial before a hostile crowd, he prays not just for himself, but for the entire "race of the righteous."[50] The hero is portrayed not as a mere individual expressing his inner convictions and facing a solitary execution but as a member of a distinct people who, collectively, embody proper religiosity. In opposition to the crowds, who represent the major peoples of the known world, Romans and Jews, Christians constitute an altogether new kind, a sort of "third race"[51] of humanity. This use of "ethnic reasoning," which may be frequently found in both the martyrological and apologetic literature of the period, was an effective tool for defining and legitimizing the various forms of Christian self-understanding.[52]

Ethnic reasoning mutually constituted religion and race in an effort to define, maintain, and defend "Christianness" in the midst of a hostile environment. However, while speaking of Christians as a distinct race had its rhetorical advantages, it also conveyed their own sense of themselves as "out of joint with the dominant values of the time."[53] As *"paroikoi,"* this marginal group were at home everywhere, but fully at home nowhere.[54] They sought to construct a new world, welcoming others into their distinct race through baptism, socializing them through teaching and worship, and sending them out to live distinctly as proper representatives of this race. Baptism, including the long and rigorous process of catechism leading up to the event, was the necessary starting point. Catechism might take up to three years, involving daily instructions in the Scriptures in order to "reform pagan people, to resocialize them, to deconstruct their own world, and reconstruct a new one, so that they would emerge as Christian people, at home in communities of freedom."[55] Baptism itself involved the adoption of a new identity.[56] Having been exorcised of evil spirits, catechumens

---

Victimhood," 236–37.

50. *Martyrdom of Polycarp*, 14–17 (ANF 1:42–43).

51. Greek: γένος. The apologist, Aristides, writing around 125 AD, listed four distinct races: Barbarians, Greeks, Jews, and Christians. Aristides, *Apology* 2 (ANF 9:264–65).

52. Buell, *Why This New Race*, 2–5.

53. Kreider, "Worship and Evangelism," 11.

54. Kreider, "Worship and Evangelism," 11.

55. Kreider, "Worship and Evangelism," 19. See also Jacobsen, "Identity Formation."

56. Johnson, *Religious Experience in Earliest Christianity*.

entered the waters naked, representing the removal of the old ways of life, and emerged a "counter-cultural religious self."[57] They could then fully participate in the mysterious gatherings of the faithful, including the Eucharist and the kiss of peace.[58] The expectation, however, was that these new members would properly live out their distinct ethnicity among a hostile society.[59] Their lives were to be ethically different, expressed in loving their enemies, caring for the oppressed and needy, and living as model citizens.[60] Ethnoracial discourse, therefore, played a key role in solidifying Christian identity during the time prior to Constantine. It not only differentiated this marginal group from its persecutors but also shaped a plausibility structure that would effectively turn pagans into Christians.

CONTEMPORARY CHRISTIAN IDENTITY IN CONTEXTS OF MARGINALIZATION

In the final section of this chapter, we will review contemporary theological and missiological conversations pertaining to Christian identity formation in contexts of marginalization. While the lived experience of Christians in the Western world is increasingly that of marginalization due to their relatively recent status as a subordinate, minority group,[61] our focus will remain primarily within majority world contexts. Even by limiting ourselves to the majority world, however, the breadth of literature within this extremely fecund and eclectic area of study is still quite extensive. Therefore, we will only introduce those topics and literature most relevant to the phenomenon under investigation. This section will review the literature pertaining

---

57. Wright, "Baptismal Community," 7–11.

58. Kreider, "Worship and Evangelism," 22–23. The kiss of peace was a sign of identification that served to reaffirm membership in the community and to exclude outsiders. Rebillard, "Becoming Christian in Carthage," 49.

59. Rebillard, "Becoming Christian in Carthage," 56–58.

60. Kreider, "Worship and Evangelism," 26–27; Buell, *Why This New Race*, 154. Aristides gives expression to this essential change in lifestyle for "the race of the Christians" in Aristides, *Apology* 15 (ANF 9:276–78).

61. One only needs to review recent publications in the fields of practical theology and Christian living to discern the increasing awareness among Western Christians of the post-Christian status and mission of the Western Church. For example, see Muehlhoff, *Winsome Persuasion*; Nichols, *Time for Confidence*; Hart, *Strangers and Pilgrims Once More*; Kreider and Kreider, *Worship and Mission*; Murray, *Church after Christendom*.

to two areas of study: qualitative studies on Christian identity formation in Asia and Christian identity formation in Thailand.[62]

Qualitative Studies on Christian Identity Formation in Asia

In this section, we will review briefly two recent works that present qualitative analyses of Christian identity formation within Asian contexts.[63] Given the similarities of these works with our phenomenon of investigation, we will evaluate each work, highlighting similarities and divergences in both topic and methodology.

Religious Identity and Social Change: Explaining Christian Conversion in a Muslim World by David Radford is a sociological study on the topic of Christian conversion and identity change in the Central Asian country of Kyrgyzstan. In a society where "to be Kyrgyz is to be Muslim" and where Christianity has historically been considered foreign (primarily Russian) and not a viable religious option, why do some Kyrgyz convert, and how do Kyrgyz Christians understand themselves as both Kyrgyz and Christian?[64] Radford explores these questions from the perspective of Kyrgyz Christians, seeking to understand how they are attempting "to transform this new religious movement into something that affirms, not diminishes, their sense of Kyrgyzness, their Kyrgyz identity, and reconstructs the normative ethic construct to show that to be Kyrgyz is to be Christian as well as to be Muslim."[65] Utilizing a broadly phenomenological approach, the author applied both qualitative and quantitative methods to uncover the meanings inherent in the 49 narrative-based interviews and 427 survey responses.[66] He then interpreted the data through the economic lens of human capital investments—social, cultural, and religious.[67]

---

62. Space constraints preclude the addition of an important third area of study pertinent to this research: contextualization. I refer the reader to the extensive literature in this area, particularly related to contextualization's significance for theological identity formation within majority world contexts. See, for example, Schreiter, *Constructing Local Theologies*; Bevans, *Models*; Mesa, "Inculturation as Pilgrimage"; Yung, *Mangoes or Bananas*; Bediako, *Theology and Identity*.

63. Another recent study that is relevant to this research is Christofferson, *Negotiating Identity*. Unfortunately, space constraints preclude our evaluation of this study.

64. Radford, *Religious Identity and Social Change*, xxv–xxvi.

65. Radford, *Religious Identity and Social Change*, 1.

66. Radford, *Religious Identity and Social Change*, 29–40.

67. Religious capital refers to the degree of mastery of, attachment to, or familiarity with a particular religious tradition. Social and cultural capital refer to the sum of

Negotiating Christian Identity

Based on his research, Radford concludes that Kyrgyz Christians convert for both religious and social reasons. Due to the interconnectedness of social, religious, and ethnic identities in Kyrgyzstan, "conversion is more likely to occur when investments by members of ethnic groups in one or more of the components of (social, religious and cultural) capital of a group have significantly declined."[68] In addition, for conversion to have lasting effects, converts require satisfactory solutions and explanations to life circumstances, formulated and reinforced within a community of like-minded people.[69] Post-conversion, Kyrgyz Christians must then negotiate their new identity within a predominantly Muslim world. Converts must make daily decisions as to what may be accepted or rejected among cultural traditions while working to maintain existing social attachments and ethnic identifications.[70] In essence, Radford concludes, Kyrgyz converts are redefining the boundaries of "Kyrgyzness"; that is, they are seeking to adjust common perceptions of "normality" and "deviance" so as to include the potentiality for being both Christian and Kyrgyz.[71]

Radford's work aligns quite closely with the research question of this book. First, the lifeworld of Kyrgyzstan somewhat parallels that of Thailand. In both contexts, ethnic, kinship, and religious identities are deeply interwoven in the fabric of society, requiring converts to negotiate their new identities in ways that both mitigates deviance and maintains group memberships. Second, the lived experience of Kyrgyz Christians is, in many ways, similar to that of Thai Christians. Referring to the experience of being marginal, one of Radford's respondents asserts, "Sometimes I feel chewed up between two cultures."[72] Interestingly, as for Thai Christians, this feeling of being marginal is most acute during funeral ceremonies, which, Radford claims, is where the "deviant" nature of Christian identity is most evident.[73] Third, the overall focus of study, namely religious conversion and the negotiation of Christian identity in a context of marginalization, aligns very closely with the topic of this book. Despite these striking similarities,

---

resources that accrue to an individual or group by virtue of their relational networks. Radford, *Religious Identity and Social Change*, 56, 78–79.

68. Radford, *Religious Identity and Social Change*, 96–97.
69. Radford, *Religious Identity and Social Change*, 100.
70. Radford, *Religious Identity and Social Change*, 125–39.
71. Radford, *Religious Identity and Social Change*, 140–65.
72. Radford, *Religious Identity and Social Change*, 125.
73. Radford, *Religious Identity and Social Change*, 132.

however, there are some divergences. First, while analogous in many ways, the sociocultural contexts of Kyrgyzstan and Thailand differ as well. The obvious distinctions between Muslim and Buddhist religious adherence combined with the unique histories of both countries make an exact parallel impossible to maintain. Second, Radford's methodology, while described as phenomenological, is more grounded in a sociological approach, which, while prioritizing an insider's point of view, is interpreted through the lens of established sociological theories. In addition, the author does not interact with phenomenological philosophy, his methodology does not include key phenomenological concepts such as bracketing or free imaginative variation, and his descriptions of interview data are not presented in a phenomenological manner. In this way, his research, while similar in scope and topic, diverges from this study in methodology, specific context, and description of findings.

The second work we will evaluate is that of Indian theologian and educator Joshua Iyadurai entitled, *Transformative Religious Experience: A Phenomenological Understanding of Religious Conversion*. Writing within the field of conversion studies for the Indian context, Iyadurai's stated purpose is two-fold: (1) "to demonstrate that religious experience—in other words, the divine-human encounter—is central to religious conversion and triggers personal transformation" and (2) "to let the reader hear the voices of converts in their own words."[74] To accomplish this task, Iyadurai designed his study from a phenomenological perspective, prioritizing "thick" descriptions of lived, religious experience while drawing insights from theology, psychology, anthropology, and sociology to assist with interpretation.[75]

The author utilized the method of in-depth interviewing to gather data from a diverse sample of South Indian converts. His findings are structured per nine metathemes. The first group of six themes deal with the specific experiences that had led to the participants' conversion: (1) visions, (2) dreams, (3) voices of God, (4) miracles, (5) prayers, and (6) mild experiences. While no single participant reports having experienced all six religious occurrences, they are considered essential in initiating one's religious transformation.[76] The last three themes deal with conversion as both event and process. Chapter 7 explains the mystical nature of

---

74. Iyadurai, *Transformative Religious Experience*, 2.
75. Iyadurai, *Transformative Religious Experience*, 4.
76. Iyadurai, *Transformative Religious Experience*, 13–142.

Negotiating Christian Identity

the transformative event; namely, the intuitive and sudden realization or spark of insight by which one meets directly with God and is, as a result, "born again."[77] Chapter 8 outlines the processual nature of conversion as transformation, including the psychological, behavioral, physical, social, and economical effects on the self.[78] Finally, chapter 9 reports how converts juggle multiple identities as they face the hostilities that arise due to their conversion.[79] Iyadurai concludes the book with a presentation of his "Step Model of transformative religious experience," which outlines seven phases of the conversion process: exposure, disenchantment, crunch, pursuit and test, hostilities, participation, and maturation.[80]

As a phenomenological study of conversion within a multi-religious context, Iyadurai's research intersects with this book in several ways. First, his attention to uncovering the lived meanings inherent in transformative religious experience via phenomenological interviewing and analysis is closely aligned with my own methodological priority. Second, as with Iyadurai, I see the value of appropriating elements of social identity theory to assist in interpreting the participants' lived experience of marginalization. Third, there exist numerous resonances between the narratives and meanings expressed by Iyadurai's participants and those of this study, especially the intimacy of mystical encounters with God, the nature of conversion as both event and process, and the navigation of hostilities via a complex negotiation of multiple social identities. Finally, it seems that the lifeworld contexts of Indian and Thai converts bear certain similarities, especially as it relates to the social hostilities they face as a result of conversion. As for divergences, we note, first of all, that conversion, not marginalization, is the subject of Iyadurai's investigation. While he dedicates one chapter to discuss how converts negotiate their identities within contexts of marginalization, the primary purpose of the book is to disclose the essential structure of the phenomenon of conversion. Second, while Iyadurai's work is the most phenomenological of the works evaluated in this section, in that it more closely follows established methods for doing phenomenological, qualitative research, there is, unfortunately, no interaction with phenomenological philosophy. For the most part, scholarly interaction is limited primarily to the fields of psychology, sociology, and anthropology. Finally,

---

77. Iyadurai, *Transformative Religious Experience*, 144.
78. Iyadurai, *Transformative Religious Experience*, 169–96.
79. Iyadurai, *Transformative Religious Experience*, 198–233.
80. Iyadurai, *Transformative Religious Experience*, 239.

we should note that there exist significant variances between the Indian and Thai contexts; for example, the relative percentage of Christians in each country, their unique histories and cultural priorities, and the greater variety of available religious options in India versus Thailand.

Christian Identity Formation in Thailand

In the final section of this chapter, we will survey literature pertaining specifically to Christian identity formation among the Thai people. Once again, we must limit our review to only those works which present a potential horizon for understanding the phenomenon under investigation. Our focus will be on concerns of evangelism, discipleship, and conversion given that the majority of scholarly work on the topic of Thai Christianity has arisen within the field of missiology.[81]

With Protestant Christianity representing a mere 0.3 percent of the population,[82] even after nearly 200 years of concerted evangelistic efforts,[83] many missionaries and Thai church leaders are wondering what has prohibited the expansion of the Christian Church in Thailand.[84] To find solutions to this dilemma, scholars and practitioners have been forced to reevaluate traditional understandings and methodologies as well as investigate new approaches for contextualizing the gospel for a Thai audience. A first step for many has been to delineate carefully the most significant barriers to Christian conversion. Missiologist Paul de Neui claims, "There is an urgent need to recognize that for most Thai Folk Buddhists the strongest barriers to Christ which they experience are not religious but social."[85]

---

81. For a sample of works related to the development of contextual theology in Thailand, see Koyama, *Waterbuffalo Theology*; Staveren, "Christian Theology in a Country of Temples"; Dinkins, "Towards Contextualized Creeds"; Haug and Holter, "No Graven Image?"; Hughes, "Theology and Culture"; Hovemyr, "Theology of the Incarnation"; Taylor, "Gaps in Beliefs"; "Prolegomena for the Thai Context"; Sorajjakool, "Religion in Thailand"; Swanson, "Dancing to the Temple."

82. As of 2010. See Bruijne, "Conversion," 3.

83. For a history of Protestant Christianity in Thailand, see Smith, *Siamese Gold*.

84. Examples abound of the frustration of Christian workers with the slow growth of the church in Thailand, but the opening line of John Davis's book, *Poles Apart*, sums up the popular sentiment well: "Anyone who has spent time in Buddhist lands attempting to communicate the 'Good News' must come up against the exasperating fact, that no matter how brilliant a linguist one may be, no matter how sincere one may be presenting the Gospel, no matter how totally saturated in the local culture, one's message seems, nevertheless, to fall on deaf ears" (Davis, "Poles Apart?").

85. Neui, "Contextualizing," 134.

Over the years, he argues, much of evangelical witness has been focused on individual conversion. However, in a context where major decisions are decided in a group, it is essential that methods are chosen that serve to bring people together into social community rather than pulling them away towards a more Western individualism.[86] Missionary-scholar Alan Johnson elaborates on Neui's thesis by demarcating some of the most common social barriers that he had discovered through a series of interviews conducted with Thai Christians. The core issue, Johnson claims, is that of Thai identity; namely, the popular belief that "to be Thai is to be Buddhist." The predominant perspective that Buddhism is for Thais and Christianity is for Westerners permeates everyday social relations, producing strong social pressure for individuals not to convert and, for those who do, to return to the fold of Buddhism.[87] Johnson comments,

> It is an irrelevant point as to how serious they are in practicing Buddhism, but what is important is that they maintain at least the minimal identification with the essence of Thainess, of which identifying oneself as Buddhist is a core part. Becoming a Christian creates problems by putting a person at odds with the broader Thai Buddhist community; it jeopardizes friendship not because people are zealous in the practice of Buddhism but because it threatens one's identity. A person can no longer join in activities that are part of defining a person as Thai.[88]

Like Neui, Johnson concludes that evangelistic and discipleship efforts must prioritize community in a way that encourages Christians to remain connected with their broader social networks.[89] Even more than that, however, he suggests that Christians must also work toward articulating a "Thai identity where religious affiliation is not solely connected with Buddhism."[90]

Besides social barriers, many scholars and practitioners have also noted, via religious comparison and worldview analysis, that there exist numerous intellectual barriers to Christian conversion and discipleship in Thailand. By comparing Thai worldview and religious practice with that of

---

86. Neui, "Contextualizing," 134–35.

87. Johnson, "Exploring Social Barriers," 138–39. Swanson, "Barriers." See also Keyes, "Why the Thai Are Not Christians."

88. Johnson, "Exploring Social Barriers," 141.

89. Johnson, "Exploring Social Barriers," 145–47.

90. Johnson, "Exploring Social Barriers," 143.

Christianity, these scholars highlight the need to produce a more contextualized model of evangelism and discipleship for the Thai people. Based on a worldview analysis of Folk Buddhism, for instance, Neui argues for an approach to evangelism that (1) is holistic in nature, that is, integrates the physical, spiritual, and social aspects of life; (2) involves all "signal systems," such as seeing, hearing, touching, etc.; (3) understands the social barriers to conversion; and (4) recognizes the reality of power in the spirit world.[91] Wan Petchsongkram, a Thai pastor and former Buddhist monk, details, in considerable depth, the primary tenets of Buddhism—such as karma, nirvana, dharma, etc.—in order to help ministers of Jesus Christ better "understand the feelings of the people they serve."[92] Throughout Thailand, he argues, Christianity is perceived as a religion of the ignorant. What is needed, therefore, is a deep cognizance of Buddhism so that Christians may more effectively present the gospel in ways that Thais will not only understand but also respect.[93] In addition, Thai theologian Nantachai Mejudhon has advanced an indigenous methodology of evangelism founded on the core Thai value of meekness.[94] While, in the past, Western missionaries have exhibited an aggressive and confrontational approach to evangelism, Mejudhon argues that a more effective method is one that is characterized by humility toward Buddhism, respect toward others, the development of long-term relationships with no strings attached, the presentation of a gospel that brings benefits not threats, sufficient time for the diffusion of the gospel, and the adoption of indigenous strategies for communication of the gospel.[95]

Related to discipleship and Christian identity, Philip Hughes compares the "soteriological patterns"[96] of both Buddhism and Christianity, concluding that many Thai Christians have effectively assimilated

---

91. Neui, "Contextualizing," 130–37. For another model of contextualization, see Johnson, "Contextualized Presentation of the Gospel."

92. Petchsongkram, "Talk in the Shade of the Bo Tree," 1.

93. Petchsongkram, "Talk in the Shade of the Bo Tree," 65.

94. Mejudhon, "Meekness [1997]." See also Mejudhon, "Meekness [2005]"; Mejudhon, "Evangelism in the New Millenium."

95. Mejudhon, "Meekness [1997]," 321–65.

96. By soteriological patterns, he means "those patterns of belief and behavior through which people seek total or partial salvation." For example, he compares the Buddhist concepts of nirvana, karma and merit, and ritual, magic, and spirits with the Christian concept of salvation from sin through the death of Christ. Hughes, "Christianity and Buddhism," 23.

Christianity to Thai cultural patterns.[97] Karl Dahlfred, writing twenty-six years later, affirms Hughes's research, arguing that syncretism indeed pervades the Thai church. Many Thai Christians, he asserts, due to the inclusivist nature of the Folk Buddhist worldview, have carried over Buddhist and animistic thinking into Christian belief and practice. This, he believes, is evidenced in their attempts to manipulate God as well as their perception that power, not the atonement, is the heart of the gospel.[98] Edwin Zehner, however, argues that a form of syncretism or "orthodox hybridity" is a necessary component to conversion in Thailand, essentially giving Christianity "a feel of the local while preserving converts' sense of being loyal to a transculturally shared set of teachings."[99] Based on data gathered from observations in urban-based churches and interviews with Thai students preparing for church ministry, Zehner contends that Thai Christians exhibit two forms of hybridity: hybridities of extension, whereby transcultural themes are clothed with local details,[100] and hybridities of transition, whereby cognitive disjunctions are minimized during the ongoing reorientations of conversion.[101] Therefore, he maintains, evangelical Christians must move beyond a simple perspective of anti-syncretism, recognizing that "conceptual overlap" is a necessary and essential component of the acculturation process.[102] Finally, Terry Muck argues that one reason why Christian witness has failed to take root in Buddhist countries such as Thailand has been because missionaries have oversimplified the complex identities of their target audience.[103] Most missionaries, Muck asserts, have historically overemphasized either elite or folk Buddhism, missing the "tricultural" nature of many Southeast Asian Buddhists; namely, the intermixture of elite Buddhism, folk Buddhism, and modernization.[104]

Despite the brevity of this survey of literature in the field of Thai Christian identity formation, we are, nevertheless, able to gain a clear perspective

97. Hughes, "Christianity and Buddhism," 39–41.

98. Dahlfred, "Animism." For another work on syncretism among Christians in Thailand, see Gustafson, "Syncretistic Thai Religion."

99. Zehner, "Orthodox Hybridities," 585. See also Zehner, "Beyond Anti-Syncretism."

100. Such as the themes of love and divine power predominant in Thai conversion narratives. Zehner, "Orthodox Hybridities," 596–604.

101. Such as the convert's perspective of heaven and hell or of the spirit world. Zehner, "Orthodox Hybridities," 605–10.

102. Zehner, "Beyond Anti-Syncretism," 177–83.

103. Muck, "Three Reasons," 110.

104. Muck, "Three Reasons," 111.

of the challenges facing evangelism and discipleship in Thailand. Referring to the social challenges that Christianity faces in Thailand, Thai theologian Ubolwan Mejudhon comments, "[This] is perhaps the core problem for Christianity in Thailand: the relational bonds between new converts and their natural social networks are broken; as a result, the new converts lose their identity as Thais and become weak Christians; the parents and relatives thus turn against the church and become strong enemies of Christian conversion."[105] Indeed, it is this problematic that forms one of the bases for this research and substantiates the need for the development of a phenomenological understanding of Christian identity formation in Thailand.

CONCLUSION

In this chapter, we have seen that Christian identity formation, whether in the early church or in contemporary Asia, requires numerous strategies that serve to affirm one's new religious identity while effectively navigating existing social identities. While the strategies may vary per context, we note that at the core of identity negotiation is the elucidation and performance of what it means to be both Christian and Roman, Asian, etc. In the face of persecution, ridicule, and misunderstanding, Christ-followers must not only discuss among themselves what it means to be Christian (as in theological discourse) but also give actual structure to Christian identity via everyday, lived performance. No matter the time period or culture, the performance of this identity is grounded in one's personal experience of God, reinforced through participation in the sacred community, and negotiated through daily decisions that may potentially enhance self-esteem and mitigate perceptions of deviance. As we will see, it is these same concerns that prompt the negotiation of Christian identity for the participants of this study. This summation of the Christian tradition, therefore, presents a significant horizon for our understanding of the Thai Christian experience of in-marginality. Before we delve into the structure of that experience, however, we must first clarify the methods and methodology that we will use to gain access to the lived meanings inherent in the phenomenon. To that discussion, we now turn.

---

105. Mejudhon, "Ritual of Reconciliation [2010]."

4

Phenomenology as Method and Methodology

INTRODUCTION

IN THIS CHAPTER, I will delineate the philosophical underpinnings informing my research methodology as well as the specific methods utilized in collecting and analyzing the research data. Terminologically, I will be following Donald Polkinghorne's distinction between methods and methodology. Methods refer to the particular procedures or plans for "going after" knowledge. They include experimental designs, sampling procedures, measuring instruments, and the statistical treatment of data. Methodology, on the other hand, is the study or examination of those procedures or plans. It deals with the philosophical principles underlying and guiding the use of particular methods in the research process.[1] The first section of this chapter will cover the methodology implemented in this book: interpretive or lifeworld phenomenology. We will survey the value of phenomenological philosophy in qualitative, human studies, argue that the interpretive framework provides the best means for uncovering lived experience within a cross-cultural context, and discuss the possibility of a distinctly theological approach to phenomenological inquiry. In the second section of this chapter, I will outline the methods utilized for data collection and analysis, specifically the in-depth interview process and the subsequent phenomenological interpretation of the data.

---

1. Polkinghorne, *Methodology for the Human Sciences*, 5.

PHENOMENOLOGY AS A RESEARCH METHODOLOGY

This book is a qualitative study of lived experience within the Thai Christian lifeworld, the findings of which may inform ecclesiological, anthropological, and missiological formulations in and for the Thai church. Before we proceed to outline the specific methodology employed in this research, therefore, it is apposite to begin with a brief *apologia* for the appropriation of human science methods in informing theological reflection and ministerial practice.

Throughout the history of the church, theologians have exploited the methods, language, and concepts of prevailing philosophical systems for theological purposes. Whether it is Justin Martyr's Platonism, Augustine's Neoplatonism, Thomas Aquinas's Aristotelianism, or Paul Tillich's Heideggerianism, philosophy has often functioned as the "handmaiden" for theological reflection. With the postmodern turn, however, a priority on the lived and local has diverted the attention of theology toward the human sciences. Increasingly, theologians are recognizing the inherently situated nature of the theological task. This is not a simple affirmation of the cultural and social situatedness of theologians as they develop their academic systematic theologies, a fact that is now readily acknowledged. Even more, theologians are recognizing that faith is first and foremost embodied in worshipping and praying communities and is lived out as a theological habitus.[2] As Clare Watkins argues, "The things Christians do together, to express their faith, are examples of 'faith seeking understanding.' To listen to these practices is to listen to works of theology. They are embodied works of theology."[3] If indeed practices are bearers of theology, and if academic theology "does not create faith, but reflects a faith that is already present,"[4] then it behooves the theologian to attend to the lived experience of the community of faith, in all its social and cultural "messiness," in pursuit of the theological task. This reflection on the "worldliness" of the faith community does not necessarily entail the replacement of the authority of revelation with an experience-based "theology from below," however. Instead, as Paul Fiddes observes,

> Since faith *is* embodied in worldly and secular forms, it is appropriate that ecclesiology should use some secular tools to analyze

---

2. Scharen, "Ecclesiology 'from the Body.'"
3. Watkins, "Practical Ecclesiology," 170.
4. McGrath, "Cultivation of Theological Vision," 107.

Phenomenology as Method and Methodology

these forms. In our age these are predominantly the tools of the human sciences, but since this is *theology*, these are not to be used as if they were autonomous disciplines; they are to be used in the service of theological reflection, to assist us to find the theological dimension in the worldly forms of life.[5]

As a tool, therefore, the human sciences connect theology to the actual practice of situated, faith communities; offer plausibility by testing theological assertions with academic rigor;[6] and pave the way toward the construction of local theologies that are sensitive to sociocultural contexts while remaining faithful to the Christian tradition.[7] It is for this purpose and in this spirit that this research seeks to contribute to theological reflection through the use of phenomenological inquiry.

Multiple methodologies are available to the qualitative researcher, each of which attempts to understand human beings from a distinct conceptual perspective. These methodologies act as theoretical paradigms, applying certain ontological and epistemological assumptions that will steer the focus of inquiry, inform the research design, and determine what qualifies as true scientific discovery and understanding.[8] As a philosophy that studies human experience and "the way things present themselves to us in and through such experience,"[9] phenomenology provides a unique methodology for accessing the pre-theoretical, lived world of participants without imposing theoretical constructs or seeking causal explanations. Research methodologist Max van Manen comments,

> It [phenomenology] differs from almost every other science in that it attempts to gain insightful descriptions of the way we experience the world pre-reflectively, without taxonomizing, classifying, or abstracting it. So phenomenology does not offer us the possibility of effective theory with which we can now explain and/or control

---

5. Fiddes, "Ecclesiology and Ethnography," 20. Kathryn Tanner makes a similar claim when she quips, "There is no point in academic theology's making a proposal for change if it does not address people where they already are theologically" (Tanner, *Theories of Culture*, 85).

6. Ward, *Perspectives*, 4–5.

7. See Schreiter, *Constructing Local Theologies*.

8. For an overview of these available research methodologies, see Polkinghorne, *Methodology for the Human Sciences*; Butler-Kisber, *Qualitative Inquiry*; Given, *Sage Encyclopedia of Qualitative Research Methods*; Denzin and Lincoln, *Sage Handbook of Qualitative Research*.

9. Sokolowski, *Introduction*, 2.

the world, but rather it offers the possibility of plausible insights that bring us in more direct contact with the world.[10]

The value of phenomenological inquiry, therefore, resides in its ability to disclose the internal meaning structures of phenomena as lived-through existentially and primordially within an intersubjective lifeworld. For this reason, phenomenology presents a useful apparatus for investigating the lived meanings of Thai Christians as they experience marginality and structure their sacred identities within a Folk Buddhist culture and society.

Phenomenology as a research methodology is as diverse as is the philosophy upon which it is based. Lester Embree identifies four distinct stages in the development of philosophical phenomenology and suggests that the discipline is on the verge of a fifth period. These stages include: (1) realistic or eidetic phenomenology which seeks to uncover the essences of a phenomenon; (2) constitutive phenomenology involving Husserl's transcendental reduction; (3) existential phenomenology that prioritizes concrete, embodied human existence in the lived world; and (4) hermeneutical phenomenology that interprets phenomena as rooted in an historical encounter. The fifth period, Embree suggests, is "cultural phenomenology," or the reflective-descriptive philosophy of collective and individual human life in the socio-historical world.[11] Each stage has its representative philosophers and unique conceptual priorities, but they all agree that the essence of phenomenology is the methodological focus on phenomena—or as Heidegger averred, "to let that which shows itself be seen from itself in the very way in which it shows itself from itself."[12]

As might be expected, this variety in philosophical phenomenology has given birth to multiple research methodologies that have been applied across a wide array of disciplines. These include Interpretative Phenomenological Analysis (IPA),[13] reflective lifeworld research,[14] phenomenology of practice,[15] descriptive phenomenology,[16] interpretive or hermeneutical

---

10. Manen, *Researching Lived Experience*, 9. See also Yanow and Schwartz-Shea, *Interpretation and Method*, 15.

11. Embree, "Continuation," 4, 6.

12. Heidegger, *Being and Time*, 58.

13. Smith et al., *Interpretative Phenomenological Analysis*.

14. Dahlberg et al., *Reflective Lifeworld Research*.

15. Manen, *Phenomenology of Practice*.

16. Giorgi, "Theory, Practice, and Evaluation."

phenomenology,[17] and empirical phenomenology[18] to name just a few. Some phenomenological commentators argue that researchers ought to avoid seeking a harmonious integration of methodologies when appropriating a method as "there are irreconcilable differences among them."[19] Others, however, advocate for a more "multi-faceted" and "holistic" approach that does not privilege one particular phenomenological theorist, but is "influenced by the core emphases ... and by a number of further elements drawn from different positions."[20] In an attempt to resolve this impasse, it is important to remember that nearly every phenomenological research methodology draws from numerous thinkers, including Husserl, Heidegger, Merleau-Ponty, Sartre, and Gadamer, among others, when constructing its methodological apparatus. This apparatus, once constructed, presents a distinct approach toward understanding a given phenomenon that ought to be followed faithfully if the outcome is going to stand up to academic scrutiny. At the same time, phenomenology's priority on an intuitive grasping of what is given demands a purposeful openness to the phenomenon when choosing and tweaking a methodology. Phenomena, especially those in the religious realm, are not one size fits all. A methodology that may work in the psychological or educational disciplines, for example, may not be appropriate when investigating the lived experience of a sacred community. What this indicates, then, is that some level of hybridization is inevitable if one is to attend appropriately to the "things themselves." Without this flexibility, a methodology becomes an ossified, mechanical process imposed on phenomena and may end up obscuring rather than revealing understanding. As Anthony Steinbock comments, "The *way* something gives itself corresponds simultaneously to the manner in which we turn to it."[21] In light of this discussion, I believe the phenomenon under investigation lends itself toward a lifeworld phenomenological approach with some level of hybridization with the phenomenology of religion.

---

17. Yanow and Schwartz-Shea, *Interpretation and Method*.

18. Aspers, "Empirical Phenomenology."

19. Giorgi, "Difficulties Encountered," 2; Laverty, "Hermeneutic Phenomenology and Phenomenology," 16.

20. Smith et al., *Interpretative Phenomenological Analysis*, 34.

21. Steinbock, *Home and Beyond*, 263. See also Vagle, *Crafting Phenomenological Research*, 75.

LIFEWORLD PHENOMENOLOGY

Numerous contemporary methodologists, such as Max van Manen, Karin Dahlberg, Mark Vagle, and Jan Bengtsson, have been advocating for a phenomenological research methodology that investigates the lifeworld within the broader category of interpretive phenomenology. While each comes to the task with a distinct voice, a common late-Husserlian and Heideggerian thread pervades their respective approaches to human science investigations. Before we clarify the specific nature of this "lifeworld phenomenology," it will be helpful if we first summarize what is known as "descriptive phenomenology," as this will provide a foil for later clarifications. Much of what is to follow will be based on the philosophical discussions of chapter 2 and, as a result, will assume that the reader has a working knowledge of the relevant phenomenological concepts.

The descriptive approach to phenomenological research takes its philosophical cues from Husserl's static phenomenology as exemplified in the eidetic and phenomenological reductions. According to J. N. Mohanty, description is fundamentally about "givenness." It seeks to uncover the non-reducible essences of what is given to consciousness without the imposition of theoretical frameworks, judgments as to the ontological status of the essences, or speculative generalizations that extend beyond the region of the phenomena.[22] For Husserl, these essential regions of subjective consciousness are only disclosed through direct grasping or intuition, allowing the researcher to "give linguistic expression to the object of any given act precisely as it appears within that act."[23] Descriptive phenomenologist Amedeo Giorgi describes a three-part method instituted by Husserl: (1) adopt the phenomenological attitude, involving the bracketing of personal past knowledge, theoretical knowledge, and the existence or non-existence of the object or state of affairs; (2) use the process of free imaginative variation[24] in order to disclose the essence(s) of the phenomenon; and (3) carefully describe the essence(s) that are discovered.[25]

---

22. Mohanty, *Transcendental Phenomenology*, 9–15.

23. Giorgi, "Theory, Practice, and Evaluation," 4; Husserl, *Ideas*, 48–50.

24. Free imaginative variation is a thought experiment proposed by Husserl for uncovering essences. According to Mohanty, the steps include (1) start with an actual or imagined instance, (2) apply an infinitely open multiplicity of variants upon it, noting what remains the same in each variation and (3) the invariant structure or essences are disclosed. Mohanty, *Transcendental Phenomenology*, 25–26.

25. Giorgi, "Difficulties Encountered," 2–3.

For human science analysis, however, Giorgi argues that an additional step is required, namely the adoption of a disciplinary attitude which "brings proper sensitivity to the analysis and provides a perspective that enables the data to be manageable."[26] Because of the focus of descriptive phenomenology on the intentional meaning structures of consciousness, many have aligned this methodology with the discipline of psychology. In fact, Paul Ricoeur argues that this alignment, and sometimes confusion, of descriptive, eidetic phenomenology with psychology is due to Husserl's own idealistic tendencies that reduced the concept of intentionality to immanence, i.e., constituting subjectivity.[27] Whatever the case, it is clear that descriptive methodology prioritizes the static, constituting "of-ness" of consciousness,[28] allowing for a psychological "description" of the ways in which phenomena are lived in the natural attitude.[29]

Many human science researchers have expressed misgivings concerning the descriptive phenomenology approach, wondering whether pure description is even possible given the historical, social, and cultural situatedness of both researcher and participants. Further, there is a desire to move away from the idealistic/psychological tendencies of Husserl since, properly speaking, the task of phenomenology is not to "get inside other people's minds" but "to contemplate and theorize the various ways things manifest and appear in and through our being-in-the-world."[30] These theoretical shifts have led researchers to look instead to Heidegger and his existential analytic of *Dasein* as being-in-the-world for inspiration in framing an interpretive research methodology. While not necessarily in opposition to Husserl, especially his conceptualization of the lifeworld,[31] interpretive or hermeneutic phenomenology seeks understanding, not explanation; lived meanings, not essences. Interpretive researchers concentrate on "historical meanings of experience and their developmental

---

26. Giorgi, "Difficulties Encountered," 2.

27. Ricoeur, "Phenomenology and Hermeneutics," 85–89.

28. "Of-ness" refers to the intentional relationship between subject and object, i.e., that consciousness is always "of" something exterior to itself. See Vagle, *Crafting Phenomenological Research*, 36.

29. Applebaum, "Intentionality and Narrativity," 10; Vagle, *Crafting Phenomenological Research*, 36.

30. Vagle, *Crafting Phenomenological Research*, 22.

31. Several commentators have argued that Husserl and Heidegger were not as divergent, conceptually, as is often assumed. See Barua, "Husserl, Heidegger"; Applebaum, "Intentionality and Narrativity"; Mohanty, *Transcendental Phenomenology*, 52–60.

and cumulative effects on individual and social levels,"[32] following Heidegger's ontological supposition that humans are always already "thrown" into a world of objects, relationships, and language. Therefore, research always begins in the lifeworld and attempts to capture the pre-reflective meaning of the "living now."[33] Mark Vagle describes this as the "in-ness" of intended meanings or the methodological pursuit of understanding how "humans *find-themselves-in* states of being" versus the "of-ness" of Husserl's eidetic phenomenology.[34] Placing the preposition "in" in front of the phenomenon directs the researcher away from consciousness and toward what it is to be in the world in various intentional ways—in-love, in-pain, in-distress, or in the case of this research, in-marginality. In order to understand better how this is accomplished, we will briefly summarize the primary components of interpretive, lifeworld research: openness, reflexivity, and the double hermeneutic.

The fundamental axiom of lifeworld research is the contention that humans are historically situated beings. In the words of Heidegger, every *Dasein* operates with a "fore-structure," or set of pre-understandings, that forms our being-in-the-world and shapes our "everyday circumspective interpretation."[35] For human science research, this means that both researcher and participant come to the phenomenon under investigation with particular fundamental attitudes and beliefs that are formed within their respective sociocultural contexts and histories.[36] If this is true, then several methodological implications follow. First, interpretive or lifeworld research is characterized by openness. Holroyd explains that hermeneutic experience is always a learning experience: the researcher does not know everything

32. Laverty, "Hermeneutic Phenomenology and Phenomenology," 15.

33. Manen, *Researching Lived Experience*, 7; Manen, *Phenomenology of Practice*, 34.

34. Vagle, *Crafting Phenomenological Research*, 39; Freeman and Vagle, "Grafting," 729.

35. Heidegger, *Being and Time*, 188–95. It should also be noted that Hans-Georg Gadamer (1900–2002) has exerted considerable influence on the formation of interpretive research methodologies, especially his conceptualizations of the role of prejudice, tradition, and language in the hermeneutic process. While the methodology of this book aligns with many of Gadamer's theorizations, I find that there is sufficient philosophical grounding in Husserl's lifeworld theory and Heidegger's fundamental ontology to support the lifeworld phenomenology used for this research. For further discussion, see Gadamer, *Philosophical Hermeneutics*; Dahlberg et al., *Reflective Lifeworld Research*, 80–85; Manen, *Phenomenology of Practice*, 132–34; Smith et al., *Interpretative Phenomenological Analysis*, 25–27.

36. Holroyd, "Interpretive Hermeneutic Phenomenology," 4–5.

and engages the phenomenon with a "genuine desire to engage in the active process of listening."[37] Similarly, Manen argues that phenomenological study compels us into the basic disposition of wonder by which we are open to the deep meanings of a given human experience: those meanings which are typically overlooked in the natural attitude.[38] Karin Dahlberg states, "Openness thus means that as researchers we make ourselves available to the world, to the phenomenon of interest, as it presents itself."[39]

Second, the researcher must not only be open to the phenomenon as it presents itself but also open to themselves in an attitude of reflexivity. No researcher is able to bracket all of their biases and presuppositions completely in order to attend to the phenomenon from a perspective of pure objectivity and neutrality. However, it is possible and indeed essential for the researcher to be critically self-aware, i.e., to be conscious of how their presuppositions might impact the research process and findings.[40] Perhaps the best term for describing this more moderate understanding of the *epoché* is "bridling." While we cannot escape our pre-understandings, we can keep them in check or bridle them so that the otherness of a phenomenon may be effectively confronted in the research process.[41]

Third, lifeworld research entails a double hermeneutic. Max van Manen makes a distinction between the "living now" and the "mediated now." The living now is the pre-reflective presence "that we are always 'in' as we live our lives from moment to moment" while the mediated now is one's reflection on previously lived experience that "turns from the subjectivity of living presence into an object of reflective presence."[42] In other words, whenever an individual reflects on a particular lived experience, he or she enters an interpretive mode of active constitution.[43] It follows, then, that the researcher is not an objective, outside observer but an actual participant in the re-presentation of lived experience through the purposeful direction of the participant's reflective process. This is the first hermeneutic. The

---

37. Holroyd, "Interpretive Hermeneutic Phenomenology," 9.

38. Manen, *Phenomenology of Practice*, 36–39.

39. Dahlberg et al., *Reflective Lifeworld Research*, 97.

40. Finlay, "Dance," 17–18.

41. Dahlberg et al., *Reflective Lifeworld Research*, 118; Dahlberg, "Essence of Essences," 16; Vagle et al., "Remaining Skeptical."

42. Manen, *Phenomenology of Practice*, 34.

43. Applebaum states, "It is our pregiven embodied life in the world—the realm of passive intentionality—that is the soil within which our reflective lives are rooted" (Applebaum, "Intentionality and Narrativity," 6).

second hermeneutic occurs as the researcher attempts to "make sense of the participant trying to make sense of what is happening to them."[44] This hermeneutic is second-order in that the researcher only has access to the participant's experience through the participant's own account of it. Stated differently, the participant interprets his or her experience emically, or as experience-near, while the researcher interprets the experience etically, or as experience-distant.[45] Given this dual-interpretive nature of phenomenological inquiry, there resides even greater importance on the role of reflexivity and bridling so that interpretation discloses experience as lived and resists conceptual imposition.

In summary, the lifeworld phenomenological approach, as a subset of interpretive phenomenology, affirms the presupposition of the lifeworld on all levels. As Swedish phenomenologist Jan Bengtsson maintains, "There is no way to escape the lifeworld."[46] Life and world are always united, meaning that any research of lived experience must take into consideration not only the immanent meanings of participants, but also their lived historical, cultural, social, and linguistic contexts. Given the cross-cultural nature of this research, the lifeworld approach provides an effective way to understand a phenomenon without artificially removing it from its surrounding environment. This does not mean, however, that lifeworld phenomenologists are performing anthropological ethnographies, nor is their purpose in research simply to understand participant experience. Instead, the goal of lifeworld research is, as Max van Manen asserts, to reveal "possible human experiences in order to reflect on the meanings that may inhere in them";[47] that is, to understand phenomena as they occur within lived and worldly contexts.[48] This does not demand that the research produce generalizable results, but simply authentic meanings.[49] To accomplish this, multiple methods are open to the lifeworld researcher, including in-depth interviews, lived experience descriptions (LED), observation, and even

---

44. Smith et al., *Interpretative Phenomenological Analysis*, 3. Similarly, Clifford Geertz remarks, "What we call our data are really our own constructions of other people's constructions of what they and their compatriots are up to" (Geertz, *Interpretation of Cultures*, 9).

45. Yanow and Schwartz-Shea, *Interpretation and Method*, 20.

46. Bengtsson, "Lifeworld as Ground," 2.

47. Manen, *Phenomenology of Practice*, 313.

48. Bengtsson, "Lifeworld as Ground," 8; Vagle, *Crafting Phenomenological Research*, 85–86.

49. Bengtsson, "Lifeworld as Ground," 11.

Phenomenology as Method and Methodology

the empathetic reading of novels and short stories.[50] For data analysis, Max van Manen suggests a "guided existential inquiry" that explores phenomena through five categories: lived relation (relationality), lived body (corporeality), lived space (spatiality), lived time (temporality), and lived things (materiality).[51] The specific methods utilized for this research will be discussed later in this chapter.

THEOLOGICAL PHENOMENOLOGY

Before we move on to the methods of this research, it is important for us to remember that the phenomenon under investigation demands an exploration into the sacred nature of the Thai Christian lifeworld. In other words, the Thai Christian experience of in-marginality occurs in religious contexts, producing a unique sacred identity that can only be understood in relation to the Holy. Therefore, it is appropriate for this research to appeal to the phenomenology of religion for methodological guidance in performing a lifeworld investigation. The questions we will answer are: (1) How does the inclusion of the sacred affect lifeworld phenomenology? (2) How should we understand bracketing or bridling as it relates to the Holy? (3) Given the interpretive nature of this research, does specifically theological presuppositions have any bearing on how we approach this phenomenon?

Referring to the application of lifeworld research for educational settings, Jan Bengtsson states, "Education takes place in a world of things, activities and interactions. The participating persons need to have a practical understanding of these things, activities and interactions. If we want to understand educational situations, we have to understand them in their lived and worldly context as this is where they have their meaning."[52] What is true for educational settings is just as true for religious settings. If we are to understand *Homo religiosus*, we must understand her within her sacred lifeworld. This means that her existential being-in-the-world is not just characterized by temporality, materiality, spatiality, relationality, and corporeality, but by the infusion of the sacred into every one of these lived categories. At the same time, this research is not conducting a general typology of religious phenomena such as was performed by Leeuw or Eliade. Instead, while

---

50. Manen, *Phenomenology of Practice*, 312–19. Bengtsson argues that the choice of methods in lifeworld phenomenology demands creativity and eschews any universal, rigid procedure. Bengtsson, "Lifeworld as Ground," 10.

51. Manen, *Phenomenology of Practice*, 302–7.

52. Bengtsson, "Lifeworld as Ground," 8.

admitting that the phenomenon under investigation may have certain similarities to related phenomena in other religions, it is a distinctly Christian phenomenon that we are interested in disclosing. Therefore, the "regional lifeworld"[53] that is to be investigated is that of Thai Christianity, which takes place not only in a particular sociocultural setting but also in a generative tradition rooted in the historical events of Jesus of Nazareth and carried on communally in particular forms as *ecclesia*.

What does this mean for an interpretive methodological approach to sacred phenomena? In order to answer this question, we must recall the nature and role of the double hermeneutic in lifeworld research. During the interview process, the researcher guides participants in reflecting upon past, lived experience. This necessarily involves a process of selective position-taking "that includes some details and omits others, frames events and their sense in a particular way, and . . . represents the narrator as protagonist in a particular light, highlighting certain characteristics and not others."[54] This is not a process of active theorizing but of tacit interpreting that allows an event to be re-presented in a particular manner. The sacred self, therefore, will inevitably interpret events according to a "living theology," or an immanent, mundane understanding of the workings of the Holy in the everydayness of the natural attitude. As British theologian Alister McGrath asserts, "Christians reflect theologically, whether they are aware of doing this or not."[55] In addition, I come to this research with my own biases and pre-understandings that will shape the interview process and data analysis. As a Christian, I share many of the same convictions and experiences as those of the participants. Therefore, I am certainly "invested" in this research in ways that would differ from if I had investigated Buddhist religious experience, for example. The question, therefore, becomes how to approach this phenomenon phenomenologically; that is, how am I to perform the important methodological *epoché* while, at the same time, giving due weight to the nature of the phenomenon as it presents itself in all of its verticality?

---

53. For a discussion on regional ontologies as they relate to lifeworld phenomenology, see Bengtsson, "Lifeworld as Ground."

54. Applebaum, "Intentionality and Narrativity," 8.

55. McGrath, "Cultivation of Theological Vision," 115.

Phenomenology as Method and Methodology

One answer might be Heidegger's methodological atheism, which is often utilized in the phenomenology of religion.[56] In defense of this position, James Cox argues,

> The phenomenologist wants to observe the phenomena of religion as they appear rather than as they are understood through opinions formed prior to their being observed. This means suspending *personal beliefs* and withholding judgements on *academic theories* about religion. If, for example, the observer is a committed Christian who believes that Jesus Christ is the true and complete revelation of God, acting as a phenomenologist, the student of religion must suspend that judgement and try to allow the phenomena under observation to speak for themselves without their being filtered through Christian presuppositions.[57]

Certainly, the imposition of academic theories, whether religious or non-religious, is anathema to phenomenological research. However, is religious commitment an academic theory? Is it even possible for a committed Christian to suspend their judgment that "Jesus Christ is the true and complete revelation of God" without essentially removing their very self from the research process? In addition, does not suspending this judgment entail adopting certain atheistic assumptions in its stead in order to conform to supposed academic or phenomenological standards? In response to this, Ninian Smart advocates instead for a softer approach, which he calls "methodological agnosticism." For Smart, the researcher neither affirms nor denies the actual existence of sacred entities and experiences but treats them as real whatever his or her personal convictions might be.[58] This approach does not commit the phenomenologist to indifference but simply to a purposeful avoidance of the existence question. While this approach certainly seems better than methodological atheism, especially for cross-religious or multi-religious studies, is it necessary for cases like this one where both researcher and participants share the same faith?

As we attempt to present an alternative to methodological atheism or agnosticism in phenomenological research, it is important to remember the fundamental axiom of interpretive research: everyone enters the research process already embedded within a particular lifeworld. For how

---

56. This is also the methodology used by phenomenological sociologist, Peter Berger. See Berger, *Sacred Canopy*, 100, 180.

57. Cox, *Introduction*, 49–50.

58. Smart, *Science of Religion*, 49–58; *Phenomenon of Religion*, 61–66.

this relates to one's choice of methodology, Christian theologian John Swinton reminds us,

> The decision to choose particular methods reflects the way in which the researcher understands the world to be. This being so, the apparently simple act of choosing to use certain methods over and against others already implies a philosophical and epistemological positioning and, as I will suggest later, an implicit or explicit theological position.[59]

Later in the article, Swinton argues that when Christians engage in scientific research, they often do so as Deists. Instead of adopting atheistic or secular assumptions for conducting ecclesiastical research, he contends, why not purposefully approach the phenomenon from a distinctively theological perspective?[60] Hermeneutically speaking, it is impossible and, indeed, undesirable for the researcher to attempt a complete bracketing of all biases and pre-understandings. In fact, research phenomenologist Susann Laverty claims that in a hermeneutical approach "the biases and assumptions of the research are not bracketed or set aside, but rather are embedded and essential to interpretive process (*sic*). The researcher is called, on an ongoing basis, to give considerable thought to their own experience and to explicitly claim the ways in which their position or experience relates to the issues being researched."[61] Coming back to the double hermeneutic, this necessitates a "fusion of horizons" between the researcher's lifeworld and the participant's lifeworld. Not only ought presuppositions be made explicit when conducting lifeworld research, but also they should be understood as contributing to the interpretive process, especially when both researcher and participants share the same religious convictions.[62] What I would propose, therefore, is a "theological phenomenology" or "methodological theism" that bridles second-order theological imposition but allows for the assumption of first-order theological convictions as part of the research process. This methodological perspective, I believe, is most faithful to the phenomenon under investigation as it presents itself, and it allows for the findings of this research to be best tailored for the intended audience: that of the Christian community in Thailand and in other regions of the globe.

59. Swinton, "'Where Is Your Church?,'" 78.
60. Swinton, "'Where Is Your Church?,'" 79, 87.
61. Laverty, "Hermeneutic Phenomenology and Phenomenology," 17.
62. Holroyd, "Interpretive Hermeneutic Phenomenology," 5; Bradfield, "Examining the Lived World," 3; Bengtsson, "Lifeworld as Ground," 9.

METHODS

In the previous section, we looked at the methodological principles underpinning this research. I argued that lifeworld phenomenology, combined with an allowance for first-order theological presuppositions to inform the interpretive process, is an appropriate methodology for investigating the lived experience of marginality among Thai Christians. In this section, I will delineate the specific methods utilized for approaching, gathering, and interpreting the research data. After a brief overview of my approach and a disclosure regarding germane pre-understandings, I will describe the interview process and how the data gathered during the interviews was transcribed, analyzed, and collated into interpretive themes.

Overall Approach

This research is an applied, qualitative study in the field of the philosophy of religious experience, namely interpretive phenomenology. The goal of the study is to reveal the lived experience of marginality among Thai Christians for the purpose of disclosing possible human experiences and the meanings that inhere in them. With this aim in mind, I recognize the limitations inherent in this research. First, the findings of this study are not appropriate for empirical or statistical generalization for the population of Thai Christians at large. The small sampling size, the nature of phenomenological inquiry, and the reality of the researcher's own interpretation of meanings restrict the generalizability of results. Second, the findings of this study are not intended, in themselves, to constitute theoretical constructs for "explaining" the phenomenon. While the data presented may contribute to theoretical formulations across multiple disciplines, the goal of this study is, rather, to provide a depth of understanding of the lived meanings inherent within the Thai Christian lifeworld.[63] Finally, despite the cross-cultural nature of this research, namely the disparity of worlds between researcher and participants, neither the research processes nor the results should be considered ethnographic in nature. My intention in this study is not to analyze the cultural "stuff" of the Thai Christian world from the perspective of an "expert" but to reveal and describe the phenomenon as lived through by the participants themselves.

---

63. For a discussion on depth as an appropriate evaluative appraisal to phenomenological studies, see Manen, *Phenomenology of Practice*, 355.

Impact of Researcher and Participant Pre-understandings

As an interpretive analysis, it is imperative that I remain critically self-aware throughout the research process so that I may effectively bridle my biases and maintain openness to how the phenomenon reveals itself. I have reserved this section for a brief disclosure of my pre-understandings and how my involvement may have shaped the study.[64] First, related to the impact of the researcher, I recognize that participants framed their responses to my questions, at least in part, based on their perceptions of me. These perceptions include the fact that I am a white, American male (that is, non-Thai), pursuing an advanced educational degree (highly respected in Thai society), employed as a seminary professor (carrying with it a certain level of spiritual authority), and resident in Thailand (with an awareness of Thai Christianity but limited in language ability and apprehension of cultural norms and values). As a result of these perceptions, participants may have, at times, withheld deep, emotional responses and/or may have tailored their responses based on what they believed I wanted to hear. While I attempted to mitigate these potential problems through an attitude of deep listening and casual friendliness, I did recognize times when participants seemed uncomfortable or hesitant to disclose fully their affective responses to situations of marginalization. Also, on occasion, I sensed that participants were withholding narratives or perspectives that might present themselves in a negative light. This may have been motivated, in part, by a desire for a positive self-image before a foreigner.

Jan Bengtsson asserts, "If the presuppositions of research are not open to examination, the research's contribution to scientific knowledge could be brought into question."[65] Therefore, it is essential that I briefly state the pre-understandings that may have guided or influenced my approach to the research topic. First, one of my motivations for choosing this particular phenomenon is the fact that I am a Protestant Christian, and I desire to understand further the nature of Protestant Christian experience. As a consequence, all of the participants chosen were in line with my broadly Protestant, ecclesiastical position. While an alignment of religious commitments between researcher and participants can be beneficial for

---

64. However, as Linda Finlay reminds us, we must also keep in mind that reflexivity is not simply a one-time activity but a "constant striving" that allows the researcher "to move beyond the partiality of our previous understandings and our investment in particular research outcomes" (Finlay, "Dance," 17).

65. Bengtsson, "Lifeworld as Ground," 3.

producing empathy and may, as argued above, assist in the interpretive process, I recognize that this alignment also carries with it the possibility that I have assumed more than is present in the data due to my prior understanding of Protestant Christian lived experience. In addition, I recognize the fact that by choosing to remain within the Protestant tradition, I have neglected the lived experience of others within the broader Christian tradition (such as Roman Catholic). Second, I am a trained theologian, having earned previous graduate-level degrees in theology and having taught theology in a graduate-level, ministry-training institution for nearly twenty years. This training may have caused me to seek alignment of participant data with certain theological positions on Christian identity and/or may have led to the imposition of theological constructs on the interview and data analysis processes. Finally, I am a Western missionary who has lived in Southeast Asia for over fifteen years. This history may have produced in me a sense of "expertise" related to matters of Asian culture and Asian Christian experience, prohibiting me, to some extent, from approaching the topic in a manner of openness.

In order to bridle my pre-understandings effectively and to allow me to be open to the phenomenon as it presents itself, I maintained a series of three personal logs as a reflexive activity. The interview and data analysis logs were maintained to record the processes followed, my personal impressions, and incipient themes related to and emerging from the interviews and data analysis. A third log, which I entitled "bridling log," was reserved for recording pre-understandings, personal limitations, or affective responses that came to the fore during the research process. While these logs proved useful in bridling or bracketing my pre-understandings, I agree with the perspective of Karin Dahlberg who asserts that bridling is less a methodological technique and more of a phenomenological attitude of "non-willing" or "dwelling" with the phenomenon.[66] I have attempted to maintain this attitude, to the best of my ability, throughout this study.

The Interview as Method

My research question is: "What is the experience of in-marginality among late-convert Christians of Northern Thailand who have transferred from the Thai Buddhist lifeworld into the new sociocultural 'world' of Christian belief and identity?" In order to disclose the phenomenon of in-marginality as

---

66. Dahlberg, "Essence of Essences," 16.

lived, I decided to adopt the interview, namely the "semi-structured lifeworld interview," as my primary method for data gathering. Kvale defines the semi-structured lifeworld interview as "an interview whose purpose is to obtain descriptions of the life world of the interviewee with respect to interpreting the meaning of the described phenomena."[67] This style of interview utilizes a rough outline of questions to guide the interview, but it prioritizes a conversational, open-ended approach by which the interviewer uses their judgment and tact to guide the conversation toward elucidating the phenomenon.[68] The "data" to be gathered during the interview are primarily pre-reflective, uninterpreted experiential accounts in narrative form.[69]

Selecting Participants

Seven participants were selected for this study. This number was sufficiently within the range recommended by the literature and seemed reasonable for allowing for in-depth interviewing while still keeping the quantity of data manageable.[70] Six of the participants were referred to me via informal gatekeepers and one was recommended by another participant. After initial communication by email, I made a contact visit in person with each candidate to (1) determine whether he/she met my selection criteria, (2) have him/her read and sign the consent form, (3) evaluate his/her ability to converse in English, and (4) set up the first interview. My selection criteria were as follows:

1. *Ethnic Thai*: By limiting the participants to ethnic Thais, I purposefully excluded the tribal peoples of Northern Thailand. The reasons for this exclusion are (1) many tribal peoples have animistic, not Buddhist, backgrounds; (2) Christianity is more prevalent among the tribal peoples, often serving as the predominant plausibility structure for those ethnic groups; and (3) in many ways, tribal identity is significantly divergent and separate from traditional Thai identity.

---

67. Kvale, *Interviews*, 5–6.
68. Kvale, *Interviews*, 129–35.
69. Manen, *Phenomenology of Practice*, 314.
70. Because phenomenological qualitative research is more concerned with depth than generalizability, recommended sample sizes tend to be much smaller than other methodologies. Smith, Flowers, and Larkin recommend four to ten participants, while others, like Churchill, suggest that just one in-depth case study is sufficient for a proper phenomenological analysis. Smith et al., *Interpretative Phenomenological Analysis*, 51–52; Churchill, "Considerations for Teaching," 58–59.

2. *Primary socialization in a Thai-Buddhist family*: Given the variety of Buddhism and levels of adherence in Thailand, I relied on self-categorizations for determining whether an individual's background met this criterion.

3. *Adult converts (late teen or older)*: "Adult converts" here refers to both (1) converted as an adult and (2) all participants were of adult age. This stipulation allowed for each participant to have undergone a significant period of socialization within the Thai Buddhist lifeworld and provided a level of maturity among participants such that they could effectively communicate their experiences.

4. *Self-identified as a Christian for at least two years*: Self-identification was the primary means for determining participants' Christian identity. The purpose of the two-year requirement was to allow enough time for narratives of marginalization to emerge in the lives of participants.

5. *Active in a local, Protestant church*: This was utilized as one means for determining participants' Christian identity.

6. *Representation from numerous denominations within the Protestant tradition*: I found that, to a limited extent, coping strategies for marginalization vary among denominations due to theological and ministerial priorities.

7. *Equal or near-equal representation of males and females*: While not strictly required for phenomenological studies, I decided this was an important criterion for more fully exploring the Thai Christian lifeworld.

8. *Resident in Chiang Mai or within forty kilometers of Chiang Mai city*: This criterion was established for the sake of convenience as well as to focus the geographical pool. Chiang Mai is known to contain the largest percentage of Christians in Thailand.

9. *No prior relationship with the researcher*: This criterion was implemented for ethics clearance and to prevent the manipulation or distortion of responses.

10. *Conversant in English*: Due to my limitations with the Thai language, performing the interviews in English was more conducive to exploring deep nuances of meaning with participants. I recognize, however, that the choice of English-speakers limited the sample to more educated individuals.

The first criterion presented some difficulties with several of the participants who self-identified as either partially or fully Chinese. However, in discussing this with them, I determined that they adequately met my criteria since (1) many, if not most, Thai Christians have some percentage of Chinese descent; (2) all of the families of the participants have lived as citizens of Thailand throughout multiple generations; (3) Thai is the primary language of all the participants; and (4) all participants were socialized within Thai culture and society, including some level of adherence to Thai Buddhism. While those with Chinese heritage displayed some divergences from other Thais, such as the practice of ancestor veneration or the ability to speak a Chinese language, the convergences were significant enough to justify their inclusion in this study.

In addition, during the early conceptualization phases, I had anticipated choosing participants who could be considered lay members of a local church as opposed to clergy. It was thought that lay members would represent a less developed theological legitimating apparatus, thereby allowing more direct access to actual lived experience and subjective meaning structures. In addition, lay members would likely be more active than professional clergy in the Thai Buddhist environment due to work obligations. As I began my search for participants, however, I quickly discovered that many Thai Christians, especially those connected with certain denominations or ministry groups, have gone through periods of training and "professional" ministry service at one point in their lives. Therefore, since producing an adequate definition of "lay member" for Thai Christians presented considerable difficulty, I removed this criterion from the list while purposefully avoiding participants who were currently employed as clergy.

Interview Procedure

During the early conceptualization phase, and after having obtained ethics clearance,[71] I performed pilot interviews in order to determine which style of interview was most effective, fine-tune my list of questions, and gain experience in performing interviews. After testing both personal interviews and focus groups, I decided that personal interviews were most effective in overcoming participant anxiety and in producing a conversational atmosphere wherein participants were comfortable expressing

---

71. Ethics clearance was granted by the Australian College of Theology on February 4, 2014.

their deepest thoughts and emotions. My approach to the personal interviews was as follows:

1. Agree on a quiet, convenient location for the interview.
2. Begin with a briefing related to how the interview will proceed.
3. Set timer for ninety minutes and prepare recorder.
4. Perform the interview in a conversational style, balancing structure and openness.
5. End with a debriefing, summarizing main points, answering questions (if any), talking about purpose of interview, and setting up the next interview.
6. Immediately after the participant's departure, reflect on the interview and write down impressions in the interview log.

Each participant was interviewed twice, with each interview audio-recorded and lasting ninety minutes. There were two exceptions: (1) I performed three interviews with Ploy due to her ability to provide rich descriptions related to the Thai Buddhist lifeworld, and (2) I performed one interview with Tom due to his own uncertainty regarding his conversion experience as well as his lack of openness during the interview. I prepared a total of forty-six questions, the majority of which focused on lived experience descriptions, to guide both interviews. The questions served only as a rough guide, with no single participant answering all of them and with other questions added where required to direct the interview based on context. The questions were categorized according to nine topics: (1) conversion, (2) family, (3) village, (4) friendships, (5) festivals and ceremonies, (6) work, (7) church, (8) spirituality, and (9) nation and culture. During the interviews, I sought to disclose the temporal, narratival character of the phenomenon; namely, the movement of the participant's narrative identity via primary socialization, conversion, and post-conversion marginalization.[72] The interviews were performed in English, with a limited use of Thai as necessary. After the interviews for each participant had been completed, I wrote a two-page summary of the interviews and sent it to the participant for confirmation of accuracy and final authorization for usage in the research.

---

72. For a description of narrative identity, see Ricoeur, *Oneself as Another*, 113–68.

During the conceptualization phase, I considered having translators present in the interviews to translate occasional Thai words or phrases. However, during the focus group pilot interview, I discovered that the introduction of more than one Thai in the interview setting complicated the social situation for several reasons: (1) if a translator is present, Thais will often revert to using Thai rather than attempting to use English; (2) since Thailand is a hierarchical society, social positioning influences responses, causing participants to be less open in order to save face; and (3) a translator introduces a two-on-one scenario which can cause feelings of apprehension and may restrict open and honest responses. In lieu of a translator, I encouraged participants to use Thai words or phrases as necessary for communicating important meanings, writing them down for later analysis. Also, during the transcription phase, I utilized a translator to ensure that these phrases were accurately transcribed and translated.

Transcription

Transcription of the interviews was performed by a hired transcriber who utilized *F5transkript* software to create a semantic record of the audio material. As suggested by Smith, Flowers, and Larkin, a simplified approach to non-verbal elements was implemented, including notations for laughter, pauses, animation, or a subdued tone.[73] Additional notations were made for elements of the conversation where Thai words were used, responses were incomprehensible, or adjustment was necessary in order to convey meaning (used sparingly). A Thai translator was hired to translate the few Thai words or phrases that were spoken during the interviews.

Data Analysis

In agreement with Devenish, I found a scarcity of material in the phenomenological literature related to a procedural method for analyzing and explicating phenomena.[74] Instead, priority was often given to revealing the dangers of following a mechanistic analysis procedure or to achieving an intuitive awareness of or empathic dwelling with the meaning structures inherent in the data.[75] However, several phenomenological texts devoted to

---

73. Smith et al., *Interpretative Phenomenological Analysis*, 74.

74. Devenish, "Applied Method," 2. I found Smith, Flowers, and Larkin to contain the most detailed outline of data analysis procedures. Smith et al., *Interpretative Phenomenological Analysis*, 79–107.

75. For example, Manen states, "It should be clear that codifications, conceptual

Phenomenology as Method and Methodology

qualitative inquiry did outline some basic steps and parameters for analyzing data within a phenomenological framework. In an effort to develop my own procedural plan, I systematized those steps, chose the ones most relevant to the phenomenon under investigation, adjusted them as necessary, and then implemented those steps in my own analysis of the data.[76]

A common thread throughout the literature regarding phenomenological analysis is the theme of whole-parts-whole. Vagle explains, "In short, whole-part-whole analysis methods stem from the idea that we must always think about focal meanings (e.g., moments) in relation to the whole (e.g., broader context) from which they are situated—and once we begin to remove parts from one context and put them in dialogue with other parts, we end up creating new analytic wholes that have particular meanings in relation to the phenomena."[77] This whole-parts-whole analysis method formed the overall structure for my own analysis plan, which was as follows:

1. *Enact bridling*: While unable to remove myself completely from the research process, I purposefully sought to (1) bridle my own understanding of Christian identity based on theology, experience, or observation; (2) bridle the tentative thoughts and assumptions I had already drawn regarding the phenomenon during the proposal and interview stages; (3) develop an attitude of openness to the phenomenon as it discloses itself in the transcripts; and (4) log my pre-understandings.

2. *Holistic reading 1*: I read each participant's interview transcripts, creating a two-page summary of the content according to the categories of conversion, pre-conversion, marginality, and identity. These were sent

---

abstractions, or empirical generalizations can never adequately produce phenomenological understandings and insights as have been described in this book. None of the work of the leading proponents of the phenomenological tradition would be commensurate with abstracting, coding, and procedural approaches; developing taxonomies; looking for recurring concepts or themes; and so on" (Manen, *Phenomenology of Practice*, 319). For similar perspectives, see Vagle, *Crafting Phenomenological Research*, 97–98; Smith et al., *Interpretative Phenomenological Analysis*, 81.

76. Texts utilized to craft my own data analysis plan included Manen, *Researching Lived Experience*; *Phenomenology of Practice*; Seidman, *Interviewing as Qualitative Research*; Moustakas, *Research Methods*; Dahlberg et al., *Reflective Lifeworld Research*; Smith et al., *Interpretative Phenomenological Analysis*; Vagle, *Crafting Phenomenological Research*; Devenish, "Applied Method."

77. Vagle, *Crafting Phenomenological Research*, 97. See also Dahlberg et al., *Reflective Lifeworld Research*, 185–94; Manen, *Phenomenology of Practice*, 319–23.

to each participant for an accuracy check and to attain final authorization for usage in the research.

3. *Individual analysis:* I followed these steps with each participant, one at a time. To assist in the organization of material, I utilized *F4analyse* software.

   a. *Holistic reading 2:* I read the participant's transcripts along with the audio, making corrections and adding Thai script and translations as necessary. I constructed a one- to two-sentence phenomenological summary of the whole.

   b. *Detailed reading 1:* The transcript was read line-by-line, highlighting statements related to the Thai lifeworld and inputting phenomenological and disciplinary comments, including questions and interpretations, as appropriate. Comments were entered as memos in *F4analyse*.

   c. *Detailed reading 2:* The transcript was again read line-by-line, this time to allow for the separation of the material into natural meaning units (NMU's). I selected the NMU's that were relevant to the phenomenon and categorized them according to meaning, using the color-coding system of *F4analyse*.

   d. *Mind maps:* After completing both detailed readings, I created two mind maps for each participant which highlighted (1) the frequency of themes and (2) a tentative interpretation of how the themes may be grouped together.

   e. *Textural-structural description:* For each participant, using the memos, categorizations, and mind maps constructed earlier, I wrote a one-page, textural-structural description that followed a narrative identity paradigm: pre-conversion "home," world transfer, and confrontation or marginalization. Unlike the earlier interview summary, this description sought to disclose the idiographic, phenomenological themes arising from the data of each participant.[78] Manen's guided existential inquiry process assisted in the formulation of these descriptions.[79]

---

78. A textural-structural description is a "vocative method" that seeks to describe the meanings and essences of the phenomenon in a way that properly embodies the vividness and nearness of the lived experience. Manen, *Phenomenology of Practice*, 240–51; Moustakas, *Research Methods*, 34–35, 100, 120–22.

79. Manen, *Phenomenology of Practice*, 302–7.

4. *Synthesis*: The parts that were disclosed during the individual analyses were then synthesized into a new whole by grouping NMU's together into larger interpretive themes. A mind map assisted in this grouping process, allowing for a greater opportunity for the imaginative variation of categories. Four meta-themes or "moments" emerged from this process, which represent more of a synchronic orientation to the data: verticality, emplacement, displacement, and negotiation. I conducted further groupings at the interpretive theme and sub-theme levels, which, together, formed the basic, essential structure for the four analysis chapters. To accomplish these groupings, I utilized the phenomenological process of free imaginative variation which prioritizes the creative and intuitive search for commonalities of meaning among NMU's. I then prepared my interpretation of these themes by considering them against the backdrop of the three horizons of this research: sociocultural identity change, philosophical phenomenology, and the Christian tradition.

INTRODUCTION TO PARTICIPANTS

In the final section of this chapter, I will briefly summarize the biographical narratives of each participant. A pseudonym will be used to designate each participant, along with information on gender and age. The narratives will follow the pre-conversion, conversion, post-conversion paradigm.

Tom (male, twenty-six)

In Tom's family, Buddhism was practiced more as ritual and tradition than as a philosophy for life. Graphic portrayals of hell which were displayed in the temple, including visualizations of grotesque punishments for particular sins, produced in Tom a sense of fear and guilt. At the age of eleven, he began to study English with a "nice" and "kind" private tutor who happened to be a Christian. After a presentation of a Christian video and a discussion with his tutor about Jesus and the nature of Christian conversion, Tom made a decision to convert. His primary motivation for this decision was to go to heaven and escape the punishments of hell. While the tutor provided some limited guidance for living out his new religious identity, Tom did not immediately join a church and he continued participating in Buddhist activities. He describes this period as a time of confusion. While self-defining as a Christian, he also experienced significant social pressure to conform to traditional Buddhist practice. At the age of seventeen, however, he joined a group of Christian friends, attended a Christian camp, and made another commitment to live out a Christian identity. His immersion in the Christian community helped him grow in his understanding of the Christian faith and, as a result, created in him a sense of confidence regarding his religious identity. When he revealed his new identity to friends and family, Tom's friends considered him strange for going against Thai-Buddhist traditions, and his parents refused to accept his new identity for a period of approximately six months.

Lek (male, forty-one)

Lek's family were Buddhists, although not strong in belief and practice. Frequently, Lek noticed the contradiction between Buddhist teachings and the actual practice of monks, making him suspicious of ritualistic Buddhism; however, he still upheld Buddhism as a philosophy of life. During university, he met his wife who happened to be a Christian. He told her that Christianity was fine for her, but that he was content with being a Buddhist. However, after graduation from university, Lek had difficulties finding a job. He was insecure and anxious; unsure of how he would support his family during this time. His wife, on the other hand, displayed no signs of worry. She was calm and secure in her belief that God would take care of them. As a result of his wife's influence, Lek decided to pray to God to help resolve his situation. Soon after, Lek found a job, an occurrence which he attributed to God's power in answering his prayer. He then sought a pastor who taught him about Christianity, and, through the pastor's guidance, he converted to Christianity. Even though Lek understood very little about Christian belief and action at the time, he saw his conversion as the start to his progressive entrance into Christian identity. Lek's family did not approve of his new religious identity, questioning his motivations for conversion, but they eventually grew to accept it. He believes that by performing loving actions toward his family, he will influence them not only to accept his religious identity, but also to become Christians themselves.

Nid (female, fifty)

During primary socialization, Nid developed a hybrid religious consciousness. Her father was Chinese, enforcing ancestor veneration at home, while her mother was Buddhist, enforcing temple attendance. Since Buddhism is deeply ingrained in the Thai social identity, Nid experienced pressure from friends to adhere to Buddhist belief and practice. This pressure eventually led to her abandonment of her Chinese identity and the subsequent adoption of a full, Thai-Buddhist identity. For university, Nid left her conservative home in Northeast Thailand to attend a Christian school in Chiang Mai. During this time, she encountered other Christians for the first time and was impressed by their kindness and care for one another. She began testing a Christian identity, attending church and small groups, praying with other Christians, and reading the Bible. At times, God spoke to her directly, encouraging her to continue going to church. It was very important to Nid that she be perceived by others as responsible for making her own decisions, especially in her choice of religion. After university, she was chosen to work at a YMCA camp in the US for a period of time, during which she self-identified as a Christian. However, she perceives her entrance into Christian identity as occurring gradually. When she returned from the US, she describes her identity as being 80 percent Christian and 20 percent Buddhist, the 20 percent representative of the social pressures for conformity that she experienced from her friends and family. Eventually, she decided to become 100 percent Christian, which for Nid meant being baptized and informing friends and relatives of her new faith. She finds it difficult to live as a Christian in Thailand, though, due to the social pressures she regularly encounters.

Kay (female, thirty-three)

Kay's family adhered to a mixture of Chinese religious traditions and Thai Buddhism. Every day, she was required to perform rituals at the household altar, often under the close supervision of her father. Kay's father was extremely abusive, often beating, kicking, or berating her, sometimes publicly. This led to a deep animosity toward her parents and a distorted self-image, which culminated in a suicide attempt. At one point, while in the process of slitting her wrists, Kay happened to be watching a Christian show on television which spoke of God's love and forgiveness. Kay believed that God was speaking directly to her, so she ceased her attempt at suicide and prayed to become a Christian. Since she was still living with her family, she kept her conversion a secret. She inwardly knew that she should no longer perform Chinese or Buddhist rituals, but the pressure she experienced from her father forced her to continue these practices reluctantly. Eventually, Kay entered university and became friends with other Christians who worked for a campus ministry organization. Several members of this group mentored Kay, sometimes enforcing strict rules and penalties to assist Kay in ceasing her "bad habits." Kay entered a church community which exhibited an impressive egalitarian ethos. She describes her baptism as being like a marriage between her and God, a relationship characterized by love and forgiveness. Over time, Kay decided to join the campus ministry full-time, a decision which prompted severe reactions from her family, including a cessation of communication for six months.

Wit (male, fifty-one)

Wit's father grew up and was educated in a temple school. While this experience did not instill in him a deep commitment to Buddhist practice, it did create a deep respect for the monks who had raised him. The importance of this family connection to the temple was passed on to Wit. While in university, however, Wit's wife became influenced by Christians, and she started attending church. To make sure his wife was not involved in a cult, Wit began attending church as well. While at church, Wit developed several friendships, heard narratives of God's provision and power, and practiced several Christian rituals such as singing and prayer. At the time, he believed in the existence of God, but he believed that he was capable of taking care of himself. A family crisis, however, shook Wit's world, leaving him with feelings of anxiety and insufficiency. He began praying to God for help, which he believed came in the form of an emotional change: from anxiety to peace. He officially converted to Christianity at that time. Because of his family connection to the temple, Wit's parents did not readily accept his new religious identity. Wit's father asked him to adhere to both Buddhism and Christianity, thinking that by continuing the performance of Buddhist rituals, Wit would be able to show his ongoing respect to the monks and the family. However, Wit's strong sense of religious exclusivism made the adoption of a hybrid identity impossible. This decision led to a long period of negotiation whereby Wit sought to demonstrate his loyalty to the family while, at the same time, refusing to participate in Buddhist rituals.

Ploy (female, forty-four)

Despite growing up in a Buddhist family, Ploy's parents sent her to a Christian primary and secondary school for her education. At the Christian school, Ploy was taught Bible stories and how to pray. This exposure to Christianity, combined with the Buddhism taught to her by her mother and grandmother, produced in Ploy a hybrid, religious consciousness. She understood the religious world territorially: Christian places were the locations of the Christian God while Buddhist places were the locations of Buddha, the spirits, or deceased monks. Concomitantly, she was comfortable praying to both God and the spirits, and she would often compare the moral commands and belief systems of both religions. After marrying an American and having a child of her own, she recognized the importance of religion for instilling in her son moral standards of right and wrong. Because only Thai is spoken in the Buddhist temple, she chose Christianity as her son's religion. This decision prompted her own further investigation of the Christian belief system, eventually leading to a conversion experience, including the abandonment of her adherence to Buddhism. Out of fear of negative feedback, Ploy kept her conversion a secret from her mother and grandmother. Currently, she occasionally experiences social pressure to perform Buddhist rituals and conform to a Thai-Buddhist identity despite her self-identification as a Christian.

Nan (female, fifty-nine)

Growing up in a Chinese family in Thailand, Nan was introduced to both Thai Buddhism and Chinese ancestor veneration. However, Nan and her siblings were more interested in pursuing religion as a philosophy of life than in performing rituals or attending temple ceremonies. During her teen years, Nan sought meaning and purpose in political activism and Buddhist meditation, both of which she found ultimately unsatisfying. While in medical school, Nan encountered a group of Christians who invited her to attend their church. This began her investigation of Christianity which included small group and church attendance as well as personal study of the Bible. One night, while reading a passage of Scripture, Nan believed that God was speaking directly to her, leading her to make a decision to convert to Christianity. Her baptism, which represented the seriousness of her commitment to her new identity, sparked negative responses from her sister who believed that Nan, by converting to Christianity, was becoming an outsider. Nan upholds a strong commitment to religious exclusivism, believing that she must no longer perform Buddhist practices. Sometimes this commitment introduces situations of conflict and tension, especially at family religious ceremonies and at funerals, but she is able to manage this conflict by demonstrating her loyalty to the group and because, as a medical doctor, she maintains a respected position in society.

CONCLUSION

As I have highlighted in this chapter, our journey of exploration into the world of Thai converts will proceed via the route of interpretive or lifeworld phenomenology. By maintaining a perspective of openness and by being aware of the potential of our own pre-understandings in shaping the exploration, we will be able to unveil the complex meanings inherent in living a marginalized existence as arising from religious alternation. To venture on this path does not require us to abandon our first-order theological presuppositions, necessarily, but only to bridle purposefully our theoretical assumptions and second-order theological convictions in order to attend properly to "the thing itself." Further, the method of in-depth interviewing of seven Thai participants will be our means of access to this phenomenon. Now, with this apparatus in hand, it is time to begin our investigation into the phenomenon of in-marginality.

5

Thai Buddhist Homeworld

INTRODUCTION

ANY ATTEMPT TO REVEAL the lived world of a marginalized people must begin by defining the "normative scheme," or the expected and "normal" ways of being-in-the-world for a given society, based upon which someone may then be considered deviant or "abnormal."[1] This normative scheme is one's generative homeworld which, while adopted during primary socialization, may be dis-appropriated to some extent during secondary socialization, especially as a result of religious alternation.[2] The purpose of this chapter, therefore, is to provide a cursory overview of the Thai Buddhist homeworld in an effort to provide a baseline of sorts for understanding the participants' post-conversion experience of marginalization. My intent is not to provide a comprehensive analysis of the worldview, history, culture, religion, or psychology of the Thai people, all of which have been adequately treated in other sources.[3] Instead, I will pursue a much more modest summation of the regional lifeworld of the participants as described during the interview process. While we could safely assume that the material presented in this chapter would apply to many, if not most, Thai Buddhists, the intent is not

---

1. Duling, "Matthew and Marginality," 366.

2. Berger and Luckmann, *Social Construction*, 138–60; Steinbock, *Home and Beyond*, 196–231.

3. For example, see Mulder, *Inside Thai Society*; Tambiah, *Buddhism and the Spirit Cults*; *World Conqueror and World Renouncer*; Baker and Pasuk, *History of Thailand*; Komin, *Psychology of the Thai People*; Amara, *Traditional and Changing Thai World View*; Kirsch, "Complexity in the Thai Religious System."

to describe *the* Thai homeworld, but only that of the seven participants who were interviewed for this study. This analysis, therefore, will be phenomenological in nature, utilizing scholarly resources, primarily in the footnotes, only to explicate further the lived meanings inherent in the experiential accounts. As a heuristic device, the analysis will follow Max van Manen's five existentials, namely relationality, materiality, corporeality, temporality, and spatiality.[4] Given the religious nature of this research, priority will be given to the constituting nature of the sacred self.

RELATIONALITY (LIVED SELF-OTHER)

For the participants within this study, the self is always perceived as a self-in-relation. While they all retain a sense of the self as individual, especially regarding the responsibilities inherent in attaining adulthood and the consequent freedom to pursue one's own life goals, community remains primary in the forming, defining, and maintaining of one's identity.[5] Community may be understood as a series of concentric rings of relationship, with the inner rings bearing more significance to one's identity than the outer rings. At the very center of this concentric, intersubjective world lies the family.[6]

As a child, Ploy's home was a traditional, multi-generational home, consisting of parents, siblings, and grandparents. Her grandmother, because she was older and had more time to spare, was the family member who was most active in participating in temple rituals and events. She took upon herself the responsibility for educating Ploy in Buddhist teaching, ritual performance, and prayers. Every week, after she had spent a night at the temple for "monk day," Ploy's grandmother returned home and shared with Ploy the story she had learned at the temple that week. Often, the stories were episodic in nature, describing some event in Buddha's life which

---

4. Manen, *Researching Lived Experience*, 101–6; *Phenomenology of Practice*, 302–7.

5. A number of Thai scholars argue that a level of individualism underlies the Thai being-in-the-world. Komin explains, "Thai people have a very big ego, a deep sense of independence, pride and dignity. They cannot tolerate any violation of the 'ego' self" (Komin, *Psychology of the Thai People*, 161–62). This ego orientation is the root value for various behavioral expressions such as saving face and avoiding criticism which are so predominant in Thai intersubjective relations. However, as Mulder highlights, this independence value is not individualism as understood and expressed in Western nations, but, rather, is always rooted in "the solidarity of near persons" which serves as a refuge or "safety-net," allowing some level of personal risk-taking and opinion-making (Mulder, *Inside Thai Society*, 81–82).

6. Komin argues that for the Thai, "The kin group is the basic integrative force of one's life" (Komin, *Social Dimensions of Industrialization*, 84).

conveyed a moral for proper living. When Ploy attended the temple, she did so not with her parents, but with her grandmother. However, the family understood that one member's involvement at the temple, primarily in acts of merit-making (*bun*), effectively brought blessing to the entire family. This group-orientation toward religious ritual and its subsequent benefits meant that the family, as a collective, exhibited a shared religious identity. For Wit, the obligations inherent in this shared identity had prompted him to enter the monkhood as a novice for a period of one week, partially to negotiate successful admission into university and partially to transfer merit to the rest of his family, especially his mother.[7]

Within the family, obligation is a defining characteristic.[8] Children are obligated to not only obey and respect their parents but also present a positive family image before extended relatives and the broader community. "Yeah, my mom was concerned about gossip," Ploy explains. "If you don't do something right, people will talk about you, and that will be shameful. The family will lose face, or something like that." Conversely, parents have an obligation to provide for and nurture their children, but often this does not require verbal expressions of love or even presence.[9] Five of the seven participants reported relational strains with their fathers, ranging from emotional detachment to complete absence. For three of them, the strain was significant enough that it had prompted a personal, lifelong pursuit for love and acceptance to replace what they believed was missing in the home. Most dramatically, Kay reported incidents during which her father abused her physically and verbally, shamed her publicly, tracked her movements and activities, and even disowned her for a period of six months.

Despite the difficulties one might face in parent-child relations, obligation within the family extends well into adulthood and beyond. Nowhere

---

7. Regarding the merit involved in a son's ordination, Kirsch avers, "It is also widely believed that much of the merit acquired through ordination is gained by the ordinand's parents, particularly his mother—who is herself barred from the Sangha" (Kirsch, "Complexity in the Thai Religious System," 250). For more on the communal transfer of merit, see Tambiah, *Buddhism and the Spirit Cults*, 54; Keyes, "Millennialism," 288.

8. Dependence on the family unit creates a sense of obligation which is to be worked out via conformity and gratefulness. "The world outside the trusted home," Mulder argues, "is presented as fearsome, threatening and unreliable" (Mulder, *Inside Thai Society*, 77).

9. In Buddhist societies, Carlisle explains, the familial self is understood within a system of role-related behaviors, duties, and expectations. The focus is on visible actions, while personal thoughts and emotions are actively hidden and removed from ordinary consideration. As a result, Thai families typically exhibit a tendency toward non-expression and a reticence in displaying love. Carlisle, "Creative Sincerity," 331.

is this more evident than in the ritual of ancestor worship. Alfred Schütz argued that relationships with predecessors are always non-reciprocal relationships. The actions and experiences of ancestors are fixed and do not overlap with mine, they may influence me through their past decisions but I cannot influence them, and I may only know them indirectly as ideal types.[10] However, for many of the participants, especially the three who self-identify as either partially or fully Chinese, ancestors were encountered much more reciprocally and directly. Nid's mother was Thai, but her father was Chinese. For her father, religion was centered in the home, particularly at the family altar. Each morning, the entire family participated in presenting offerings of food and drink to the ancestors, lighting incense sticks, and praying to them to provide wealth, happiness, and protection for the family. Ancestors were perceived as ghost-like, requiring food for their afterlife, and able to curse or protect the family at will. Significantly, ancestor worship was understood as an expression of filial piety and respect for age.[11] By offering food and praying to the ancestors, one was not only appeasing the deceased, but also demonstrating respect and care for one's elders. For Nid's father, the perceived threat that his children would cease performing family altar rituals produced in him feelings of abandonment and fear for his future, signifying the intimate connection between religious ritual and proper social relations within the family.

The next concentric ring beyond the family is the village. Thai village life, whether considered in a rural context or in a circumscribed urban context, is deeply collectivistic in nature.[12] Growing up in rural Northeast Thailand, Nid's primary socialization, including the development of her self-understanding, moral awareness, and sense of belonging, was intricately

---

10. Schütz, *On Phenomenology and Social Relations*, 231–34. Clifford Geertz argues that for cultures in which ancestor worship is practiced, predecessors, because they interact with the living, should be considered contemporaries or consociates. Geertz, *Interpretation of Cultures*, 366–67.

11. Fordham asserts, "Ancestors are generally believed to have the ability to exert benevolent and/or punitive influences over the lives of the living. The attitude of the living towards them has been variously defined as *pietas,* one of filial piety; respect for age; respect and fear; and, as concerning acts of 'propitiation' and 'conciliation' directed to the deceased. Most importantly, ancestor worship is part of the wider social system. Ancestors derive their authority from parental authority and their worship is related to descent and succession within the living generation" (Fordham, "Ancestors and Christians," 118).

12. Komin describes this as the "interdependence orientation" within the Thai value system, which serves to reinforce neighborhood relations and helps facilitate the successful assimilation of other ethnic groups. Komin, *Psychology of the Thai People*, 231–32.

tied to members of her village. She relates, "Thais are very social, and they are very caring and helping of one another. The community has very much influence in your life. If you do not join or do what other people do in the community, you would be isolated, and somehow you will be isolated and they will look down on you . . . everyone knows what everyone else is doing." Within the community, each member must enact his or her specific role within a highly structured hierarchy.[13] Age predominates in the hierarchy, symbolized in an extensive vocabulary for properly addressing those who are younger or older.[14] Just behind age comes status. Certain professions, such as doctors, lawyers, teachers, and especially monks, hold great prestige within Thai society, requiring others to honor them appropriately, thereby establishing intricate relationships of obligation (*bun khun*).[15] For three of the participants, Nan, Wit, and Nid, their roles as physician, psychologist, and teacher, respectively, earned them great prestige within their village. As Wit explains, "Thai people believe the status of doctor is superior to the general people." In sum, by properly fulfilling one's role, honoring those who are superior, and conforming to socially defined norms and traditions, village harmony is achieved and one feels at home.

The nation comes next in the Thai concentric world of relationship. Many Thais readily identify three primary components that make up a proper Thai identity: monarchy, nation, and Buddhism. The king is the chief guardian of the Dharma,[16] the order of monks (*Sangha*) stands at the apex of the social order, and the faithful laity represent over 90 percent of the population.[17] Regardless of how relatively "strong" or "weak" one's actual

---

13. Komin notes, "[The] Thai social system is first and foremost a hierarchically structured society where individualism and interpersonal relationship are of utmost importance" (Komin, *Psychology of the Thai People*, 160).

14. For more on how hierarchy is expressed in the Thai language, see Bandhumedha, "Thai Views of Man as a Social Being."

15. The Thai practice of *bun khun* structures social relationships according to favors and obligations. When one receives a favor, he or she is obligated to be grateful and seek an occasion to repay the favor at an appropriate time. The expected duties performed by individuals higher on the hierarchy, such as parents and teachers, are also considered *bun khun*, requiring appropriate social obligation by the recipients. Podhisita, "Buddhism and Thai World View," 46–48.

16. Dharma primarily refers to the teachings or doctrines of Buddhism, which may or may not have come from the Buddha himself, but which form the tradition in which all Buddhists seek refuge.

17. Geertz, *Local Knowledge*, 198–200; Kirsch, "Complexity in the Thai Religious System," 244; Platz, "Buddhism and Christianity in Competition?," 476.

practice of ritualistic or philosophical Buddhism, the fact remains that in common perception, "to be Thai is to be Buddhist."[18] During his school days, Lek was required by his teachers to attend a Buddhist confirmation ritual. He and his schoolmates were rounded up for a field trip, taken to the nearby temple, and, after listening to a sermon by the monk, instructed to make a promise to "believe in Buddha." After the ceremony, Lek received a certificate confirming his Buddhist identity.[19] When asked whether he had a choice to attend the ceremony, he animatedly explained that his school had forced him to participate.[20] Tom and Kay related similar stories. Wit summarized this interweaving of religion and Thainess by suggesting that the adoption of a Buddhist identity is "just the culture." One need not ask whether a Thai is a Buddhist simply because, "many people in Thailand understand that they are Buddhist. That is strange to ask this question."[21]

Outside of one's family, village, and nation resides "the other." The other may be understood as encompassing any group that is non-Thai, such as hill tribes, other Asian ethnicities, or Westerners. Being half-Chinese, Nid faced social ridicule at school. "Back thirty to forty years ago," she explains, "when you are Chinese you get teased. They call you names." Because of this, Nid eventually decided to abandon her Chinese identity in favor of a traditional Thai identity, even changing her name in the process. Nan, on the other hand, expressed pride in her Chinese ethnicity. During

---

18. Podhisita comments, "The history of Thai culture is so dominated by Buddhism that if we take away the Buddhist component, there is little to say about it. In Thailand, the orientation toward Buddhism is important and all-pervasive" (Podhisita, "Buddhism and Thai World View," 37).

19. Also significant for many of the participants was the acquisition of their national identification card as it contains a statement of one's religious identity. Participants mentioned that the expectation among government officials is that one will self-declare as a Buddhist.

20. This sense of obligation to accede to a superior's request is known as *kreng jai*. Komin describes it as "to be considerate, to feel reluctant to impose upon another person, to take another person's feelings into account, or to take every measure not to cause discomfort or inconvenience another person" (Komin, *Psychology of the Thai People*, 164). Nearly every participant appealed to this concept of *kreng jai* at some point during the interviews.

21. "To these conventional believers, who constitute the vast majority," Mulder explains, "Buddhism is a way of life, an identity, and the key to primordial Thai-ness" (Mulder, *Inside Thai Society*, 129). Tambiah argues that, despite the voracious modernization and urbanization that Thailand has faced in recent years, the integral connection of Buddhism with Thai identity is not in decline, but actually intensifying. Tambiah, *World Conqueror and World Renouncer*, 267–68.

the interview, she differentiated between "Chinese-Thai" and "Thai-Thai," explaining that many "Thai-Thai" are "like lazy people." In response to a question regarding her Thai self-awareness, she responded, "Actually, I'm not Thai. I'm Chinese!" This is despite the fact that she was born in Thailand, speaks Thai as her first language, and bears a Thai name. Overall, however, the Chinese have been successfully assimilated into Thai culture and society with many of them identifying primarily as Thai while still retaining some Chinese traditions.[22]

In Thailand, the "other" is most fully embodied in the *farang*, or Westerners. *Farang*, which comes from the word for Frenchman, are the epitome of outsiders.[23] They are decidedly not Thai. Just as "to be Thai is to be Buddhist," Thais believe that "to be *farang* is to be Christian." Therefore, "outsiderness" is often interwoven with a non-Buddhist religious affiliation, most often Christianity. When Wit's wife initially became interested in Christianity, Wit was concerned since "Christianity is foreign; something about foreigner." When asked why he had thought Christianity was foreign, Wit's response was that he noticed the leaders of the church were staffed by foreign missionaries and the Bible talks about a foreign nation, Israel. Prior to her conversion, Kay's father told her that "Christianity is for *farang*. It is not for your family, and if you believe in Christianity you will stop respecting your parents." Her father attributed Kay's eventual conversion to the fact that she was learning English. In the process of adopting the *farang's* language, he believed, she was duped into adopting their religion as well. After her conversion, Nan was labeled an outsider by her sister and was told that she had betrayed her culture and family. The reason given was that Christianity was a *farang* religion. "If you believe in Christianity, you believe in *farang*. So, it's out of your society; so, you're different."[24]

---

22. Tobias, "Buddhism, Belonging and Detachment"; Mulder, *Inside Thai Society*, 25; Sattayanurak, "Construction of Mainstream Thought," 23.

23. Nantachai Mejudhon argues that, historically, the attitude of the Thai toward Westerners has been ambiguous. The negative impact of colonizers has led to the usage of the pronoun "it" to refer to Westerners, rather than "he" or "she." At the same time, Western missionaries have been instrumental in improving the health care and educational systems of the country and have introduced modern technology. Today, however, "the Thai remain closed communities where foreigners are not allowed, and even if they are permitted to enter, an invisible wall awaits them there, a dividing line foreigners never really cross" (Mejudhon, "Meekness [1997]," 32–35).

24. The Thai people are generally characterized as being very accommodating to the other, no matter one's beliefs or ways of life. The stereotypical picture of Thailand as "the land of smiles" suggests that Thai society, as a whole, is essentially open-minded, flexible,

Strangers in a Familiar Land

The final concentric ring in the Thai intersubjective world is the realm of spirits (*phii*).[25] The significance of one's relationship with the spirits is relatively ambiguous. On the one hand, spirits lie outside the sphere of human-to-human relations and, as a result, are distinctly other. On the other hand, spirits are encountered as possible deceased relatives, they reside in and surrounding the home and other frequented locations, and they influence the lives of individuals for good or ill almost on a daily basis.[26] In a sense, therefore, the realm of spirits resides just as close to the self as does one's home and family. Wit claims that the worship of multiple divine or spirit beings is normal for the Thai. "It's in their life," he explains. "Thai people pray to many spirits more than Buddha. You see many idols around. They pray for this. They pray for that. And if sometimes you hear that, if you lost something and you want to find, you have to pray to this idol. But, if you want more economic, you have to pray to another. Something like that. There are many specialists in the spirit realm." While spirits can provide wealth, protection, and blessing, they can also be a source of fear. Kay was taught to fear the spirits in order to please them and receive

---

and tolerant. While true to some extent, this characterization of Thai people as accommodating may only be understood within the backdrop of "social smoothing." In order to protect the ego, i.e., save face, one is expected to maintain pleasant and smooth interactions by subduing emotional responses and avoiding undue intimacy. This practice of social smoothing, therefore, presents a veneer of acceptance, a perspective which may or may not lie under the surface. As we will see in this research, social pressure remains for those who are different, but it is often enforced in other ways; usually indirectly and nonverbally. Komin, *Psychology of the Thai People*, 158, 195–207; Mulder, *Inside Thai Society*, 110.

25. Thai religion is often characterized as "Folk Buddhism," comprising diverse elements of Therevada Buddhism, animism, and Brahmanism. While many scholars have carefully identified the individual beliefs or practices that align with each of these three religious perspectives, the Thai perceives his/her religion as a single distinctive tradition that is approached very pragmatically. See Kirsch, "Complexity in the Thai Religious System"; Tambiah, *Buddhism and the Spirit Cults*; Terwiel, "Thai Buddhism."

26. Sorajjakool explains, "The unseen world is as real as the phenomenal world in which they find themselves. Within the religious psyche of Thai people, the world of gods, spirits, and karma is operative and real. On a day-to-day basis, Thai people deal with spirits and gods in the same way they interact with people. They talk to people and pray to the spirits. They placate the gods and please people. And within this religious psyche, the impacts of the gods and spirits are viewed as just as real as responses from their friends and family members. People try not to offend the spirits in the same way as they avoid hurting their friends. They are intentional about showing respect to the gods in the same way that they show respect to the elderly. The reality of the unseen world is an important part of their daily living" (Sorajjakool, "Religion in Thailand," 266). See also Cassaniti, "Encountering the Supernatural."

a blessing. For Tom and several of the other participants, this fear inspired the regular performance of certain techniques, such as *wai*-ing[27] spirit houses or offering ritualistic prayers and gifts, which would effectively and somewhat mechanically appease the spirits and access their power. For Ploy's mother, the spirits are believed to be deceased family members who must be fed and taken care of by the living. As a result, "ghosthood" was perceived as a possible future state for living family members, requiring certain ritualistic preparations in the present.

MATERIALITY (LIVED THINGS)

The Thai sacred lifeworld is very tangible. While the "nibbanic" aspect of Theravada Buddhism is known for being other-worldly, as it is largely concerned with the problem of death and its aftermath, in its "karmic" aspect the predominant concern is everyday existence in the world.[28] The ubiquitous and well-known phrase, "Do good, receive good; do bad, receive bad,"[29] adequately summarizes the average Thai's philosophy of life whereby individuals seek to accumulate merit (*bun*) for a better life now and for future reincarnations.[30] To achieve this better life, one must "make merit" (*tham bun*) through the giving of alms and gifts, and access power through the ritualistic usage of sacred images and magical objects. Certain material items, therefore, serve a sacramental purpose, bridging the worlds of the sacred and mundane and transferring merit in the process.

Central to the material world of the Thai Buddhist are sacred gifts. The pursuit of good luck was what had motivated Lek's acts of generosity. If the appropriate gifts (money and food) were given to the right people (monks) in the right way (ritual), then he would receive, almost mechanically, good

---

27. The *wai* is a traditional Thai gesture that is commonly used in society to demonstrate respect. It is used to greet one another, and in religious contexts, it conveys reverence and worship.

28. "Nibbanic Buddhism" is a term used by some scholars to refer to the practice of those Buddhists, usually monks, whose ultimate aim is to free themselves from suffering and attain Nirvana (*nibbana*) or enlightenment. "Karmic Buddhism" refers to those Buddhists, usually the laity, whose religious focus is on moral actions of merit and demerit which are required for a desirable existence here and now or in the next life. See Podhisita, "Buddhism and Thai World View," 34–36; Tambiah, *Buddhism and the Spirit Cults*, 55; Cohen, "Christianity and Buddhism," 120.

29. *Tham dii daai dii, tham chua daai chua.*

30. Cassaniti, "Agency and the Other," 305–6.

luck in return.[31] While donations to the temple often topped the list for effective merit-making, Lek would also give practical items to the monks such as toothpaste, clothes, or food. For Ploy, the ritualistic act of giving food to a monk communicated personal benefit for her own afterlife. "When you offer the food for the monk and pray," she explains, "that is the food that you prepared for your life after death." Feeding the monk, therefore, was understood to be equivalent to feeding oneself in a future, disembodied state. With her Chinese heritage, Nan was active not only in Thai Buddhist merit-making activities, but also in the traditional practices of Chinese ancestor worship. On certain Buddhist days, she would attend the local temple to present offerings to the monks and perform a ritualistic walk that involved circumnavigating the chedi[32] three times while holding a candle. On certain Chinese days, she and her family would go to the tombs of her deceased relatives to present offerings of food and to burn paper copies of material items, such as houses, money, cars, and even electronics. These offerings, it was believed, were then transferred as real items to her deceased relatives, allowing them to enjoy a more comfortable afterlife while, at the same time, demonstrating the family's filial piety.

Besides acts of gift-giving, the use of sacred images and objects are also instrumental for attaining merit, luck, and protection. Wit and Lek wore sacred amulets around their necks, each containing an image of the Buddha or other sacred figure which they believed protected them from accidents and brought good luck.[33] Larger images, such as Buddha statues or household idols, were thought to convey power, dispense prosperity, or mediate with the spirit realm. Kay had five idols in her house, each one representing an ancestor. Every morning, her father watched her as she performed the daily cleaning rituals, offered incense and food, and prayed for her ancestors' blessing and help. Nid had a spirit house (*san phraphum*) in her backyard. Constructed to look like a miniature version of a traditional Thai house, complete with figurines, the spirit house was believed to

---

31. While gift-giving is central to the action of merit-making, the merit is not acquired by the giving *per se* but by the willingness of monks to receive. The gift-taker, therefore, is superior to the gift-giver. Tambiah, *Buddhism and the Spirit Cults*, 53.

32. The chedi, or stupa, is the central structure in a temple complex that often contains a treasury of sacred objects.

33. Amulets are often inscribed with a sacred *yantra*, a form of mantra written in Sanskrit. These words, written by well-known and respected monks, are considered magical as they are able to communicate special powers to protect and bless the owner. Sorajjakool, "Religion in Thailand," 273–74.

contain the spirits of dead ancestors or territorial spirits that needed to be appeased through offerings of food and drink. By performing these rituals, the home would be protected from evil and the inhabitants would be recipients of good luck. As a child, Nan's home contained a prayer room (*hong phra*) in which resided numerous images of the Buddha. Not only did the family believe that these images protected and blessed the home, but they could also be petitioned to provide help for life's problems and circumstances. "Sometimes you can talk to them, like when you have problems," Nan recalls. "It's like talking to them, and we *wai* and ask them to help you; give you some good studying; better result for entrance exams so you can pass the exam to get into the university, like that. And if I had something that made me feel bad or troubled, I would go there and tell them that I needed help." In the Thai lifeworld, then, images are often believed to possess magical powers that assist in bringing success, protection, and blessing. As Lek explains, "I think it's uh, power. It's power. It can give something to me. To success; to get happy. To protect."

CORPOREALITY (LIVED BODY)

Within the Thai Buddhist lifeworld, one's body is a sacred body. Through the appropriate enactment of certain postures and gestures, one's body becomes the means of worship and communication with the realm of spirits and deities.[34] The most common gesture utilized in intersubjective and religious contexts is the *wai*. The *wai* is expressed by raising one's hands to the face, palms together and fingers up, with a slight bow of the head and a lowering of the eyes. It is the most common greeting in Thailand, in lieu of a handshake, but is also used in religious contexts to convey reverence, honor, and submission.

When Ploy visited the temple with her grandmother, the *wai* was a central component of worship. She would *wai* the monks, *wai* the Buddha, and, during the two-hour period of chanting, she would sit on the floor with feet facing backward and hold the position of the *wai* for most of the service. "I felt like it was challenging," Ploy recalls. "I would see if I can hold the position as long as I can without adjusting my body too much." When asked what the *wai* meant in this context, she explains, "We respect the monk, so we *wai* them. It is like we are supposed to *wai* older people. And it is the manner when the monk is chanting or praying. You have to *wai* all

---

34. Sorajjakool, "Religion in Thailand," 266.

Strangers in a Familiar Land

the time."[35] A funeral is another location where the *wai* is commonly used as a religious gesture. During funerals, Ploy explains, one will *wai* at the picture or coffin of the deceased, *wai* the Buddha image that is present, and *wai* during the chanting of the monks. While the gestures performed before the deceased and the Buddha are individual in nature, the *wai* that is to be maintained throughout the chanting ceremony is communal. The entire audience is expected to hold their *wai* position in unison until the monks finish this portion of the service. Finally, the *wai* is an important gesture of worship before images, shrines, and spirit houses. The daily rituals that Kay performed at the family altar always involved a period of *wai*-ing her ancestors, the posture most appropriate for conveying respect and communicating prayer. For Wit, even driving near a sacred shrine or temple required a *wai* as a gesture of respect.

TEMPORALITY (LIVED TIME)

Sacred time for the Thai is largely measured by the lunar calendar and often involves temple attendance.[36] Festivals and holy days not only provide an opportunity for individual and family merit-making, but also serve as occasions for community socializing. Ceremonial occasions, such as weddings, engagements, or the groundbreaking for a new construction, are calculated to occur on days that are considered auspicious by monks or fortune-tellers.[37] Days, months, and years, therefore, are perceived as neither homogeneous nor continuous in the Thai world, but as intervals of sacred and mundane.[38] Beyond earthly time resides transcendent time: the afterlife, the realm of heaven and hell, and a nearly endless cycle of birth and rebirth. Transcendent time significantly imposes itself upon the present, requiring the regular performance of rituals and proper moral actions now in order to ensure a prosperous and comfortable future later.

As a youth, Nid attended the temple every Sunday with her mother. She would prepare food for the monks, spend time with her friends, and

---

35. Cassaniti's research indicates that the primary reason why Thais *wai* images is to achieve a desired mental and emotional state, especially a feeling of calm. As one of her research participants explains, "I *wai* to make merit for myself, to calm my heart and not be like a monkey running around in the trees. To be quiet." Cassaniti, "Agency and the Other," 307. See also Tongprateep, "Essential Elements of Spirituality," 200.
36. Sorajjakool, "Religion in Thailand," 270.
37. Komin, *Psychology of the Thai People*, 221.
38. See Eliade, *Sacred and the Profane*, 68–113.

perform ritualistic activities. This regular attendance, she believed, made her a "strong Buddhist."[39] Later in her life, she dedicated herself to a temple for a period of seven days. During this time, she focused on meditation and followed a strict daily schedule, including starting the day at 5:00 am with prayers. Nan did not attend the temple every week, but she did follow the typical Buddhist calendar of holy days and festivals. During Buddhist lent,[40] Nan and her family would visit the temple several times to offer food for the monks. The entire community contributed to supplying the temple with food, following a carefully scheduled rotation. She describes this time as "kind of like a party. You go and many people just bring their food in." Nan also observed a Chinese calendar, consisting of three special days per year during which time the family would set up a special altar and burn offerings to their ancestors. Ploy remembers the times she spent in the temple with great fondness. During major holidays and Buddhist days, she would attend temple ceremonies with her grandmother and steal opportunities to play with her neighborhood friends. "Maybe that's why I looked forward to those days," she recalls, "because I could see my friends."

Besides following the lunar calendar of special events and festivals, time within the Thai lifeworld is also perceived according to life transitions, especially regarding the entrance into adulthood and the transition from life to death. For most of the participants, the university period signaled their entrance into adulthood. It was a time when family ties were loosened, although not separated, allowing for relative freedom to consider alternative identities and life goals. Graduation from university, Wit explains, is when one becomes an adult. Within the Buddhist symbolic universe, this life is understood as just one in a series of reincarnations, potentially moving one toward the ultimate goal of Nirvana, or enlightenment.[41] Between reincarnations, one enters a period of liminality, during which time he or she may enjoy the bliss of heaven, the pains of hell, or the ambiguity of becoming a ghost. Ploy's mother was obsessed with ensuring that Ploy's afterlife was well-provided for, offering food at the temple on a regular basis so that Ploy would enjoy food in the afterlife. Tom recalls seeing paintings

---

39. This idea of "strong" versus "weak" Buddhist identity was a common point of discussion during the interviews. Many of the participants highlighted regular ritual activity or temple attendance as representative of a strong Buddhist identity, while those who only visited the temple on occasion were considered nominal in their religious adherence. For discussion, see Mulder, *Inside Thai Society*, 125–30.

40. Known as the period of *khao phansaa*.

41. Podhisita, "Buddhism and Thai World View," 34.

at the temple depicting the various forms of punishments that would be inflicted on wrongdoers in hell. One image showed people climbing up a tree of thorns while another was a visualization of sinners being fried in a pan like eggs. "It was very scary," he recalls. The intent of the paintings was to bridge transcendent and earthly time, instilling fear in the viewer to encourage proper moral action in the present.[42]

SPATIALITY (LIVED SPACE)

Lived space in the Thai sacred world is not uniform. Space is perceived territorially, with certain spirts, deities, or powers inhabiting and ruling over certain locations. When preparing for a university entrance exam, Ploy visited a famous shrine at the base of the nearby mountain, Doi Suthep. The shrine is believed to be the home of the territorial spirit of an especially powerful monk who conveys success and blessing for major life events. Blessing is communicated transactionally: Ploy offers flowers to the deceased monk and the monk responds by answering her request. Indeed, territoriality was central to Ploy's being-in-the-world prior to her conversion. While attending a Christian university, she viewed the campus as the home of the territorial spirit of the Christians, Jesus. While on campus, Ploy would pray to Jesus, seeking help for success on her exams; but as soon as she left the campus, she would seek out Buddha or other spirits for help with her other requests. She carried on this territorial perspective even after she had accepted a position on the university's faculty. She explains it this way:

> RES:[43] And I belong there as I am a Ploy, I belong to Buddha territory. But if I am a Ploy who work in (name of university), I belong to God's land. That is my belief.
>
> INT: Explain that a little bit more. You mean, when you are somewhere else, you belong to Buddha?

---

42. Proper moral action is very important within the Thai Buddhist lifeworld. Many participants alluded to the "five commandments" of Buddhism which serve to guide one's moral life: (1) abstain from taking lives, (2) abstain from stealing, (3) abstain from sexual misconduct, (4) abstain from telling lies, (5) abstain from alcohol and drugs. While the laity are expected to follow these five commandments, novices must follow ten and monks must follow a total of 227. Sorajjakool, "Religion in Thailand," 269; Hughes, "Theology and Culture," 48.

43. RES refers to respondent while INT refers to interviewer.

RES: Oh. When I do something that is related to the responsibility as a faculty . . . working at nursing school, I belong to God and belong to God's land. But, if I live my life in general, I belong to Buddha. Yeah, this is how I separate.

INT: Yeah, and is it like before, was there no conflict there?

RES: Actually, there was no conflict. I think it's blended in myself. It is just (pause) ah, I don't know how to explain, it is . . . for example, if we have a meeting, and we know that there are some difficulties in our work, I would pray to God to help solve that problem. But I did not pray to God for like ok, I want to have good life; I'm going to travel to somewhere and I need some protection. I did not pray to God, but I pray to Buddha.[44]

Wit displayed a similar perspective on sacred space. "I think maybe Thai people like the same as me," he explains. "Because they think this is the house of . . . you do not worship other spirits in this spiritual house, something like that." The Thai term for this concept of territoriality literally translates as "lord of the house" or "landlord."[45]

The locus of each Thai village is the parish temple or *wat*. The *wat* serves as the community center for devotional and recreational activities, it is built, maintained, and staffed by village members, and it may even function as a village school, especially for children from poorer families.[46] Because his grandparents were very poor, Wit's father grew up in the village temple as a *dek wat* (child of the temple). He received his schooling, accommodation, food, and general care from the monks, which instilled in him a deep sense of obligation toward the temple community. This sense of obligation was experienced multi-generationally, with Wit and his siblings expected to convey gratitude and allegiance to the temple as well. Every year, the entire extended family met at this same temple to perform rituals, express gratitude to the monks, and reunite with one another. As a child, Nid perceived the temple as a place of happiness. It was the central location where the community gathered to chat, eat, and perform merit-making rituals together. "The temple is the center for everything,"

---

44. It should be noted that this perspective on the territoriality of the Christian God was prior to her conversion and baptism. After her baptism, Ploy adopted an exclusivist position whereby she considered it "inappropriate" and even "sinful" to pray to or worship another deity or spirit.

45. *Jaaw khong baan*.

46. Tambiah, *Buddhism and the Spirit Cults*, 11.

Strangers in a Familiar Land

she explains. "My mother will go to the temple, which is very nearby the house, so I often go with her because I have to carry the food along with her to the temple. And there I have seen that what they do is listen to the monk chanting, and after the monk eat, we get to eat. And I feel like this is just a very good feeling; to see them chit chat, talking, and eating a variety of food at the temple. And then my mother is happy. So, I think, oh, this is what the Buddhist is: happiness." Ploy and Nan expressed a similar fondness regarding their childhood memories of the temple. Nan describes those experiences as "happy times" since "it's like meeting people and eating." Likewise, Ploy exclaims, "It was fun!" While at the temple, she enjoyed spending time with her grandmother, meeting friends, bringing flowers, and eating with the community.[47]

CONCLUSION

For the participants of this study, home is comprised of a complex network of intersubjective relations, both natural and supernatural, occurring within a setting that is thoroughly infused with the sacred. Thus, one's identity is always a sacred identity. It is formed and maintained through a hierarchical and deeply collectivistic plausibility structure, understood within a symbolic universe that is governed by magic, spirits, and the law of karma, and enacted through the daily fulfillment of one's social, moral, and sacred obligations to the family, village, and nation. Indeed, within the Thai lifeworld, religious, ethnic, and social identities are intricately interwoven. The phrase, "to be Thai is to be Buddhist," therefore, is not a simple statement expressing a community's preference for one's choice of religion. It is, instead, a mantra about belonging and identity. Buddhism ties the individual to kin groups, villages, the king, and even a nation. It creates a social identity by which one is empowered to face the exigencies of life, and it effectively structures one's being-in-the-world. Indeed, we may even say that Buddhism serves as the unifying thread in the fabric of the Thai homeworld. As Mulder avers, "Buddhism is therefore the greatest of Thai

---

47. It should also be noted that while many participants alluded to the temple as a happy place, given its role in the community, it could also be perceived as the source of significant social pressure. Nid remarks that failure to appear at certain events or ceremonies would raise questions since the community knew each other well and attendance was expected.

institutions, expressive of and perpetuating the Thai nation, its traditions, its ritual, and its identity."[48]

Based on this understanding of Thainess, therefore, it becomes readily apparent that any aberration from a Thai Buddhist identity will likely present significant possibilities for marginalization within the Thai lifeworld. By transferring worlds, which is the central action of conversion as discussed in chapter 1, complete with a new symbolic universe, plausibility structure, and sacred allegiance, Christian converts effectively become "marginal men"; strangers in a familiar land. Their conversion both threatens their sense of belonging within the family, community, and nation, and aligns them with what is perceived as a foreign religion, thus requiring the constant separation and re-integration of their social and religious identities. In a land where "to be Thai is to be Buddhist," therefore, the Christian believing self is always, to a greater or lesser extent, a marginalized self. To the adumbration of this experience of in-marginality we now turn.

---

48. Mulder, *Inside Thai Society*, 113.

6

Verticality

INTRODUCTION

THIS CHAPTER MARKS A turning point in our investigation. In this and the next three chapters, I will present the heart of the research, namely a phenomenological explication of the Thai Christian experience of in-marginality. The chapters are structured according to what I interpret to be the four primary moments of the phenomenon: verticality, emplacement, displacement, and negotiation.[1] For each moment, the categories that were disclosed during the data analysis phase will be collated and discussed as three or four interpretive themes. The discussion of each interpretive theme will begin with experiential accounts from participants that will allow the reader to re-experience reflectively and empathically the lived meanings that belong to the phenomenon. These accounts will be edited for grammar and literary flow. Following the experiential accounts, I will present a phenomenological analysis of the interpretive theme as set against the horizons of this research.

In his work *Phenomenology and Mysticism*, Anthony Steinbock describes verticality as consisting of the dynamic vectors of experience that

---

1. Sokolowski defines moments as "parts that cannot subsist or be presented apart from the whole to which they belong; they cannot be detached." For example, in mechanics, a body in motion possesses the moments of mass, velocity, momentum, and acceleration. While each moment may be abstracted and analyzed on its own, the moment only truly exists as blended with its complementary parts. In this research, I am perceiving the phenomenon of in-marginality which arises from religious alternation as a whole, comprised of the necessary and complementary moments of verticality, emplacement, displacement, and negotiation. Sokolowski, *Introduction*, 23–24.

Verticality

take us beyond ourselves. Vertical experiences, he argues, are dangerous, spontaneous, and unpredictable. They incite awe and, as a result, wonder. They are "testimony to the radical presence of 'absolutes' *within* the field of human experience," pertaining primarily to the spheres of the religious, the moral, and the ecological.[2] Verticality, therefore, refers to that realm of human experience which exists beyond the presentation of objects and the rationality of doctrines. It is the locale of one's encounter with the "wholly Other"; an overpowering and suprarational experience that, as Rudolf Otto maintained, is characterized by both mystery and fascination.[3] This vertical dimension functions as the founding moment of the Thai Christian experience of in-marginality. Other moments, such as emplacement, displacement, and negotiation, revolve around one's primordial encounter with God. In other words, for participants, one's intersubjective encounters with the divine Other both introduce states of marginalization and produce the means by which one may then cope with and negotiate marginal situations. This chapter, therefore, while not strictly concerned with marginalization *per se*, provides the necessary substratum for understanding the formation of Thai Christian identity as occurring within the Thai Buddhist contexture.

This chapter is divided into three interpretive themes which had arisen from the data analysis phase of this research.[4] (1) *Yearning* refers to the pre-conversion religious and existential factors that prompted one's pursuit of the Sacred. This theme includes the data analysis categories of "external world shaken," "internal world shaken," "resolution after world is shaken," "former self as inferior," and "former self as searching." The second interpretive theme is (2) *event and process* which discloses the participants' direct and intuitive hierophanic encounter with God as well as the gradual and often lengthy process by which an individual "becomes Christian." Within this theme, we will explore the categories of "direct encounter with the Sacred," "attunement with the Sacred," "intervention of the Sacred," "identity transformation as processual," "growth in Christian identity," "testing Christian identity," "hybrid religious identity," and "self-awareness of Christian identity." The final theme of this chapter is (3) *reorientation* or the cognitive, affective, and behavioral restructuring toward the Sacred that occurs consequent to conversion. This theme will cover the categories

---

2. Steinbock, *Phenomenology and Mysticism*, 12–15.

3. Otto, *Idea of the Holy*, 20–34.

4. See chapter 4 for more details regarding the processes enacted in theme categorization.

of "exclusivist convictions," "Sacred as relational," "world-transfer as reorientation to the Sacred," "affective responses to world transfer," and "understanding of Christian identity."

YEARNING

Lek: The Search for Power

Here I was with a master's degree in Southeast Asian studies. I had experience doing research on projects, but, so far, all the projects were short term. No one would hire me full-time. I kept searching for a job, but to no avail. I was starting to get worried. Would I ever find a job? When you are unemployed, the days, weeks and months seem like an eternity. I couldn't afford our rent. I barely had enough money for food. The weight of responsibility was overwhelming. I needed to provide food and shelter not only for myself, but also for my new wife. We had only been married a couple of years. What was she thinking? Was she disappointed in me? What about my parents? They must be so ashamed.

I tried all the typical, Buddhist avenues for resolving my problems. I went to many shrines and temples throughout the city. I tried temple after temple, shrine after shrine, praying to many different images that were believed to possess great power. But nothing ever happened. I still had my problems. I still felt the weight of stress and anxiety. I still believed I could do nothing to make my life better. I thought to myself, "Where can I find real power? Is it even out there?" I felt helpless. No, not just helpless; I felt hopeless.

Amid the chaos, my wife was a refuge of calm. She was always happy and at peace. She never worried about the situation, or at least, if she did, she never expressed it. I would often vent to her my restless frustrations: "I will never find a job. This is useless!" She listened to my endless grumblings, but, in response, her voice was always like a cool breeze on a steamy, summer afternoon. "Don't worry," she would say. "God has a plan for us." Who is this God? Does he have the power that I seek? Is he more powerful than the Buddha images in the temples and shrines? Yes, I wanted more power, but, to tell you the truth, what I really yearned for was what my wife had. Sure, I wanted a job. I wanted someone to help me, and I needed a higher power to make that happen. But, in the end, it wasn't really about the power. What I yearned for was the cool breeze of a peaceful life. I wanted a Power who loved me, who cared for me, and who would release me from the burdens of a destitute life.

Kay: The Search for Love

I was never good enough for my father. "You are stupid and lazy," he would often tell me. I remember one time in school my teacher had given me an A for the subject. My dad couldn't believe it. As soon as he found out, he went with me to the school and talked to my teachers. "How can this be?" he asked them. "Kay never studies, she never completes her homework. She probably cheated. I want her to have an F." He did this in front of everyone: not just my teachers, but my friends, too. My friends would ask me, "Is your dad crazy?" I felt like no matter how hard I worked or how much I achieved, it was never good enough for him. I felt like he didn't love me.

I began hating my father. If I could never be good enough for him, why even try? I skipped class, started drinking alcohol, and gambled with my friends. Honestly, I wanted to kill my parents. Sometimes, I would slip small amounts of poison in their food. I didn't want their deaths to seem obvious or sudden, so I did it very gradually. Nothing ever happened though. Buddhism taught me that disrespecting one's parents would result in severe punishments in hell. But I didn't care. I just wanted them gone.

I not only hated my parents, I hated myself. I figured the reason why I had such horrible parents was due to my own bad karma. I would go to the temple and offer flowers, food, and money to the monks, hoping that the merit I earned would take care of my bad deeds. In the end, though, I felt helpless. I was so tired: tired of my parents, tired of home, tired of myself. It was at this low point in my life when I decided to commit suicide. I felt like I was nothing; that I was the cause of my horrible situation; that I would never be able to leave the prison of my home. I needed to experience love, but I didn't think true love even existed. Maybe if I just ended my life, I would finally make my father happy. I would rid him of the burden of Kay.

Interpretation

Prior to alternation, converts encounter diverse life situations that serve to initiate their personal search for new religious solutions. This search, which is existential and pragmatic in nature, is expressed as a yearning of the soul, not only for a resolution to a specific crisis, but, even more, for the restoration and integration of the self. Available cultural and religious resources are often tapped in the pursuit of resolution and fulfillment, but usually to no avail. Consequently, seekers reach a point of abject despair, helplessness, and dissatisfaction. They experience the inferiority and failure of the self in approaching a world that has become chaotic and antagonistic. This is the end of self.

Many converts refer to their pre-conversion period as a time of searching, and they often self-identify as a "seeker."[5] Rather than referring to this period as a search, however, the data indicates that a better term might be "yearn." What does it mean to yearn? Is it the same as searching? To search for something entails the sense of having lost with the hope of re-discovery. Searching seems to imply a prior having, or at least a clear sense of the object of the search. Yearning, on the other hand, is quite different. Rather than conveying a sense of finding what had been lost, yearning implies a restless, painful longing for what one has never had or what only seems to exist beyond reach. Maybe, at some point in the past, one has tasted of the fruit of one's yearnings, but full satisfaction is always elusive. If anything, the taste only intensifies the yearning. To yearn is to crave, in the deep, visceral, emotive sense of the term. When I search for a precious object that is now lost, I am anxious, I become stressed, and my world may become chaotic until I find it again. But I don't yearn for this object. I don't crave it as I would a lost love, or an unfulfilled desire. Yearning is much deeper; much more existential. It encompasses one's entire being: the mind, the emotions, and even the body. The pursuit for what one yearns may drive one to great heights, but the almost inevitable failure in finding fulfillment may engulf one in great despair.

Yearning is at the heart of the self's existential pursuit of the Sacred. The immediate object of one's yearning may be love, meaning, power, forgiveness, belonging, truth, hope, among others. Indeed, the object of yearning varies just as much as do the circumstances that prompt it. But whatever the case, the yearning always exceeds a momentary emotional or cognitive need. It defines one's world as the ultimate *telos* of the self. For Lek, the loneliness he had experienced as a child only intensified his response to his later crisis. As a child, he had learned to rely on himself to solve his own problems. In the absence of parental care, he necessarily developed a strong

---

5. Many qualitative studies on conversion indicate that a recurring theme among conversion narratives is a period of "seeking after truth," often due to life crises or emotional and psychological needs. While not universal among all converts, the "search" does appear to be a common feature regardless of nationality or ethnicity. For samples from Kyrgyzstan, India, and Australia, respectively, see Radford, *Religious Identity and Social Change*, 100–102. Iyadurai, *Transformative Religious Experience*, 70, 99–100, 112; Devenish, *Knowing Otherwise*, 216–20.

Verticality

sense of self-sufficiency and independence. He could tackle life's problems on his own, and he knew that no one would come to his side should difficult circumstances arise. The crisis of being unemployed, however, shattered his self-sufficient world. He experienced the complete disempowerment of the self which, as a result, instilled in him a yearning for power. He was longing for someone or something with the capacity to resolve his problems. But as we look closer, we find that the yearning was neither for raw power nor detached power. Instead, he was longing for a personal Power that would convey love and care, effectively bestowing peace to his chaotic world.[6] For Kay, the yearning for love was prompted by an abusive home situation. She internalized her father's abusive words and actions to such an extent that she considered herself as a no-thing. If love makes someone a some-thing, it's absence essentially erases the self. Her yearning for love, therefore, went beyond a resolution to her circumstances. Instead, it encompassed the pursuit of her identity: to belong, to be accepted, to be one's self. Other participants expressed similar yearnings. In each case, however, the yearning was for what seemed to exist just beyond reach. It encompassed one's entire self, and it arose from a perceived lack in one's being-in-the-world. Anxiety produced yearnings for peace, fear produced yearnings for joy, helplessness produced yearnings for power, shame produced yearnings for honor, etc. The yearning defines the individual, and it prompts one's ongoing search for resolution and fulfillment.

In their pursuit of fulfillment, participants first attempted culturally and religiously prescribed solutions. Many of these solutions were religious in nature. Both Lek and Kay turned to traditional Buddhist rituals, offering gifts and prayers to seek good luck and absolution. Nid practiced meditation at a local monastery, while Wit entered the monkhood as an initiate for a one-week period. Established religious avenues were pursued to seek fulfillment for one's existential yearnings. Within the Buddhist lifeworld, the self is understood as a sacred self whose well-being and success depends on the enactment of proper methods for manipulating higher powers. In the end, though, these prescribed solutions were deemed ineffective. Lek noticed inconsistencies and hypocrisies within the temple and among the monks which made him wonder whether their communication of power would be effective. His doubts were confirmed when his circumstances were not

---

6. Of course, this reminds us of Leeuw's conception of the Transcendent as Power. He states, "Man, however, cannot rest content with mere life: he must seek sacred life, replete with Power" (Leeuw, *Religion*, 195).

altered. The sacred had failed to enter and alter the world of the mundane, leaving Lek both disillusioned and frustrated. Other solutions for finding fulfilment are non-religious in nature. Nan's yearning was to find meaning, truth, and purpose. "Why are we born on this earth," she would wonder. "What are we to do for the next life?" She described herself as a seeker and philosophy was her path to resolution. Buddhist philosophical thought and meditative practice represented her first attempt at fulfillment. While providing a temporary sense of calm and peace, they failed to truly satisfy her yearnings. In lieu of religious solutions, she next sought resolution by immersing herself in political Marxism. During turbulent times in Thailand's history, Nan believed that by empowering the proletariat one could transform the country into a Utopia and find personal meaning and purpose on the way. Her yearnings were unfulfilled, however, when she discovered that the common people did not want to change. Her being-in-the-world then shifted from hope to disillusionment, from action to apathy.

When prescribed solutions fail, the end of self begins. Disillusionment turns to despair, one's existential bearings become contorted, and home transmutes into homelessness. If one exhausts all the typical solutions to satisfy one's yearning, then what possible recourse is left? During the interviews, several of the participants mentioned that at their deepest point of despair, they simply did not know about other religious solutions. Speaking about the fear she had of her parents and how Buddhism only served to exacerbate that fear, Kay explains, "At that time, I had no choice because I didn't have any ideas about other religions." Her being-in-the-world had become characterized by hopelessness: without options and, therefore, without choice. When it comes to yearning, choice is essential to hope. To avoid despair, one must believe there is always another possible solution that will resolve the crisis, restore love, cease the pain, or make one whole again. If one believes that all the options are exhausted, yearning transforms into despair, resulting in the possible destruction of one's world.

Participants vary in how they cope with despair. For several, their low points were relatively mild. Ploy and Nid both gradually transitioned from a Buddhist identity to a Christian identity, meaning that their sense of despair did not culminate in a crisis event but rather existed under the surface like magma under a dormant volcano. While yearning for love, peace, and guidance, they did not experience the end of self, partly due to mitigating circumstances within their lifeworlds and partly due to their processual emplacement in the Christian intersubjective lifeworld.

On the other end of the spectrum, Kay had experienced the end of self in literal, not figurative, terms. She perceived the self as inferior: as causing her desperate situation and as unable to acquire an adequate solution. Not only that, she adopted an ossified and unmalleable identity. "I wanted to change," she describes, "but when I went back home, the situation was the same. I pretended to be a good person, but inside I knew I wasn't. I could not change." Home, for Kay, was fixed in a state of despair. Outside of the home, Kay could try on new identities, perceive herself as malleable, and convince herself that there still existed possible fulfillment for her yearnings. In the home, however, her identity was immovable, constantly acting contrary to its wishes. Her lived experience may be compared to that of the Apostle Paul's who, in Romans 7:15, proclaimed, "For what I am doing, I do not understand; for I am not practicing what I would like to do, but I am doing the very thing I hate." As Heidegger would say, she was "falling" into a state of anxiety. Her being-in-the-world entered the existential mode of being-not-at-home.[7] Home should be a place of belonging, love, and hope. A place where one can be oneself. By bearing the quality of despair, Kay's home ironically was intended in the mode of homelessness. Consequently, suicide was perceived as the only possible resolution to her existential state. She was a no-thing. She was "tired," mainly of herself, and living in a world that was without hope or meaning. Therefore, suicide was believed to be the only possible means to bodily reflect the reality of her inner state.

While Kay's suicide attempt represents the extreme end of unfulfilled yearnings, her perception of the self at this low point was common among the participants. Amid their efforts to resolve life crises or replenish affective and psychological needs, participants frequently encountered themselves as morally inferior or sinful. Nan states, "I thought I was a good person, but somehow I couldn't perform my goodness. I knew that I should behave well with my parents, but when I went back to my hometown I would say something to hurt my mom. I felt so sorry for that. I felt like, even though I want to be a good person, I can't. I felt guilty." Similarly, when Wit came to the end of self, realizing that he was impotent to resolve his economic crisis, he also became aware of his own moral impotence. The need for a power to resolve a seemingly uncontrollable life circumstance also revealed a parallel and deeper need for a Power to resolve his uncontrollable moral ineptitude.

---

7. Heidegger, *Being and Time*, 233.

Strangers in a Familiar Land

These examples highlight the essentially religious nature of the yearning period. While seekers typically yearn for the immediate object that will meet their affective, psychological, and situational needs, for example love, power, peace, etc., the deep existential nature of the yearning also pulls them away from themselves and moves them toward the Beyond. The end of self in resolving crises simultaneously communicates the contingency of one's world, the failure of the moral self, and one's necessary dependence on a divine Other. In other words, for the participants, this period of yearning is not simply pragmatic but primordially religious. Our deepest desires and longings define who we are, govern our vision of the good life, mold our being-in-the-world, evoke worship, and, when left unfulfilled, ultimately drive us toward the Transcendent.[8] As Augustine famously described it, "It is yearning that makes the heart deep."[9] However, while we may perceive our yearnings as driving us toward the Transcendent, a striving from below as it were, the actual crossing of the threshold into the Beyond is only experienced as a gift. Twentieth-century Catholic theologian Henri de Lubac described it this way: "Sometimes we think we are looking for God. But it is always God who is looking for us, and he often allows himself to be found by those who are not looking for him."[10] To this external, even mystical, experience of God as both event and process we now turn.

EVENT AND PROCESS

Kay: Restoration of Self

> My sister was sleeping in the bed next to me. It was late, and I was the only one in the family who was still awake. Tears were streaming down my face as I held the razor blade in my right hand. The television was on, broadcasting some video about a guy from the past named Jesus. I wasn't watching the show, though. Instead, I was thinking about the bad luck in my life: why I had such horrible parents and how my negative karma had caused it all. I slit my left wrist. Nothing happened. Did I do something wrong? I'm so stupid that I can't even kill myself correctly. My dad would have a good laugh about that one for sure. I was preparing for the second cut when the words streaming from the television suddenly caught my attention. No, it was more than that. The television was speaking to

---

8. Smith, *Desiring the Kingdom*, 50–51.

9. Or, "Longing is the very bosom of the heart." See Augustine, *Tractates* 40.10 (NPNF 7:374).

10. Lubac, *Discovery of God*, 168.

Verticality

me. It said, "Forgive them, for they know not what they do." I looked up to see a figure of a man, bloody, bruised, and nearly naked, dying on a tree. That dying person had just spoken to me. I stopped what I was doing and glued my attention to the show. The words were like water, satiating my desperate thirst.

The next scene shifted to the modern day. A person was talking about how bad his life used to be: how he had been involved in a gang and had committed many crimes. He spoke of his encounter with Jesus, and how he had experienced complete forgiveness with no strings attached. He described the Heavenly Father as kind and loving; a Being who was apparently the polar opposite of my earthly father. Another person shared a similar testimony. After that, the announcer asked me if I wanted to receive forgiveness from this loving God. Looking back on it, I know he was speaking generally to everyone who happened to be watching the show, but at the time, he was speaking only to me. I wanted forgiveness. I needed hope. I yearned for love. I decided to pray with him for Jesus to come into my life. I figured, if God is real, he can help me. If not, there is no risk. After that my tears immediately ceased. This concerned me since just a few minutes prior I could not stop sobbing. I even tried to start crying again, but I couldn't. I felt a strange wave of emotion flow in and over me. It was an emotion I had not experienced for a long time. Finally, I was happy.

Ploy: Hybrid Consciousness

I had attended a Christian school throughout my entire childhood. I remember singing Christian songs, listening to sermons, and studying materials that explained about the Bible. Later, when I had entered university, I joined a Christian activity group. We would do community service together, but we would also spend time in small groups, praying and singing. Even though I was a Buddhist, I would pray and sing along with them. For me, there was no conflict. Christianity and Buddhism were very similar. They both taught me how to be a good person, and they both could help guide me throughout life. Even more, I believed that the Christian God was the territorial spirit of the school. This was a Christian school, so Buddha has no authority here. Why wouldn't I pray to the Christian spirit while I'm at this school? When I was not at school, though, I would always pray to Buddha or some other spirits. This was how I thought for a long time. There was no conflict in my mind. I realized that I could not belong to two religions at the same time, so I remained Buddhist and prayed to the Christian God only when in his territory.

Eventually, I even started attending church. I was looking for a moral standard for my son, and I chose Christianity because much of the church's teaching was in English. However, if I wanted my son to follow Christianity, I figured I should probably try to learn some more myself. I went to church every Sunday, and I encouraged my husband and son to go as well. I joined a small group and began formal study of the Christian faith. It was like being in university again: just a lot of boring information. One day, though, something happened. I can't fully explain it. Suddenly, I just had this strong feeling that God loves me. I was convinced that he is there, and that he is the leader of my life. As soon as that happened, I recognized that God is the biggest God. No, not only that. He is the only God.

Interpretation

Religious alternation may be understood as both event and process. First, converts often report experiencing a sudden and transformative event whereby the Sacred enters the world of the profane, which is typically perceived as conversion proper.[11] During the event, one becomes, as William James described it, "a passive spectator or undergoer of an astounding process performed upon him from above."[12] Among participants, it is this hierophanic event that effectively transitions one out of the world of Thai Buddhism and into the world of Christian belief and identity. However, religious identity transformation is not only a singular, momentary activity, but also a processual transfer of worlds whereby one gradually "becomes Christian." The hierophanic event is typically preceded by a gradual immersion in the Christian lifeworld and symbolic universe and is proceeded by incremental periods of growth and reversion in the pursuit of what is considered an ideal Christian identity. Therefore, while conversion proper clearly marks a before and after in one's narrative identity, the processual nature of Christian identity formation blurs those boundaries, creating greater or lesser periods of hybridity. How, then, may we understand religious alternation as both event and process?

---

11. This is what Eliade referred to as an "hierophany" (Eliade, *Sacred and the Profane*, 11). See also Berger, *Heretical Imperative*, 88; Flinn, "Conversion," 56–60.

12. James, *Varieties of Religious Experience*, 169.

Verticality

Foundational to one's Christian identity is a direct and personal encounter with the Holy. During this event, converts mystically meet with God, and it is this meeting, not simply a conveyance of new knowledge, that is transformative. What is the structure of this divine-human encounter? First, we may say that the encounter is sudden and unexpected. For Nan, the day of her hierophany was like any other. She had no reason to believe that this particular day would be special or set apart from the rest. She went about performing her normal, daily, and very corporeal tasks within her routine, mundane home environment. As she sat on her bed to read the Bible, she suspected nothing unusual as this has been her habitual practice for six months. "On that particular day though," Nan remembers, "the words became real to me. It was like someone was talking to me. I was so amazed because while it was the simple words that I read every day, this time it was something special." Implicit in the suddenness of this event was the passivity of the hierophant. There was an inevitability to the encounter. God was the one who was active; Nan's participation was passive. As Steinbock explains, "We do not cause or provoke epiphanic givenness; it is experienced as grace. Our 'activity,' as it were, is receiving."[13]

Secondly, the encounter is both revelatory and relational. Amid the mystical experience, hierophants have an overwhelming sense that God is speaking or otherwise revealing himself to them. However, the communication that they receive always exceeds that of a transmission of intellectual content. It reveals God's very presence via what Alfred Schütz called a "we-relationship." Speaking about human to human encounters, Schütz described the we-relation as a reciprocal orientation whereby two or more people share in the consciousness of the other. They encounter each other as a "Thou" in the immediacy of a concrete experience.[14] In a similar sense, participants often speak of God's presence or "thereness" during the hierophany. The hierophant immediately apprehends, and feels apprehended by, the divine Other. Nan, in relating her experience, repeatedly exclaimed, "I felt like he was there." For her, the "thereness" of God was both an intuition and a visualization. She sensed God's presence as she read the words of the story, but she also experienced the presence of a bright light. For her, God was the ultimate *Dasein*: no longer simply "out-there" in the general space of the Beyond, but the supreme "Being-there," or even better, the "Being-here," right now, in this room.

13. Steinbock, *Phenomenology and Mysticism*, 139.
14. Schütz and Luckmann, *Structures 1*, 62–64.

Concomitant to God's "thereness" is his "mineness." In one sense, God is the actor and initiator who overwhelms the hierophant by his strange presence and pointed communication. He is truly "Other": untamed and powerful. However, in another sense, the hierophant intuits the encounter as profoundly intimate; as a revealing of God-for-me. In the hierophany, God enters the world of the mundane, not in a general sense, but as a specific and personal fulfillment of one's yearnings. Nan found release, Kay found love, Nid found guidance, Lek found power, etc. In other words, the communication they had received and the knowledge they had gained was both deeply personal and convictional. The experience was their "transforming moment," which, as James Loder argues, awakens and tells them, "Don't be afraid—trust and live. Live beyond the boundaries and shelters you have built up against the void. Live in the transparency of the self with the Holy."[15] Further, the revelation of God that participants receive during the hierophany is, at the same time, both direct and mediate. Kay heard the voice of God, but it was via the mediation of a television program. That which is normally intended in the mode of anonymity was, instead, the vehicle for a direct, personal revelation of the Sacred. In fact, the vehicle, the program itself as program, entirely disappeared to clear the way or open up the space for God's communication to Kay.[16]

A final element of the hierophanic event structure is the responsive transformation of the convert. During the event, participants experience a range of affective responses that, while not unusual in themselves, were conspicuously sudden and instantaneously transformative. Prior to her hierophany, Kay was crying, situated in a state of despair and facing the end of self. As the words of the show were thematized in her stream of consciousness, she spontaneously and unwittingly ceased her crying and became overwhelmed with the emotion of happiness. The shift in her emotion was so sudden that she performed a test to see if the suspicious transition was indeed real. "I tried to think of something sad," she reports, "but no crying; no tears. I feel like, 'Oh! I'm so happy!' I wasn't sure whether God did this, so I prayed, 'If you are real, if this is not by my emotion, then show me.'" Both Wit and Lek encountered the Sacred in response to economic

15. Loder, *Transforming Moment*, 122.

16. William James claimed, "Personal religious experience has its root and centre in mystical states of consciousness." By "mystical states of consciousness," James meant that the experience is characterized by (1) ineffability, (2) noetic quality, (3) transiency, and (4) passivity. I have found all four qualities to be present in the hierophanic experiences of the participants of this study. James, *Varieties of Religious Experience*, 281–83.

life crises. After praying to the Christian God, they both experienced an unusual sense of peace and calm even though the situation itself was not resolved. Wit had prayed to Buddha numerous times, but it was only his prayer to the Christian God that effectively and immediately communicated the peace for which he yearned.

In addition to immediate affective responses, the hierophany also restructures one's personal identity and biography via the in-breaking of the sacred into profane time. Mircea Eliade argues that for *Homo religiosus*, time is essentially non-homogenous. Temporality is experienced as intervals of the sacred and profane, structured per the liturgical calendar to re-actualize sacred events that had occurred in the mythical past.[17] While Eliade had prioritized cyclical, liturgical time in his analysis, we may say that conversion introduces a radical and singular in-breaking of the sacred into personal, biographical time. The event transforms a normal, mundane day into a sacred day or, better, *the* sacred day, for the hierophant. Thus, the day of one's conversion serves as the point of transition, or the fulcrum, of one's narrative identity.[18] Post-event, one begins to make a clear delineation between before and after and between one's former self and one's new self. Before the event, participants were Buddhists, yearning but without hope. After the event, participants become Christians, altered in both their religious allegiance and belief structure. In this way, the hierophanic event marks one's "switching of worlds." It immediately transforms one's self-understanding and initiates him or her into a processual journey of "becoming Christian." As Nan explains, "After that, I didn't exist to Buddhism anymore. I existed to Christianity. I stepped across to something different. From that point on, I was changed. I was not the same."

Besides being an event, religious alternation is also experienced as a process. For converts, Christian identity is always in tension between being and becoming, already and not yet. The processual nature of this tension begins prior to conversion as "seekers" are gradually immersed in the Christian intersubjective lifeworld and symbolic universe.[19] During my

17. Eliade, *Sacred and the Profane*, 68–72, 104–5.
18. See Berger and Luckmann, *Social Construction*, 159–60.
19. Asian theologian Simon Chan comments regarding the processual nature of conversion among Asians: "The complexity and variations of conversion in Asia show that the traditional Protestant concept of conversion, which identifies 'being saved' by means of a standard *ordo salutis*, cannot be readily applied. Rather, conversion is a gradual process that may begin with a hazy awareness and understanding of the person of Christ and progress to where certain essential Christian truths are more formed over time" (Chan,

interview with her, Nid repeatedly referred to her conversion as slow and gradual. "Step by step," is how she described it. The process was so gradual, in fact, that, in reflection, she can attribute percentages to how much of her identity was Christian and how much was Buddhist during specific times of her life. Likewise, Ploy clearly experienced a lengthy period of hybridity due to her Christian education and intersubjective involvement. She speaks of her identity at the time in territorial terms. When she was at work, she was in "God's land" and, therefore, belonged to God. However, when she left the university she entered the land of Buddha and, therefore, belonged to Buddha. "There was no conflict," she explains. "I think it was blended in myself." Both Nid and Ploy demonstrate that converts often experience a period of hybrid consciousness prior to their conversion. How should we understand this period of hybridity?

First, we notice that hybridity is introduced via one's immersion in the Christian intersubjective lifeworld. All the participants, save Kay, established relationships with Christian significant others prior to their conversion, and it was these relationships that initiated a process whereby one's self became the other. Peter Berger notes that this processual transfer of worlds occurs as one enters a new plausibility structure, or a specific social base and social processes required for the maintenance of one's subjective reality.[20] Given the tenuous nature of secondary socialization, significant others are essential for transmitting and legitimizing the new symbolic universe. "They are particularly important," Berger explains, "for the ongoing confirmation of that crucial element of reality we call identity."[21] In other words, as Anthony Steinbock avers, "We become other through others."[22] This "emplacement" of a seeker or convert into a new social world, while certainly an element of the process of becoming Christian, is also an essential moment of the phenomenon under investigation. Therefore, we will treat this topic more thoroughly in the following chapter.

Second, the period of hybridity is often characterized by an internalization of the Christian symbolic universe. During this period, one straddles two worlds, as it were. One may continue to pray to Buddha or make merit at the temple, but, at the same time, he or she may attend church, pray to the Christian God, or read the Bible. This period of hybridity

---

Grassroots Asian Theology, 122).

20. Berger and Luckmann, *Social Construction*, 154.
21. Berger and Luckmann, *Social Construction*, 150.
22. Steinbock, *Home and Beyond*, 196.

represents an essential moment whereby one tests out the Christian God and "tries on" a Christian identity. Nid had prayed to God for his help to secure a spot on the YMCA team to the US. "I had heard many times, 'Don't challenge God,'" she recalls. "But, just to myself, I challenged him. When I prayed, I said, 'If it's really your plan for my life, let it happen that I can go.' Amazingly, I went through the entire process and was accepted." The idea that God answers prayer was both modeled and transmitted by her new Christian friends. This period of testing, while characterized by a trying out of the Christian symbolic universe, is, however, not merely cognitive. The self, as an embodied self, begins to take on the religious habitus of the Christian lifeworld. One prays differently (closed-fisted rather than in a *wai* position), re-defines sacred time and place (entering the church on Sundays rather than only attending the temple), and forms new habits (reading the Bible, worship, and fellowship). These transformations do not occur suddenly, but represent the slow, and sometimes unconscious, transition of the self into a Christian sacred self.[23]

Immediately prior to conversion, participants often experience a liminal period during which they are neither Buddhist nor Christian. They have progressed far in their adoption of a Christian identity, but, up to that point, they have yet to formalize that identity via ritual or hierophany. Victor Turner defined liminality as the period of anti-structure whereby one is "betwixt and between" two social structures.[24] It is a state of limbo, as it were, during which one's identity is ambiguous. For participants, this period often occurs during formalized training in preparation for baptism. Nid and Ploy both went through such periods. Prior to their baptism, they were reluctant to identify fully as Christian even though their belief structures were already significantly altered. This explains why Nid could speak of herself as 80 percent Christian. The other 20 percent, as she understood it, represented her need to undergo the formal ritual processes which would not only initiate her into the community of saints, but also publicly proclaim her new religious identity to friends and family. As she explains this period, "I was almost to the line where I completely became a Christian." Nan's liminal period was in anticipation of her hierophany. Prior to her conversion, she was frequently reading the Bible,

23. Regarding the body's unconscious habitation of a world, Merleau-Ponty avers, "My body has its world, or understands its world, without having to make use of my 'symbolic' or 'objectifying function'" (Merleau-Ponty, *Phenomenology of Perception*, 140–41).

24. Turner, *Ritual Process*, 95, 107.

attending church, and, in all but name, living out a normal Christian identity. She would not self-identify as a Christian yet, but neither was she a Buddhist. The hierophany served to seal the transition from a Buddhist identity to a Christian identity.

While we may say that a hybrid consciousness typifies the pre-conversion self *en route* to conversion, another form of hybridity ensues post-conversion. This hybridity is no longer characterized by the maintenance of two religious identities, however, but is, instead, characterized by growth, learning, and possible relapse. Post-conversion, the self is perceived as a Christian self, but one's religious being-in-the-world may be experienced as weak or strong, confused or confident, lazy or active. Tom, for example, expressed confusion regarding his conversion. Despite having a conversion experience at the age of eleven, he did not enter the church, did not have any Christian friends, and would occasionally take part in Buddhist rituals. "I felt like I was a Christian, but I wasn't sure," he recalls. "In my heart I believed, but I didn't do religious activities like a Christian. I was confused." Ten times throughout the interview, Tom alluded to his "confusion" during this period. Later, when he experienced another conversion moment at the age of seventeen, he transitioned into a "confident," Christian identity. "After that day," he explains, "I became confident about my salvation and about being a Christian." In a similar manner, Kay described her periods of relapse as "laziness" while Nan used the phrase "not a very good Christian." In all these cases, participants experienced periods of being an inferior, sacred self, requiring, therefore, a certain level of growth to attain fully one's newly acquired religious identity.

In sum, one's transition from a Buddhist identity to a Christian religious identity is experienced as both event and process, being and becoming, already and not yet. Understood processually, the gradual embodiment of a Christian identity involves periods of hybridity. Prior to conversion, this hybridity is often displayed in the straddling of two religious worlds, while post-conversion, the hybridity is tied to a sense of the self as inferior, growing, or in-process. The processual hybridity of converts post-conversion, therefore, begs the question as to what has changed in one's religious outlook. To this topic we now turn.

REORIENTATION

Lek: Change in Allegiance

My mind was focused as I entered the idol room in my house. I knew what I had to do. I walked in and looked at the shelf stacked with about a dozen images representing Buddha and other famous monks. As I examined each one, the memories of my past suddenly flooded over me. I remembered praying to this image when I needed help in school, and this other one when I was looking for a job. I used to believe that this Buddha image, which was handed down to me from my grandfather, not only answered my prayers, but also protected me and my house. These idols represented the power I needed to get through life. They were my hope, my security, and my protection. But, now, all I see are just blocks of wood, metal, and stone. How could I ever have thought otherwise?

After I had scrutinized each image, I began throwing them away. Strangely, I felt nothing but satisfaction. A Buddhist monk would be appalled at what I'm doing, but I don't care. These things are now worthless to me. The idols that had family significance I decided to give back to my father. It is not my place to throw them out. I gathered them together and drove over to my father's house. As I gave him the bag full of idols, he was not terribly surprised. He knew that I was a Christian now. He asked, "Why are you getting rid of these? Don't you know that they protect you? This is very dangerous." "I don't need them anymore," I replied. "I have changed. My God is greater than these idols."

Sometimes, it's hard for me to believe how much my life has changed in such a short amount of time. What I told my dad was true, but it was only part of the story. Yes, my God is greater than those idols, but that doesn't mean he will necessarily fix all my problems. That's what I used to think. My idols were there for me to manipulate to get what I wanted, whether it was money, success, or relationships. If I prayed the right prayer, they had the power to give me the right answers. But God is different. He is not just a power that gives me what I want; instead, he is my Father who loves me and cares for me, even when I go through difficult times. God doesn't solve all my problems, and, yes, I still do fear at times. But in the end, I am confident that I have God. He has a plan for me, and I can talk to Him like a close friend. That is certainly much better than praying to a block of wood.

Strangers in a Familiar Land

Ploy: Everyday Miracle

This was the worst trip of my life. A day before my flight from Bangkok to Dallas was scheduled to leave, I got sick. I did alright on the fourteen-hour flight to the US, but by the time we arrived in Dallas, I was exhausted. I just wanted a bed, but the trip wasn't over yet. Our destination was St. Louis, and we still had two more flights to get there. The plane out of Dallas was delayed. When we were finally in the air, I realized that we weren't going to make our connection flight to St. Louis. I was getting very worried.

Anxiety had always been a problem for me. I used to worry about everything: school, boyfriends, family, you name it. Believe it or not, I even worried about praying to the right spirit to help me with my worries. As I sat on the plane, I could feel my pulse quickening and my forehead sweating. Here comes the anxiety. I decided to take out my Bible. I bring it with me wherever I go, so it was in my backpack in the overhead compartment. I held the Bible in my hands and began reading Philippians 4:6 which says, "Do not be anxious about anything, but in every situation, by prayer and petition, with thanksgiving, present your requests to God." I thought, yes, that's what I need to do. This circumstance is out of my control, but it is not out of God's control. I just need to trust Him. I closed my eyes and prayed, "God, I can't take this anymore, but there is nothing I can do. I want a miracle." Immediately, I felt better, but I still wasn't sure if even God could do anything with this circumstance. After all, I'm stuck in an airplane 25,000 feet above the ground. What could he possibly do?

As we were nearing our destination, I flagged a nearby flight attendant. I told her, "Because the flight was delayed, we are going to miss our connection to St. Louis. We'll have only five minutes to reach the next flight. Is there anything you can do?" "Don't worry," she replied. "The crew on this plane will be transitioning to that same plane. We will be the attendants on that flight as well. They won't leave without us." I couldn't believe it. It was a miracle! Only God could make this happen. I know that this wasn't a major miracle. He didn't part the Red Sea or anything, but it was a major miracle for me. I have learned over the years that, unlike the shrines and spirits, my God will always take care of me. I don't need to resolve my own problems or worry about praying to the correct spirit. I just need to wait on Him. He is the God of everyday miracles.

Interpretation

Post-conversion, converts undergo a radical reorientation to their lived world. Their hierophanic experience of God, combined with their processual inhabitation of the Christian mythos and lifeworld, effects a transformation in how converts perceive the Sacred, themselves, and their world. This reorientation is a paradigm shift, a spiritual revolution wherein one abandons one's former religious identity and belief structure in favor of a new vision of reality and mode of being-in-the-world.[25] As a result, converts now perceive circumstances per a revised interpretive schema and behave in line with a modified ethic and religiosity.

Phenomenologist Jan van den Berg reminds us, "The subject's qualities are the aspects of a world, physiognomies of the objects of everyday existence."[26] He provides this example: two people might live in the same village, but depending on their health, cultural background, sex, or age, they may perceive their world quite differently. They unwittingly and inevitably see their own qualities and characteristics in the environment around them; therefore, the village streets, buildings, and people take on a unique flavor for each person. For example, a child might see the physical structures of his village as imposing and forbidding while an adult might see them as familiar places of business, work, or leisure. In a sense, therefore, even though they live in the same village, they inhabit two very different worlds.[27] Likewise, since religious alternation is a thorough transformation of one's being-in-the-world, converts will perceive their surrounding environment differently post-conversion than they once did pre-conversion. The same places, people, and material objects which once comprised "home," take on a new mode of being and, consequently, a new meaning, in light of one's transformed identity. How may we understand this radical shift in one's being-in-the-world?

The touchstone of one's religious reorientation is a revised apprehension of the Sacred as both exclusive and relational. As a convert directly and intuitively encounters the divine Other, a convictional knowledge is conveyed that reveals both the God-who-is-alone and the God-who-is-there-for-me.

---

25. I'm thinking here, especially, of Thomas Kuhn's well-known work on scientific revolutions, a phenomenon which bears certain similarities to personal, spiritual revolutions. See Kuhn, *Structure of Scientific Revolutions*.

26. Berg, *Different Existence*, 47.

27. Berg, *Different Existence*, 45–48.

This dual orientation toward the Sacred effects a transformation in one's perception of the self and one's world. Let's investigate this further.

First, we notice that participants perceive God in religiously exclusive terms. Previously, as members of the Thai Buddhist lifeworld, participants upheld an inclusivist worldview whereby multiple divine beings competed, often territorially, for one's reverence and allegiance. The spirit world was understood pragmatically, with temporary loyalty conferred for purposes of manipulation, appeasement, or personal benefit. Post-conversion, however, a dramatic reorientation transpires that reduces the realm of the sacred to one, all-encompassing and all-knowing divine Being who demands the self's singular allegiance. Prior to Kay's conversion, she would follow a daily routine that involved cleaning the family shrine, offering food and drink to the idols, and praying to them in a *wai* position. Her father enforced this practice of ancestor veneration as it was an expression of the family's filial piety. However, the day after her suicide attempt and subsequent conversion, Kay was compelled to cease paying respect at the shrine. "I didn't know why, but inside my heart I knew that I should stop showing respect to any idols or gods," she recalls. "I stopped feeling fear or anything. Instead, I felt confidence in God. I have my own God, and I don't have to fear anymore." This intuitive sense of the exclusivity of the Christian God is universal among the participants. Pre-conversion, Wit referred to his religious adherence as two relationships: Buddhism and Christianity. However, post-conversion, in response to his father's request that Wit continue these relationships, Wit refused. For him, the essence of Christianity is founded on the singularity of the Christian God, thus demanding his exclusive worship and allegiance. Likewise, Ploy, who had spent over twenty years navigating a hybrid consciousness, suddenly came to an awareness of God's exclusive superiority. While she may still fear evil spirits at times, she now knows that her God is "bigger" and that he exercises sole authority over both the natural and supernatural realms. For converts, therefore, the singular presence of God is an irresistible irruption into the lived world that not only reveals his sole authority and power, but also, and concomitantly, reduces the authority and power of competing deities. Thus, converts experience a transfer of religious allegiance concurrent with their transfer of religious identity. Like the Deuteronomist, participants are compelled to proclaim, "The Lord, he is God in heaven above and on the earth below; there is no other" (Deut 4:39).

Verticality

This compelling exclusivity of the Christian God enacts a transformation of one's view of the self. The demand of this God on the self is exclusive: either worship Him alone or worship idols. The inclusivity which predominates in the Thai Buddhist lifeworld is not an option for the transformed sacred self. Previously, Lek's religious outlook consisted of a pantheon of spirits and deities who existed for purposes of manipulation. Lek understood himself as the center of the sacred world, demanding of the spirits their power to assist him in navigating life's problems. Post-conversion, however, he not only abandoned his polytheistic worldview, which was represented in the disposal of his collection of idols, but he also willingly submitted to the authority and purposes of the one God. "After I became a Christian, I didn't give food to monks or pray to idols anymore. I prayed to God. I know God. I know Jesus is alive." Even more to the point, Nan descriptively describes her exclusive religious identity in this way: "I do not exist to Buddhism anymore. I exist to Christianity."[28]

Concomitant with exclusive worship is a renewed cognitive and affective perspective of the self. The knowledge of the "thereness" of God removes the priority and potency of the self. During his encounter with God during a time of crisis, Wit intended himself in the mode of dependence. The exclusive sufficiency and potency of the Sacred had both confronted and eradicated his entrenched self-confidence. The self, as it were, receded or became a minimal self to open up space for the radical in-breaking of the all-encompassing, all-powerful divine Being. Further, participants refer to the removal of fear, anxiety, or self-doubt in light of their new religious allegiance. Both Tom and Kay describe their former religious identities as shrouded in fear: fear of punishment, fear of evil spirits, and fear of their own inferiority. However, post-conversion, this fear was removed. God, as the only God, not only removed their feelings of guilt and shame, but also removed their sense of uncertainty in encountering a polytheistic world. Ploy describes this experience as a healing of the mind: "I think it's easier because we Christians have only one God. I don't have to worry about whether I should go to this statue or this certain Chinese temple. There are too many statues that I had to go and worship! I think it (conversion) has helped with my mental health."

---

28. Therefore, we may say that conversion not only entails the adoption of a new identity and belief structure but also a "deconversion" from former religious identities and beliefs. Barbour, *Versions of Deconversion*.

Strangers in a Familiar Land

A final transformation of the self in response to God's exclusivity is the embodied habitation in a God-ordained and God-ruled universe. Because God is one, the self becomes a sacred self who must live *coram deo*: a bodily, daily enactment of whole-hearted submission and service "before the face of God." Kay's decision to join a Christian organization was, in many ways, just as significant to her being-in-the-world as was her initial decision to convert. Whereas her job as a secretary was believed to represent selfish pursuits, service was perceived as submission to the Divine will. "When I stand in front of God and look into his eyes," she explains, "I want to say, 'I did this for you because of what you did for me.'" A simple change of mind or mental awareness of the Holy would not be a sufficient response to God's activity in her life. Instead, her embodied self had to become a "living sacrifice" (Rom 12:1) a physical, outward, everyday enactment of a new, inner reality. Since Kay's universe is now ruled by a singular Sovereign, only such a holistic expression of submission would be adequate for conveying her unswerving and exclusive allegiance.

In addition to a change of self, a convictional understanding of the Sacred as monotheistic also results in a transformed world. First, the world is disclosed via the revelation of the one God, the Bible. For participants, the Bible is not a static record of past events, but rather is given, in the phenomenological sense, as the communication of the Sacred for day-to-day living. When Ploy experienced intense anxiety amid her flights, the Bible became a source of calm, comfort, and direction. The book that was in her backpack in the overhead compartment was transmuted into living communication from the Holy that was particular to Ploy and her current circumstance. As she reflected on the verse, her interest was neither in the historical background of the text nor in the literary intent of the author. In fact, the "pastness" or "otherness" of the Bible had entirely receded, allowing the text to speak only to her current situation. What Ploy was reading was God's "voice," founded on the belief that the all-encompassing, all-present, singular God was *there* in that plane and was concerned for her well-being.

Second, the world of things is transformed. If God is exclusively God, then a transfiguration of sacred materiality must take place. Lek's narrative above highlights this transition of materiality from sacred to profane, from valued to junk. The idols in his house were once believed to represent power. They were not just inert objects, but entities from another realm. They provided supernatural protection, answered prayers, and, sometimes, demanded appeasement. Post-conversion, however, these sacred objects transmuted into blocks of wood, stone, and metal. In Lek's new world, these objects had become disempowered and desacralized. Even more, they were given in the mode of "less than": less valuable even than everyday, household items. In other words, they became garbage.[29]

Finally, the religiously exclusive world of the sacred self entails a revision of one's sense of sacred space. While the church may take on a special significance as a place for sacred activity, for the most part, the singular presence of God demands of participants a view of the entire world as his domain. God cannot be confined to a temple or to a wooden image. The God who is there, is also the God who is everywhere. Therefore, this God may be accessed at any time and at any place via the medium of prayer. Ploy no longer needs to pray at certain locations to have her prayers answered. She can pray anywhere, even on an airplane, because even when she is 25,000 feet in the air, God is there.[30]

Besides the exclusivity of the Christian God, the second reorientation of the participants' view of the Sacred is of the God-who-is-there-for-me. As we have seen, the yearning of the seeker is for existential or situational fulfillment. The seeker is pursuing power, hope, joy, love, or meaning amid a world imbued with anxiety, crisis, and hopelessness. Inherent in this pursuit, however, is not a yearning for raw, detached, impersonal power, but for a relationship with a Power who is loving, forgiving, and present. One's conversion experience, therefore, is characterized by a theological-existential encounter with the God who is relational, with love being the most commonly experienced attribute of this relational God.[31] Kay's childhood was one of abuse, shame, and fear. Her father's incessant berating and lack of affection wore on Kay's sense of self-worth. Despair defined her being-in-the-world. "I felt like no one loved me; like, if I die then this family will be better without me. My life was nothing." However, on the day of her conversion, she encountered a God who was a loving Father. Unlike her earthly father, this relational God forgives, cares, and does not condemn. He loves "with no strings attached." God as love also characterized

---

29. Lek's perspective here parallels that of the prophet Isaiah, who boldly argued against the folly of producing and worshipping idols by demonstrating their mundane materiality. See Isaiah 44:9–20.

30. This reminds us of Jesus' comments to the woman at the well regarding the role of the temple for prayer and worship. See John 4:20–24.

31. This theological motivation, namely the pursuit of a God who is love, was also a primary motivation for first-century converts. For discussion, see Hurtado, *Why on Earth*, 124–26.

Lek's conversion experience. As part of her presentation of the Gospel, Lek's pastor had discussed with him about the love of God. For Lek, who had never experienced love in his family, this concept was welcomed as truly "good news." "As soon as I came to know Jesus," he recalls, "I thought, I now have someone to care for me, to love me. Even if no one in the community loves me, God loves me. Jesus loves me." Perhaps the best way to describe this aspect of the participants' intentionality of the Sacred is of God-as-friend. While, on the one hand, the exclusivity of God highlights his power, authority, and right to be worshipped, on the other hand, this same God is experienced as close and friendly. As Kay avers, "Even if I don't have friends, I know that Jesus is with me."

The convert's intentionality of God as relational reorients one's perception of self. If God is love, I am beloved; if God is friend, I am befriended. More than just a feeling or change of mind, the experience of being beloved or befriended defines one's identity. For Kay, this renewed sense of self was most powerfully experienced at her baptism. She describes it this way:

> So, you know, before knowing God my life was chasing love, right? (quiet) My parents, my family, they never showed love, and I tried to make people love me. (emotional) When I was baptized, I felt like I was getting married, you know. Married to someone who will love me as I am no matter what. So, for me, baptism meant that Jesus died for me. We will always stay together, and I will have his love . . . forever. I was so excited. When I was standing in the line to go to the waterfall, I felt . . . excited. It felt like the same day that I was married.

Conversion, for Kay, was her entrance into an all-encompassing love relationship with the God who is love. Her baptism, which she likened to a marriage, exemplified the intimacy of this relationship: a mystical and personal union of the self with the Sacred. Therefore, love now defines the self. Because God loves her, Kay has transitioned from a no-thing to a someone, and from being homeless to being at-home. This union has re-defined Kay's narrative identity. Since her conversion, Kay's existence is now characterized by a love obligation. Kay imagines God as asking, "I love you. That's why I died on the cross for you, but do you love me?" Kay's reciprocation of love is understood as nothing other than her willingness to devote her entire existence to the service of God. In other words, the God who had delivered her from self-destruction, uniting her to himself, introduces an obligation for reciprocation which is motivated by love itself. This obligation defines one's being-in-the-world. As Kay explains, "I don't want to disappoint him." This radical reorientation of the self in light of the God-who-is-there-for-me is universal among participants. For Wit, the relational God is perceived as in-control, meaning that Wit must respond appropriately with humility and dependence. God may not resolve all his problems, but, no matter what happens, he is always kind, present, and available. For Nan, the personal presence of God instills in her a deep sense of satisfaction. "God knows me better than I know myself," she proclaims. "I always pray that he will keep me from straying. If I do stray, I hope he takes my life. Only God satisfies me. I prefer death over abandonment from God."

Finally, we notice that not only is the self altered in response to the relational God, but so is one's entire world. One's former world, which was characterized by fear, loneliness, and despair, is now re-framed as a sacred "with-world" (*Mitwelt*).[32] It is a world permeated with the loving and caring presence of a God who is no longer solely intended in the mode of "Other." He is now *with* me: lovingly present through the exigencies of life, readily available for direct communication, and genuinely committed to my holistic well-being. For Nid, God was her personal counselor. Prior to her baptism, Nid heard God's voice, telling her to go to church and even helping her understand the Bible. However, after her baptism, the voice ceased. Did God abandon her? She remembers, "I no longer had a sense of confidence. It felt like I had lost my counselor." Despite the immediate sense of loss, Nid remained unwavering in her belief that God has been and always will be guiding her. From her acceptance to the YMCA camp in the US to her miraculous survival in the mountains after being separated from the group, Nid believes that God is responsible for directing her life. She sees the world as a stage, with life events playing out under the loving and caring direction of the Divine author and director. Even in the face of suffering and marginalization, and even without the presence of an audible voice, she proclaims, "God is the one who is with me, guiding me. He has taken me to this new land; to this new life."

This perspective of the relational God who intervenes transforms one's interpretation of life events. In the story above, Ploy perceives the flight attendant's "chance" transition to the exact same flight as nothing but divine intervention. It was a "miracle," as she calls it. For Wit, even a crisis event, such as finding out that his daughter is autistic, falls under the loving guidance and purposes of the Sacred. As a doctor, he is accustomed to resolving

---

32. Heidegger, *Being and Time*, 155.

problems, but this crisis reminded him once again of his utter dependence and humility. "God gave this to me so that I know I am not powerful," he explains. "My life is in God's hands." To understand this radical, and seemingly strange, alteration in one's interpretive schema, Devenish explains,

> When we "see" into the spiritual dimension to discern God at work in our lives, we do not actually see him with our physical eyes. Rather, we discern his invisible presence at work in the visible world by "reading" circumstances in such a way that we attribute events and circumstances to the purposeful actions of a loving God rather than to the meaningless unfolding of random events.[33]

In other words, "chance" is not an operative concept in the convert's world. Indeed, the world of the convert is neither arbitrary nor chaotic, but is one governed by a loving and all-powerful divine ruler for whom "there is no creature hidden from His sight, but all things are open and laid bare" (Heb 4:13).

CONCLUSION

As we have seen in this chapter, the convert's vertical orientation, experienced as yearning, event and process, and reorientation, redefines one's being-in-the-world. The divine-human encounter that initiates one's ongoing and intimate relationship with God is experienced as compelling, inevitable, direct, relational, and transformative. The self, indeed the very world, recedes to clear space for God's immense but loving presence. As a result, the world in which a convert awakens is a radically different world. Old allegiances, fears, certainties, and attachments suddenly and decisively disappear, paving the way for the creation of new meanings and new perspectives. However, and with some irony, it is this radical reorientation, grounded in the exclusivity of the Christian God, that introduces the convert to situations of marginalization. The same conversion experience that revolutionizes one's world, providing hope, love, meaning, and intimacy, at the same time, divides families, severs friendships, and threatens social identities. That is to say, by entering a new homeworld, that of Christian belief and identity, one necessarily becomes estranged from one's previous homeworld, that of Thai Buddhism. However, as we will see, one's new identity as friend-of-God not only introduces states of marginalization,

---

33. Devenish, *Seeing and Believing*, 12–13.

Verticality

but also orients, sustains, and guides during situations of marginalization. Verticality, therefore, may be understood as both the source of and the power for negotiating the experience of in-marginality. This vertical orientation, however, is not only an individual affair, but also essentially communal in nature. We will now investigate this primordial emplacement of the sacred self within a sacred community.

7

Emplacement

INTRODUCTION

IN THE PREVIOUS CHAPTER, we investigated verticality, or one's direct, intuitive, and powerful "meeting with God," which serves as the founding moment for the phenomenon of in-marginality. Vertical experiences transform the self into a sacred self via the irruption of the Sacred into the world of the mundane. As a result of these encounters, identities are transformed, yearnings are fulfilled, and allegiances are transferred. However, as we have seen, vertical experiences are never without a horizontal dimension. The sacred self requires a determinate social world to embody these sacred realities, to maintain their plausibility, and to protect the self under its "sacred canopy."[1] Therefore, it is difficult, if not impossible, to understand the meanings inherent in conversion without, at the same time, disclosing the primordial, everyday intersubjectivity that takes place among sacred selves.

In this chapter, we will investigate this emplacement of the convert within an intersubjective place-world. Emplacement, Edward Casey explains, refers to where I find myself in the world. As a situated being, I am always "in place," or localized somewhere in particular. More than just a background for concrete actions or thoughts, place anchors and orients me, shapes what and who I am, and delimits what I call "home."[2] Further, place determines not just where I am but how I am together with others. "This implacement is as social as it is personal," Casey argues. "The idiolocal is not merely

---

1. Berger, *Sacred Canopy*.
2. Casey, *Getting Back into Place*, xii, 23.

Emplacement

idiosyncratic or individual; it is also collective in character."[3] For Thai converts, this collectivity of place is integral to the proper formation and maintenance of their new religious identities. While hierophanies may introduce converts to a new, sacred reality, we may say that it is the community of saints that effectively "makes" them Christian. The *ecclesia* becomes their new social reality: a place where faith pervades and alters one's self and one's lifeworld, where deep intersubjective bonds are formed, and where the Sacred is encountered in worship, prayer, and redemptive imagery.[4]

How may we understand this emplacement of the self within a sacred community? How does one's self become the other? To answer these questions, we will explore the moment of emplacement both genetically and generatively as the movement of the self from outsider to insider or from alien to "homecomrade." We will follow this movement through the adumbration of three interpretive themes which were disclosed during the interviews. (1) *Entrance* refers to the convert's attraction to and immersion in a new and idealized social reality. This theme includes the data analysis categories of "immersion in community," "community as alternate world," and "significant others as exemplary." (2) *Membership* includes the formal and informal processes by which the convert imbibes the sedminented tradition and becomes a full-fledged, contributing member of the community. Included are the categories of "learning as identity formation," "significant other as mentor," "baptism as official entrance into new identity," "Christian identity as ritual," and "narrative as exemplary." Finally, the theme of (3) *reimagining*, which covers the categories of "world transfer as reimagining lifeworld," "community as mediating world transfer," and "disillusionment with Christian lifeworld," refers to the convert's revised vision of one's self and the world as motivated by the adoption of the sacred community's social imaginary.

ENTRANCE

Nid: Lost and Found

> I was lost, alone, and frightened. I had lost sight of the group, and now even the trail had disappeared. It was evening, and darkness

---

3. Casey, *Getting Back into Place*, 23, 31. In a similar vein, Craig Bartholomew states, "Place is furthermore never individualistic; rather, it 'insinuates itself into a collectivity.' There is inevitably a *social* dimension to place; humans are placed in relationship, and in relationship they form and fashion places" (Bartholomew, *Where Mortals Dwell*, 3).

4. Farley, *Ecclesial Man*, 106–8.

was rapidly descending on this lonely mountain. I thought I was going to die.

My friends and I came to this place to help kids from a poor mountain village. As members of a Christian activity team from a local university, we often did things like this together. I wasn't a Christian yet, but this group had accepted me anyway. I was afraid they would pressure me to become a Christian, but, to my great surprise, they didn't. Instead, they just prayed for me and showed me care. The entire time, I was observing them. I watched how they loved one another, and how they loved me. I had never experienced anything like this before.

That's why I was here, on this mountain. I remembered what my new friends had taught me. They told me that God is everywhere, and he listens to our prayers. If that is true, then God is here in this forest, and he can help me. I stopped walking, sat down on a stump, and prayed, "God, if you are there, then please help me!" My fear subsided, and I began walking again. Suddenly, I heard a whistle in the distance. I stood on the edge of a cliff and shouted as loud as I could. Thankfully, the group was in the valley below, and they heard me. I don't know how, but they found me! I was saved! Later, I found out that my friends were praying for me, too. They didn't give up on me, and neither did their God. From that point on, I knew that these people were not just my friends, they were my family.

Kay: An Alternate Reality

The only churches I had ever seen were in movies. They were always so beautiful and majestic, with stained glass and exquisite sculptures. I suppose that's what I was expecting as I sat in my friend's car on the way to my very first church service. But when we pulled into the parking lot, I was sorely disappointed. This isn't a church, I thought. It's just an old house.

The door had barely opened when a group of people swarmed around me like bees on honey. They all had huge smiles on their faces, and they each greeted me individually. I thought, "These people are weird!"

When I went to this church, I was very suspicious. My family abused me, my friends were shallow, and I even hated myself. Things were changing now that I had encountered God, but I still had no idea what love was. I just assumed that everyone was out there for themselves, and that no one would have the time or desire to love and care for me. They were just too happy and friendly.

This is silly, but I actually wondered whether they were on drugs. But, at the end of the day, my perspective had completely changed. These people were genuine. They accepted me, and they loved one another. Not only that, they were overflowing with life. Unlike at the temple where everyone wears drab white and is respectfully quiet, the members of this church were fun, vibrant, and colorful. When I walked into church on that day, it was like I had entered an alternate reality . . . and I loved it!

Interpretation

Alternation encompasses not only a transfer of one's personal, religious identity and orientation, but also a transfer of social worlds. Throughout the conversion process, a determinate and proximal community, which may represent either certain individuals or an entire group, impinges itself upon the biography of the convert. After an initial period of observation, one becomes enamored with the group's alternate modes of being-with. Group attributes such as love, care, acceptance, and friendship become compelling and attractive, leading to deep, face-to-face we-relationships and, finally, to the full immersion of the individual within the community. Critically, the sacred self understands these horizontal relationships as permeated with verticality: not only is the Sacred perceived as a member of the community, but also the community is perceived as the embodied incarnation of the Sacred. This section will investigate how it is that one enters and inhabits a new sacred community which, prior to conversion, was primarily understood in the mode of suspicion as a subordinate and alien sub-group. We will adumbrate this interpretive theme per the temporal structure of observation, attraction, and immersion.

Early twentieth-century phenomenologist Edith Stein (1891–1942) contrasted the essence of community with what she had termed "association." Association, Stein argued, is a union of individuals that is founded on a rational and mechanical intentionality of the other. One person approaches another as subject to object for purposes of examination, methodical "dealing with," or coaxed reactions. Conversely, community is the "natural, organic union of individuals" wherein one accepts the other as subject, does not confront them but lives with them, and is infiltrated by their "lifepower."[5] Therefore, community is a solidarity of individuals: an openness to one another such that each one contributes to the energy

---

5. For more on lifepower and its deployment for sentient abilities and properties, see Stein, *Philosophy of Psychology*, 197–200.

and attitude of the group, thus forming a common life and a common "current of experience."[6] This sense of community, or togetherness, is a primordial and essential experience in the participants' transition to a sacred self. Friends, mentors, church or small group members, and pastors are integral in forming the religious identity of converts, uniting them to a communal energy, attitude, and current of experience that is uniquely characterized by the presence and qualities of the Sacred. How does one enter this sacred community?

The entrance of participants into the sacred community often begins with a period of observation. Initially, participants perceive Christians in the mode of suspicion, representatives of a foreign religion, or perhaps a cult, who believe and act contrary to "normal" ways of being-in-the-world. This suspicion inhibits one from "leaping" into a determinate sacred community, instead requiring a distanced stance wherein one can observe, consider, and evaluate. When Wit's wife began attending church, Wit initially believed she was involved in a cult. He noticed that foreigners were always leading churches, and he was concerned that these leaders were taking advantage of or brainwashing Thais. "I was concerned about cheating," he explains, "that she was getting involved in a cult like the one Tom Cruise is a part of." Because of this fear, and his desire to protect his wife, Wit began attending church services to "monitor whether this foreign belief was okay or not." The first time he attended a service, he was uncomfortable since the music was foreign, and he experienced pressure from church members to convert. After several weeks of observation, however, Wit concluded that the teachings were not dangerous. "I realized I don't have to be paranoid since the teaching is good," he recalls, "but I decided that it is good for believers, not for me." Observation also characterized Nid's initial encounters with the sacred community. While attending a Christian university, Nid joined a campus activity club, which consisted mostly of individuals who were preparing to enter pastoral ministry. She enjoyed these friendships, but she was wary of their religious stance and worried that they would pressure her to convert. She explains, "I feared that they would try to convert me or talk about Christianity with me. I felt in my heart that they were going to do something. They seemed nice, but I wondered if they were pretending. So, I observed them a long time."

Observation, therefore, is a distanced stance wherein one is both present and absent to the community. While the participant may be physically

---

6. Stein, *Philosophy of Psychology*, 130, 171, 195, 211–14.

present within the group, perhaps even participating in group activities and conversation, due to suspicion, lack of trust, or curiosity, she purposefully absents herself or "holds back" from the community's common life and form of togetherness.[7] As Jean-Paul Sartre (1905–1980) highlighted, this act of observation apprehends the other in the modality of "object-ness." Under one's gaze, the other is reduced to an object in the world, precluding the formation of subject-to-subject, or I-Thou relationships.[8] As an object, the other is subsequently typified as a representative of a given group.[9] The actions, words, and qualities of the individual are perceived as representing the group as a whole; therefore, the observer draws conclusions about the group by watching, tracking, and evaluating the specific actions of each member. Since Christianity is perceived as a foreign religion, participants initially approach Christians with both suspicion and curiosity. Christians are "alien" members of an obscure sub-group, representatives of Western ways of being-in-the-world. Because of this, participants must first observe Christian behavior. What they observe are not the idiosyncrasies of certain individuals, but typifications of the group-category, "Christians." Every encounter, conversation, activity, and prayer, therefore, contributes to the participant's overall understanding of the character and qualities of the Christian community, broadly speaking. Depending on how these interactions transpire, the individual is either attracted to or repelled by the group's form of togetherness. Of course, for converts, the group becomes attractive, a phenomenon that we will now investigate further.

What attracts participants to a determinate Christian community is a form of togetherness that aligns with one's imagined preconception of an idealized community. Participants observe in Christian intersubjectivity the possible fulfillment of their social and existential yearnings and integration of the self. As a result, they desire to join the in-group: to participate and reciprocate in this new and attractive form of togetherness. When Kay first entered the church, she was overwhelmed not only by their outgoing and friendly manner, but also by their apparent egalitarianism. It was a small church of around thirty members, but included among them were doctors, lawyers, and businessmen; in other words, people who command

---

7. Alfred Schütz calls this a "they-relation" that occurs in certain face-to-face encounters. He states, "The possibility arises that, even when one meets his fellow-man, one may 'hold back' from the living we-relation and replace it, so to speak, with a they-relation" (Schütz and Luckmann, *Structures 1*, 77).

8. Sartre, *Being and Nothingness*, 340–45.

9. Schütz and Luckmann, *Structures 1*, 73–79.

an elevated position within the Thai social hierarchy. Kay observed that these high-ranking individuals did not elevate themselves, but, rather, interacted with her in a casual and friendly manner. No matter one's position, everyone was accepted as equals within this sacred community. This came as a huge shock and was considered as almost too good to be true. In addition, she noticed that underlying this egalitarian mood was what Kay had desired the most: a common current of love and acceptance. Other participants refer to intersubjective displays of kindness, humility, concern, practical care, or fun as what had initially attracted them to Christians. Nid was impressed with how members "hold on to each other" through active displays of affection. She explains,

> Christians share love and care in action. Buddhists may love and care, but they don't show it in action. They keep quiet. They don't hug or say, "Oh, I love you and care for you." They just give money; they don't show their love. But Christians show their love in action. They will visit you, pray for you, and talk with you. They hold on to each other and help each other. That is what I have observed.

For many participants, this "holding on to" was not only experienced in a large community of members, but also in individual friendships. Spouses, girlfriends and boyfriends, university classmates, or other friends displayed attractive qualities within the relationship, leading to the participant's attraction to Christianity. In this way, significant others serve as exemplars of the Christian faith, embodying God's love via their interpersonal demonstrations of care, affection, acceptance, and loyalty within a proximal we-relationship.[10]

Based on these descriptions, we may say that what had initially attracted participants to the Christian community was a social phenomenon known as "communitas." As a subordinate, liminal group suspended betwixt and between the established social structures of Thai society, Christians often, in response, form existential and spontaneous I-Thou relationships with one another that may be characterized by the perspective of "each for one and one for each." Within these concrete social bonds, structural differentiation is eliminated, resulting in sentiments of egalitarianism and comradeship.[11] For participants, communitas is compelling as it exhibits an idealized

---

10. For more on a phenomenology of friendship, see Sokolowski, "Phenomenology of Friendship."

11. Turner, "Betwixt and Between," 49–53. Bible passages such as Acts 2:42–47 suggest that the early church also experienced a form of communitas. See also Bechtler,

form of togetherness that may potentially fulfill one's yearnings. For Kay, who was yearning for love and acceptance, the togetherness of the Christian community was a balm to her soul. In a sense, the Christian community was the unexpected embodiment of what she had always longed for and envisioned as an ideal community. As another Thai convert explains, "This was my dream community. My dream was to be in a community that loves one another without lies and without hate. When I first attended church, I was surprised that this kind of community actually exists."[12]

Once one is attracted to the Christian in-group, he or she desires to spend time with them via conversation, activity, and friendship. We may call this moment, "immersion." Immersion is understood as a practical, everyday, embodied participation in the attitudes, actions, and experiences of the group. It is the comportment of the self into the community's with-world in the mode of "doing-with." Immersion transitions the self from external observer, wherein one treats the other as object and alien, to internal participant, wherein one recognizes the other as subject and friend.[13] After a period of observation, Nid began to realize that her new friends' demonstrations of love and care were genuine. She desired to spend more time with them by joining group meetings and travelling to various locations to perform acts of service together. While on these excursions, team members would pray for one another, discuss religious topics, and provide help and encouragement to those who were struggling. Friendships developed on-the-way, as it were, as Nid interacted with others via joint activity and common experience. Nid describes this period as "coming into a new world." She was immersed in a new vision of "we" based upon friendship and commonality.

Another form of doing-with that is essential to the immersion experience is church attendance. During the immersion phase, participants often join formal Christian services and small groups, first as observers and later as participating members. Within this formal setting, participants may observe uniquely Christian ways of being-with, participate in ritualistic activity while, to some extent, remaining anonymous, and listen to and evaluate formalized Christian teachings. For individuals like Wit, Nan, and Ploy, church attendance was part of their weekly routines, a primary intersubjective component of their burgeoning religious habitus. Wit, for example,

---

Following in His Steps, 109–78.

12. Personal conversation with the author, April 20, 2016.
13. Sartre, *Being and Nothingness*, 535.

prior to his conversion, had spent four hours per week at cell group, three hours on Sundays attending the worship service and a fellowship meal afterward, and several hours per week informally meeting with church members. What we notice, therefore, is that immersion entails the temporal, spatial, and embodied comportment of the self into a community's shared world via activity and we-relationship. During this phase, the self opens oneself up to the community, entering reciprocal relationships such that one becomes a part of the community's common current of experience.

Before we move on, we should note that the religious self's experience of sacred community is always "more than" a mere being-with. Unlike other forms of community, the sacred community bears the unique distinction of "presencing" the Holy. God is not only a member of the in-group, but he is also embodied in the group's personal and interpersonal attitudes, actions, and rituals. Therefore, by means of observation, attraction, and immersion, converts are not only introduced to horizontal intersubjectivity, but they are also mysteriously and immediately engaging with the realm of verticality. As Wit avers, "When we had fellowship, I felt that God was in the group." The most common medium for the community's presencing of God is prayer. For all the participants, prayer was an integral component to their entrance in the sacred community. Nid sensed her friend's companionship, care, and love via prayer. Prayer not only communicated Nid's importance to the group, but also, because prayer was always specific to Nid's circumstances, it demonstrated their and God's concern for her daily well-being. When Nid was lost on the mountain, she implemented a ritual that she had learned from the community. When she was rescued, she learned that her friends were praying for her as well. She attributes her rescue, therefore, to the miraculous intervention of God, but, at the same time, she recognizes that the medium for that miracle was the intercession of her friends. The community had accessed God's presence specifically for her and her difficult circumstance. "I was really touched," she recalls. "Their prayers gave me confidence. I knew God was with me. Even if no one else was with me, God was with me."

MEMBERSHIP

Nan: A Church Home

> As I sat in the pew, listening to the pastor preach from the book of Romans, an overwhelming sense of relief washed over me. What he was saying made a lot of sense: I don't have to do anything to

earn God's favor. His grace comes to me only because of Jesus. I thought to myself, "I have been a Christian for over twenty years, and, only now is the truth of God's grace starting to make sense." Ever since I joined this church a month ago, I've been learning so much. Our small group studies God's Word in depth, we have wonderful discussions on who God is and what it means to be a Christian, and the sermons are both thoughtful and relevant. I have been a member of several churches in the past, but this time it is different. Finally, I feel like a Christian.

After my conversion, I had joined a church but never developed close relationships with the members. The leader was charismatic and godly. Our church was growing rapidly, and I was involved with many different ministries as one of the leaders. However, I didn't grow much in my understanding of God during those years. I was busy with church activities, but I didn't feel like a better Christian. I was very immature in my faith at that time.

Now, as a member of this new church, I have learned more about my faith in one month than I had in the previous twenty years combined. When I was baptized many years ago, I knew at the time that I was taking a serious step. Only now, though, can I say for sure that I won't move away from God. He is the One holding me, and he won't let me go. It feels good to be home.

Kay: Almost Lost

I had turned mentor avoidance into an art form, but sometimes it didn't work. My mentor during my university days was very strict, and I was very stubborn. She would call or text message me every day to see if I had read the Bible that morning. If I said no, she would ask why. I didn't like the pressure, so I began lying to her just to get her off my back. One day, I had an appointment with my mentor to study the Bible. As I was preparing to leave, one of my friends called and asked if I'd like to go with him to see a movie. Hmm, should I go to Bible study or go out and have fun with my friends? It didn't take long for me to decide to skip Bible study. I joined my friends, and we headed down to the bus stop. The bus pulled up, and we jumped on board. Suddenly, I heard a voice yelling from outside the bus, "Kay, come back now!" My stomach lurched. It was my mentor!

Many times, I wondered what it would have been like to have a nice, caring, and understanding mentor. Someone who would affirm me rather than fine me. I would tell my friends, "Why is my mentor so strict? I don't like her." As I look back on it though,

> I think my mentor had saved my life. At the time, I was very stubborn and lazy. After experiencing incessant abuse and hatred in my home for so many years, I just didn't care anymore. My mentor, though, had a vision of a better Kay. She was tough, but I needed tough love. I thank God that he knew what I needed. You know, if my mentor did not show up at my door that day, maybe I would have been lost. I thank God for her.

Interpretation

Religious alternation, as a form of secondary socialization, is always tenuous in nature. While the entrance of the convert into an idealized community is an essential component to the acquisition and formation of a new religious identity, it is the process of resocialization within that community that effectively "makes" one Christian. The specific social base, or plausibility structure, immerses converts in a new world. Through ritual, teaching, emulation, narrative, and conversation, converts slowly adopt the community's habitus, find belonging among its members, and inhabit its sedimented tradition and mythos. When successful, this process of resocialization transforms individuals into full-fledged and contributing members of the community. They become stabilized under a new and eminently real sacred canopy, allowing them to face the exigencies of a marginalized existence. However, should the resocialization process prove ineffective, converts then face the threat of identity loss or reversion. In this section, we will investigate the social processes involved in "making" one Christian. To aid our investigation, we will structure this interpretive theme per three primary components: ritual, emulation, and conformity.

"Membership" is a relatively ambiguous term. In everyday language, we use this expression to convey the state of belonging to or associating with a determinate social community or organization. Membership, however, occurs at varying levels. I may belong to several groups, for example, but certain groups may carry more prominence, more influence, or more consequence in my life. Some memberships exist primarily for the development of friendships, while others thoroughly shape how I view the world. Some are only salient during occasional or brief periods of time, while others are salient in every activity of life. Some shape portions of my identity, while others transform my identity in its entirety. Religious membership may acquire any of these potentialities. I may be a "nominal" member of a religious community such that my religious membership is only "turned on" during Sunday church activities. However, and as we will discuss later

Emplacement

in this section, I may also be defined by my religious membership, entirely re-socialized into the group's subjective reality. In these cases, I am re-formed and trans-formed through my participation in the community. I adopt the community's social identity and religious perspective: I live as members ought to live and see as members ought to see. Through membership, therefore, one truly becomes the other. How may we understand this process of membership as resocialization?

First, we notice that religious affiliation is often formalized through the enactment of ritual. Ritual, as Clifford Geertz reminds us, is consecrated behavior or ceremonial form which serves to fuse the symbolic moods, motivations, and metaphysical conceptions of a sacred community.[14] By re-enacting the mythic past, ritual shapes members by recreating a sacred order out of the profanity of chaotic space and time.[15] In this way, Christian rituals saturate the community with Christological images and stories that essentially modify human existence toward redemption.[16] For participants, baptism is the ritual *par excellence*. Baptism, including both the act itself as well as the catechetical period of study prior to it, is the formal and public initiation of converts into the institutionalized community. As such, baptism carries a perlocutionary force, solidifying one's burgeoning religious identity and signaling one's official membership within the sacred community. For many years, Nid had been progressively entering the world of Christian belief and identity. She had self-identified as a Christian, she was reading the Bible and performing other Christian activities, and she was immersed in the Christian community. However, prior to her baptism, she perceived herself as only 80 percent Christian. "I began studying the Bible because I wanted to be a Christian. I was ready to get serious," she recalls. "Before I made my last decision (baptism), I wanted to make sure that I fully understood Christianity." Her church then guided her in a three-year period of intensive study, which included the acquisition of basic Bible knowledge and church doctrines, as well as practical guidance for navigating marginalization. When the study had finished, she was "almost to the line where I completely become a Christian." This line was her moment of baptism, a formal affair presided over by the highest official of her denomination. After the event, Nid received a certificate that formally affirmed her membership in the local church and in the denomination. She remembers, "I felt like, oh, I'm a real Christian now. I'm

---

14. Geertz, *Interpretation of Cultures*, 112.
15. Eliade, *Sacred and the Profane*, 68–113; Cox, *Introduction*, 92–94.
16. Farley, *Ecclesial Man*, 106–28.

not hiding anymore. I can tell people that I am a Christian. I can eat bread and drink wine at the church now."

Baptism was a significant ritual for other participants as well. For Nan, even though she repeatedly alludes to her hierophany as the most significant event in transforming her identity, her baptism signified the seriousness of her new identity and the reality of group transfer. Even her sister recognized the severity of this decision. Nan explains, "Before, my sister didn't think I was serious about Christianity. I was just attending church services, but I was not a part of them. When I told her that I was going to be baptized, she thought she was going to lose me. So, she asked me to delay the baptism." Baptism, therefore, is understood as a formal and public display of one's new religious identification and one's new group membership. It transforms the self into a fully functioning member of the community, such that one abandons one's former allegiances and formally adopts the Christian mode of being-in-the-world. As Ploy explains, "Baptism is a symbol that says, ok, now I'm a Christian. I will live my life as a Christian. I can't say anymore, oh, I'm not sure or something like that." This perspective on the ritual of baptism echoes the beliefs and practices of the early church. Baptism and the catechetical process leading up to it were perceived by early Christians as creating a "counter-cultural religious self." It re-socialized and re-formed pagan people, deconstructing their former world and reconstructing a new one, "so that they would emerge as Christian people, at home in communities of freedom."[17] For participants, therefore, as for the Christians of the early church, baptism is the preeminent ritual of membership. It is the official transference of the self into the religious identity and imaginary of the redemptive community.

Other rituals are also formative for assimilating converts into the symbolic world of the *ecclesia*. Nid mentions her post-baptismal participation in the Eucharist, a ritual that is replete with Christological imagery, as symbolic of her full entrance into the Christian in-group. Less formal rituals, or what we might term "liturgies," also carry transformative significance. Church attendance on Sundays and the performance of service roles within the church are perceived as indicative of one's new identity. Worship in the form of singing, for example, is frequently mentioned by participants as especially significant. Both Tom and Nan were initially drawn to the Christian community via song. Prior to her conversion, Ploy could not understand why other Christians were so emotional during the worship portion of Sunday services.

17. Kreider, "Worship and Evangelism," 19.

Emplacement

However, since her conversion, communal singing now evokes in her deep emotive responses based upon an intuitive awareness of God's powerful presence. Music, as Husserl once argued, is experienced in the "living now," a constitutive flux within one's stream of consciousness.[18] I move with the flow of the song, retaining what had already been played and anticipating what is to come in such a way that I may constitute the song's unity. In congregational singing, however, I experience music in the mode of togetherness.[19] My consciousness is united with those singing along with me. The song moves us through the flow of time together, focusing our thoughts on the same words, affecting our emotions through the same "musical motion,"[20] and orienting us to the same divine Being. In the process, the horizontal and vertical dimensions of existence are fused and my membership with this community and with its God is re-affirmed.

The second means of assimilating members is through emulation, or the process of absorbing and internalizing the community's subjective reality via everyday, intersubjective encounters. Significant others, Berger and Luckmann explain, are the principal agents for the formation and ongoing maintenance of an individual's subjective reality. Close relations within the community, such as friends, family members, religious leaders, and other church members, serve to confirm one's identity, legitimate a symbolic universe, and define what is taken for granted.[21] One way this occurs is through narrative. Wit's religious outlook changed dramatically after hearing narratives about God's intervention in the lives of others. Based on these stories, Wit perceived possibilities for inhabiting a new religious world in which God is active and concerned for his daily well-being. Likewise, Nid was shaped by communal narratives, or testimonies, that were shared in a small group setting. "We heard about how God was working in each life. It was good to hear them discuss this." As narrative selves, we thrive on and are formed by stories. Stories, Paul Ricoeur argues, are 'imaginative variations" for the self. They are laboratories for conducting thought experiments regarding potentialities for one's identity.[22] Further, within a community, narratives constitute and re-constitute a homeworld. They shape a tradition and the "normal" or

18. See Husserl, *Phenomenology of Internal Time-Consciousness*.
19. Schütz, *On Phenomenology and Social Relations*, 214–17.
20. For more on this idea of musical motion, see Johnson, *Meaning of the Body*, 235–62.
21. Berger and Luckmann, *Social Construction*, 149–52.
22. Ricoeur, *Oneself as Another*, 148.

expected ways of being-in-the-world. As Steinbock explains, "Through narrative, homepeople are guided by the same thoughts, as it were, and these thoughts give rise to the shared historical narrative."[23]

Besides narrative, emulation also includes the phenomenon of modeling. In modeling, significant others influence the self through their enactment of an alternate and attractive identity. They function as prototypes for the self; that is, through their behavior, they display the ideal features of an in-group member.[24] They are living examples to which one aspires. Lek's wife modeled for him calm amid chaos, a missionary friend was Wit's inspiration for humility, and Kay's mentor modeled spiritual discipline. The power of modeling is well-summarized in Wit's statement about his mentor, "His character is what was influential. He showed by example how to be a Christian. He didn't teach me how to pray, he showed me how to pray. He didn't teach me how to believe, he showed me how to believe." Another form of emulation is conversation. Conversation is, according to Berger and Luckmann, "the most important vehicle of reality-maintenance."[25] While speech may directly and formally legitimate a world, such as in sermons or catechism class, more often than not its effect is implicit and subtle. "It takes place against the background of a world, that is silently taken for granted."[26] In other words, casual conversation creates and assumes a taken-for-granted world in which the conversation partners live. Nid, for example, by joining her friends in service activities and small groups was, at the same time, being formed by their casual conversations. She was speaking and listening her way into their world, so to speak, sometimes consciously and sometimes unconsciously.

Finally, besides ritual and emulation, members are assimilated into the sacred community via conformity. To maintain the plausibility of its social world, a group will exert pressure on its members, both implicitly and explicitly, to conform to accepted ways of being-in-the-world and to inhabit its sedimented tradition. Conformity seeks to produce what Alfred Schütz called the community's "thinking as usual." Every member reared in the group requires a ready-made, standardized set of "trustworthy recipes for interpreting the social world and for handling things and men in order to obtain the best results in every situation with a minimum

---

23. Steinbock, *Home and Beyond*, 217.
24. Hornsey, "Social Identity Theory," 208–11.
25. Berger and Luckmann, *Social Construction*, 152.
26. Berger and Luckmann, *Social Construction*, 152.

of effort by avoiding undesirable consequences."[27] These recipes are part of the cultural pattern of the group, handed down by ancestors, teachers, and authorities as an unquestionable guide for everyday thinking and behavior. Members, then, must appropriate this tradition, or adopt the sense inherent in one's generative homeworld, in order to be perceived as a "normal" homecomrade.[28]

How is this thinking as usual transmitted within the sacred community? First, formal training or education is a common means for both transmitting and legitimating a set of recipes. Education may include periods of intensive and focused training in the faith or common learning that takes place weekly at Sunday services, Bible studies, and small groups. As a new Christian, Lek had initially perceived God in a similar way as the spirits of folk Buddhism. He believed that God as power existed to provide for his needs and wants, and, therefore, could be manipulated to provide these things. He states,

> At first, I wanted the same power as in Buddhism. I thought God was more power, so I could pray to Him to get me everything. But after I studied Christian lessons more, I learned that my life is part of God's plan. God has a purpose for my life. So, sometimes I get happy, and sometimes I get bad. It is up to God. I think my thinking has changed.

Ploy, who had previously understood the Sacred in territorial terms prior to her conversion, assumed an exclusivist perspective after a period of formal training in the church. Consequently, she now uses communal terms to describe her new belief structure, "I have only one God. That is what Christians believe, that we have only one God, the biggest God. We don't believe in any other God."

Mentorship is also an important means for instilling conformity. Mentors serve as both teachers and models of the community's thinking as usual. As we see in Kay's case, mentors may sometimes exert significant pressure in order to transform initiates into fully-functioning, "normal" members of the community. Much of this pressure seeks to instill in the convert habits for performing spiritual disciplines, such as Bible reading, prayer, and church attendance. These disciplines are perceived by the community as essential to the maturation of one's religious identity and, thus, to maintaining a sense of group belonging. Further, mentorship provides

---

27. Schütz, *On Phenomenology and Social Relations*, 81.
28. Steinbock, *Home and Beyond*, 186–99.

day-to-day accountability and guidance for the enactment of the Christian ethic. Kay's mentor not only enforced attendance at group activities, but also sought to reform Kay's speech and study habits. Kay explains the reason for this, "Sometimes, I felt like I wanted to do things that everyone else does. I wanted to enjoy my life besides my Christian life. I just wanted to enjoy the world." Mentors, therefore, serve on the front lines of the plausibility structure, providing day-to-day services that effectively displace converts from their former worlds while immersing them more fully in the community's mode of being-in-the-world.[29]

Religious alternation, as we have already mentioned, is a tenuous phenomenon. The internalization of a new world requires significant and ongoing social processes that seek to annihilate one's former worlds while, at the same time, making the new world both cognitively and affectively plausible. To quote Berger and Luckmann, "To have a conversion experience is nothing much. The real thing is to be able to keep on taking it seriously; to retain a sense of its plausibility. This is where the religious community comes in. It provides the indispensable plausibility structure for the new reality."[30] The more one is conformed to the community's thinking as usual, i.e., the more he or she sees as the community sees and behaves as the community behaves, the more likely the convert is to truly inhabit this new world. Tom's story exemplifies the tenuous nature of Christian identity. His conversion experience at the age of eleven amounted to very little until he eventually joined a Christian community. Likewise, as Kay explained, without her mentor showing up at her door that day, she might have been lost. This sense of lostness was not just to herself, but to the entire Christian lifeworld and system of belief. Another Thai convert describes it this way, "If I'm not with Christians, I'll die. What I mean is that my spiritual life will die. I will go back to Buddhism again because no one would encourage me. I would not listen to sermons, not worship in the church, and not have fellowship. I would go back because my (non-Christian) friends are powerful, and they may influence me."[31] Conversion, therefore, requires the comprehensive inhabitation of a new lifeworld. Converts must become part of a new family in which they find intersubjective belonging, existential meaning, and the tools they need to face social marginalization. To the nature of this new lifeworld we now turn.

29. Berger and Luckmann, *Social Construction*, 157–58.
30. Berger and Luckmann, *Social Construction*, 158.
31. Personal conversation with the author, April 20, 2016.

Emplacement

REIMAGINING

Nid: Still Family

There she is again, sitting in the pew in front of me. Why can't she move to the other side of the sanctuary? This is awkward. Last week, I had finally confronted her. She is a leader in our church, but so many times I heard her gossiping about other church members. The Bible says, "Do not gossip," but she does it anyway. Christians should not do that. What she was doing was hurting the testimony of Christians. Finally, I told her that she needs to stop and apologize. She didn't take it too well. I wish she would leave.

I always knew Christians were not perfect. Even before I had converted, I saw my Christian friends get angry, tell lies, or gossip about others. Yes, I was impressed by their love and care, generally, but I knew they weren't perfect. Sometimes, I think about leaving the church when issues like this arise. I wonder where God is in all of this. But, whenever I start thinking like this, my next thought is always, "These people are my family." Christians in Thailand are very small in number. We need to stick together. We are related in Jesus, so these are my brothers and sisters. This church is my family. I can't imagine living my life without them.

Ploy: Not Alone

We are here because the father of one of our colleagues has passed away. When I go to funerals by myself, I'm never sure what to do. Do I *wai*? Do I pay my respects to the deceased? Do I give gifts to the monks? As a Christian, it is confusing to know what to do and what not to do in these situations, but this time it is easy.

I have been to many funerals before. Prior to my conversion, I would participate in all the activities, thinking that the Buddha images, the chanting of the monks, and the gifts I gave earned me merit. Things are different now. Since my conversion, what I once thought was so important, I now see as empty. However, I still find funerals difficult. I'm worried about offending people or sticking out. When I'm by myself, I feel like everyone is staring at me when I don't participate in the Buddhist rituals. Usually, at those times, I just do what everyone else is doing. When you are alone, you just have to conform, right?

I'm here with Christian friends, so we can go through this together. As we walk into the crematorium, we all sit together in one row and chat until the service starts. Soon, the usual Buddhist activities begin. The monks start chanting and everyone in attendance assumes the *wai* position; everyone, that is, except my friends and me. We are the only ones not participating, but I don't feel uncomfortable at all. That is because I'm not alone!

Interpretation

As we have seen, membership in the sacred community entails a process of resocialization whereby one's self becomes the other. Ritual, emulation, and conformity serve effectively to transform Buddhists into Christians, thereby immersing them in an entirely new, and generatively deep, religious homeworld. This new homeworld transforms their perception of life and reality. While remaining within their existing lifeworld contexts, converts reimagine their world through a revised interpretive schema of sacred time, place, self, and other. They inhabit a new social identity and social imaginary wherein that which was alien is now home and that which was home is now alien. In this section, we will briefly investigate the nature of this reimagined homeworld. To structure our investigation, we will again follow Max van Manen's five existentials: relationality, materiality, corporeality, temporality, and spatiality.

Relationality

Upon entering the sacred community, converts become members of a minority people who exist betwixt and between the normal social structures of Thai society. However, as we discovered earlier, the liminal experience of Thai Christians also produces within the group the social phenomenon of communitas, or the spontaneous formation of immediate, concrete, and undifferentiated I-Thou relationships.[32] This egalitarian ethos within the *ecclesia* is solidified in the social imaginary via kinship discourse, a pattern both introduced and exemplified in New Testament literature.[33] Members of the sacred community are not merely friends or associates, therefore, but brothers and sisters in a family whose father is God and whose older brother is Jesus. Nid's frustrations with the church did not negate her felt connection with and dependence upon members of the sacred community. Fellow members were still apprehended as spiritual relatives, united by a bond that was, by nature, indispensable and inseverable, but which may also at times incorporate family feuds. The utilization of familial terminology within the

---

32. Turner, *Dramas, Fields, and Metaphors*, 45–53.

33. For more on the role of family terminology in the New Testament, see Sandnes, *New Family*; Trebilco, *Self-Designations and Group Identity*, 16–67.

sacred community, however, is not entirely metaphorical. As we will see in the next chapter, conversion often displaces individuals from existing kinship relations, thus requiring the Christian community to replace those bonds. As Nan recalls, "After my conversion, I told my small group that now I am a Christian; I believe in God. They were so happy. They congratulated me and said that now we are in the same family. In the past, I was just a guest, but, now, I feel like a member of the family."

Kinship discourse is the linguistic symbolization of the everyday mode of being-with for a determinate Christian community. Implicit in Christian intersubjectivity is a being-for-another such that one bears an ethical responsibility to the other as subject.[34] A generalized reciprocity,[35] based on principles of caring and sharing, characterize in-group relationality, demonstrating that members are not strangers or acquaintances but, indeed, relatives. Converts become "one of us." They enter a new clan and, thus, find a new form of belonging and acceptance wherein each one is for the other. Founding this form of intersubjectivity, however, is something even more basic. Within the *ecclesia*, members co-intend one another in the mode of redemption; that is, as fellow recipients of God's grace.[36] I apperceive the other as like me: a sinner, replete with faults, but, at the same time, redemptively re-oriented via an hierophanic encounter with the Holy. My own experience of God's acceptance, therefore, motivates my acceptance of others, and my spiritual adoption as son or daughter motivates my intention of the other as "brother" or "sister." "We love because he first loved us" (1 John 4:19), as the Apostle John phrased it. Therefore, we may say that sacred relationality is both religious and social. Within the "family of God," one finds a sheltering home characterized by belonging, acceptance, and love, both with God and with others. This new home transmutes one's identity from alien to friend and from stranger to brother.

Materiality

The former lifeworld of participants was replete with sacred things: images, gifts, pendants, spirit houses, etc. These sacred items were believed to possess an almost magical power, a conduit into the world of the sacred to

---

34. For more on a Levinasian interpretation of familial relationality, see Knapp, "Ethical Phenomenology of Emmanuel Levinas."

35. General reciprocity refers to transactions that are putatively altruistic without the expectation of direct material return. Sandnes, *New Family*, 178–79.

36. Farley, *Ecclesial Man*, 209.

mobilize merit, protection, and blessing in the world of the profane. However, as we saw in the last chapter, conversion initiates the desacralization of these religious objects, transmuting them into everyday items of stone, wood, metal, and, sometimes, even trash. Concomitantly, converts are immersed in an entirely new world of sacramentally significant things. Ordinary bread and wine are intended as the body and blood of Jesus. Money is both a gift of God and a gift to God. The pages of an ordinary book contain the very words of God for his people. However, significantly, within the Christian lifeworld, sacred objects are no longer intended as magical talisman or supernatural sources of merit and material blessing. Instead, their power resides in their symbolic significance, connection with the provision of God, or in their potential use for religious service. When Kay received her first Bible, prior to her conversion, she treated it as an ordinary book. Rather than reading it, however, she perceived only its material value and, consequently, sold it as a source of income. Post-conversion, Kay received another Bible from her mentor. "This time it was different," she explains. "I wanted this Bible, and I began to read it. Surprisingly, it made sense. I could understand it." The transition in the book's sacrality was a consequence of Kay's altered religious outlook. Following her conversion, this ordinary book became the Holy Bible, replete with generative symbolism and bearing an almost mystical quality in its ability to communicate the words of the Sacred and, thus, transform the identity of the reader.

Further, even everyday material objects are perceived as bearing the mark of the Sacred. The purchase of larger items, such as a house or car, are understood as spiritual decisions since God is both the source and the ultimate owner of one's material goods. Those goods, therefore, are to be utilized in a wise and grateful manner, perhaps even offered up for sacrificial use within the community of faith: e.g., a home as the locale for small groups, or a car to transport individuals to church services. Even everyday objects, such as food, are perceived as sacred things. Nid's practice of praying before meals, thanking God for his provision, effectively transfigures ordinary food into a gift of God that, when eaten, empowers her for divine service. "Thus the 'things,' with which man comes into contact," Leeuw explains, "are either receptacles which he must fill with power or wheels that he must set in motion . . . they are connected with God directly and immediately, and God can at any moment breathe into them new life and grant them fresh potency; He makes instruments of His Power out of 'things,' He creates and renews them."[37]

Corporeality

"The body is our general medium for having a world," Merleau-Ponty observed.[38] Inherent in this statement is the fact that humans are not simply cognitive machines, or disembodied minds that thrive solely on the nourishment of ideas and propositions, but thinking, feeling, and acting selves who corporeally encounter the material world via the mode of "I can."[39] For sacred selves who now inhabit an alternate religious place-world, therefore, religious behavior and existence is primordially corporeal in nature. One's body is offered as a "living sacrifice" (Rom 12:1): a breathing, moving, and acting "performance" of devotion to the Sacred and of service within the sacred community. He or she is an instrument of Divine use, a vessel for the enactment of God's purposes and sovereign will. As Devenish avers, "The mechanism through which the soul's new allegiance can be displayed is the body."[40] Embodied, religious performance had motivated Kay's decision to join the staff of a Christian ministry organization. While walking across the street one day, she suddenly and spontaneously perceived the masses of people in terms of biblical imagery: as sheep without a shepherd. This prompted a question in her mind, "What is my purpose here on earth? Am I wasting my life?" In response, she fasted and prayed for forty days, then finally concluded that she would "invest her life" by entering Christian service full-time. This investment implied not only that her embodied "I can" would be daily engaged in what she perceived as Divine service, but also that these performances would reap dividends in a future, post-mortem state of existence. Kay's body as instrument, therefore, implies the contiguity between the earthly and transcendent planes of personal existence.

Embodied liturgical activity is also characteristic of the sacred self's inhabitation of a new religious lifeworld. Prayer was a common practice among participants prior to their conversion. However, post-conversion the practice is transformed, even at the level of physical gestures. Buddhists, Kay explains, utilize the *wai* position, with palms pressed flat together, at nose level, and

37. Leeuw, *Religion*, 361–62.
38. Merleau-Ponty, *Phenomenology of Perception*, 146.
39. Smith, *Desiring the Kingdom*, 42; Merleau-Ponty, *Phenomenology of Perception*, 137.
40. Devenish, *Ordinary Saints*, 98.

fingers facing upward. However, Christians, she asserts, pray with hands in a locked, close-fisted position. The difference is more than surface-level. The variance in prayer gestures convey the divergent intentionalities inherent in these two prayer acts: one to earn merit or gain blessing and the other to commune with the Sacred. Another liturgical expression of religiosity is one's physical presence at church on Sundays. This includes the activities of sitting, standing, kneeling, reading, singing, reciting, listening, and even tasting, all of which are physical expressions of devotion and allegiance. Many other examples could be cited, but, overall, we may say that, like sacred objects, one's own body is an instrument with sacramental significance. It is, as Eliade argued, a microcosm of the sacred cosmos and the source of communication with a plane that is transcendent to it.[41]

Temporality

The Thai Buddhist liturgical calendar revolves around a temporal rhythm of the sacred and profane, rooted in the re-actualization of its sacred myths. Personal and communal existence in the Thai lifeworld, therefore, moves along like flotsam and jetsam within this sacred flow of time. Festivals, monk days, and temple visits structure one's biography, strengthen community solidarity, and recover the sacred dimension of life. To withdraw from sacred time, therefore, is essentially to withdraw from the sacred cosmos, the result of which is anomy.[42] For converts, the abandonment of Buddhist time requires the concomitant adoption of a new temporal rhythm that will effectively structure their altered religious habitation. They must indwell the liturgical calendar of the historical church, centered in the re-actualization of myths surrounding the person and work of Jesus of Nazareth. Easter is especially significant for Kay: "It reminds me of what Jesus is doing here, and what he is doing in my life." For her, the festival reenacts the sacred myth and, by doing so, both reasserts God's immediate presence and rekindles Kay's embodied performance of her altered religious identity. Weekly observance of a sacred day is also constitutive of one's new temporal rhythm. Each Sunday, the historical existence of Jesus Christ, especially his resurrection, is reenacted and made present among the sacred community. For Ploy, Sundays are set apart from every other day of the week. Church attendance, fellowship meals, and other forms of Christian service structure her day, reinvigorating her religious allegiance and empowering her to tackle another

---

41. Eliade, *Sacred and the Profane*, 172–77.
42. Berger, *Sacred Canopy*, 49–50.

Emplacement

week of profane activity. Even Ploy's parents recognize this rhythm, having deduced their daughter's new religious identity via her temporal habits of religious activity. Sacred time, therefore, is indicative of a new sacred identity and the habitation of a new religious homeworld. "For religious man," Eliade argues, "reactualization of the same mythical events constitutes his greatest hope; for with each reactualization he again has the opportunity to transfigure his existence, to make it like its divine model."[43]

Spatiality

"Sacred space is, in all religions, a place to step outside of the humdrum world and commune with the sublime," phenomenologist, Archana Barua, explains. "The need to create sacred space is also the need to find stability in a restless and dehumanized world."[44] Spaces are sacred because they are the earthly residences of the transcendent and, therefore, set apart for religious activity. Prior to their conversion, participants had structured their world territorially, with sacred locations being the domain of certain spirits or deities. Further, the temple (*wat*) comprised the sacred site *par excellence*, centering a given community's social, religious, and biographical activities. Folk Buddhist shrines, temples, and other sacred places, therefore, stabilized participants, founding their world and, thus, orienting their identities.[45] At conversion, however, participants become displaced from Buddhist space. To avert the threat of atopia, therefore, converts must quickly and concomitantly inhabit Christianity's new divine world. They must reorient within Christian sacred space, a process that essentially founds a new world and, as a result, establishes a new home. Post-conversion, Ploy finds her religious life easier than it was previously. While she was once burdened by the need to travel to various locations in order to seek the favor of territorial spirits, she now perceives the entire world as God's domain. For Ploy, world is sacred space. No matter where she is, she is always under the benevolent watch and care of the omnipresent God. While the entire world may be considered sacred, the church building is perceived as a special and powerful place wherein one meets with the Holy. In describing the importance of church attendance, Kay explains that, after a long week of work, it takes discipline to attend the Sunday church service instead of going to the mall or the movie theater. "It is important to stand up and say, 'Ok, I will go to

---

43. Eliade, *Sacred and the Profane*, 106–7.
44. Barua, *Phenomenology of Religion*, 105.
45. Eliade, *Sacred and the Profane*, 64.

church first.'" This is because weekly church attendance, according to Kay, parallels temple attendance in the Thai lifeworld. Like the temple, the church is the center for community and religious activities. Performing religious ritual at a sacred location is perceived as indicative of one's religious identity. Consequently, Kay explains, even Buddhists are impressed when they notice the regular and faithful attendance of Christians at weekly church services. The church as sacred location, therefore, replaces the temple or shrine as the center of one's intersubjective and platial world. It orients the convert around an absolute fixed point wherein God is present and wherein the self is meaningfully and protectively situated.[46]

CONCLUSION

The emplacement of the convert in a new homeworld is, as we have seen, a complicated and lengthy process by which one enters and inhabits a new intersubjective and platial reality. The seeker first observes sacred relationality, becoming attracted to its form of togetherness and, eventually, becoming immersed in the community's egalitarian mode of being-with. The sacred community becomes the convert's new plausibility structure, mediating a new world through processes of ritual, emulation, and conformity. As a result, a lifeworld transformation occurs whereby the convert reimagines sacred time, space, things, self, and other. In the end, the convert, then, adopts a new and favorable social identity. He or she belongs to the group, and that sense of belonging shapes his or her being-in-the-world. The convert now makes salient the new sacred we, thus maximizing both out-group differences and in-group similarities. This new sense of "we" boosts one's self-esteem, enhances group cohesion, and shapes how one behaves and self-identifies in the world.[47] However, as we will see in the next chapter, this new social identity also marginalizes the convert from existing, dominant group memberships. To this experience of displacement, we now turn.

---

46. Eliade, "World, the City, the House," 192–94.

47. Tajfel and Turner, "Integrated Theory," 38–44; Turner et al., "Self and Collective," 454–58.

8

Displacement

INTRODUCTION

In his book *Totality and Infinity*, Emmanuel Levinas claimed, "Man abides in the world as having come to it from a private domain, from being at home with himself, to which at each moment he can retire."[1] The home is not the end of human activity, he argued, but its very condition. In other words, one goes forth from the inwardness of home. As we have seen in the last two chapters, the experience of conversion is essentially the process of emplacement or re-habitation. Thai converts have met with God, have been incorporated into the sacred community's unique mode of togetherness, and have drunken deeply from the well of Christian generativity. They are now comfortably "in place" and "at home," re-situated in a new "private domain" from which they may then go forth into the world. However, converts quickly discover that the world they re-enter is stranger than it used to be. While still recognizable as the familiar locale of their childhood socialization, the Thai Folk Buddhist lifeworld is no longer amenable to converts' circumspective and embodied comportment. Their conversion has introduced a "border crossing,"[2] the reversal of that which is home and that which is alien, resulting in a Janus-like duality in one's being-in-the-world. Stated differently, converts have become strangers in a familiar land. They increasingly find that they no longer fit; they don't belong. They are deviants, or what the Apostle Peter described as

---

1. Levinas, *Totality and Infinity*, 152.
2. Giroux, *Border Crossings*.

"aliens and strangers" (1 Pet 2:11). This is the experience of displacement, or the sudden and disturbing "finding-oneself-out-of-place" in a world that was once considered home.³

In this chapter, we will investigate the lived experience of displacement as occurring within the lifeworld of Thai converts. This investigation finally brings us face-to-face with marginalization *per se*, the core phenomenon being explored in this research. The moment of displacement will be structured per four interpretive themes as disclosed during the interviews. (1) *Dis-belonging*, or the social effects of conversion that result in perceptions of abandonment, deviance, and disruption, is the ground for the convert's experience of displacement. Included in this theme are the data analysis categories of "group departure or marginalization," "social roles or requirements as marginalization," "social pressure as obstacle," "groupality as substratum," and "social identity tied to religion." (2) *Misunderstanding* refers to experiences of mild marginalization arising from presumptions of "normality" or from ignorance of Christian belief and behavior. This theme will cover the categories of "foreignness of Christianity," "misunderstanding about Christian identity," and "physical gesture as conveying religious identity." More severe experiences of marginalization, such as disapproval and "the look," will be examined under the theme of (3) *antagonism*. Categories include "sensing disapproval," "family disapproval," and "experience of being observed." Finally, (4) *strangerness* refers to the consequences of marginalization on the self, or the emotional and psychological internalization of displacement. This theme covers the data analysis categories of "self as stranger," "disillusionment with former world," "affective response to marginalization," "dual identities," and "displacement from home."

DIS-BELONGING

Wit: Family Obligation

> Each year, our family performs a service at this temple, and I knew I had to go. Now that I was a Christian, I simply had to show my family that I was still part of the group. As the oldest son, I had special duties to perform. It was my job to give the gifts to the monk, and everyone would expect me to do it just as I have for the past twenty years. What should I do?

---

3. For more on the relationship between home and displacement, see Casey, *Getting Back into Place*, 34–37, 293–303.

For many of us, this is the only time of the year when we see each other. It is like a family reunion. The ceremony started, and I was feeling nervous. I decided to sit in the back where I hoped I may not be noticed. But it was impossible. I had a religious duty to perform, but I knew I couldn't do it. The time for my performance drew near. I know the service rituals like the back of my hand, and it was nearing my time. I left right in the middle of the service, went to the toilet, and didn't come back until I knew that my portion of the service was finished. Whew! I was glad that was over, but the real difficulty was only beginning.

After the service, my father approached me. With a look of anger on his face, he demanded, "Wit, where were you?" I told him that I had left because I am now a Christian. I couldn't perform these rituals anymore. "Why not?" he asked. "You used to perform them, even though you were going to church. Why can't you do them now? You know how important this event is. What you are doing is disrespectful." I didn't know what to say, so I remained quiet. "Wit, you may worship your God, but please continue to worship Buddha as well. Don't disrespect your family." What he said shook me to the core. I felt so uncomfortable, but I knew what I had to do. In a quiet voice, I simply replied, "I love my family, and I will never leave the pack. But, I cannot worship Buddha. Sorry, Dad." He said no more.

Nan: The Outsider

The most difficult conversation I ever had was with my sister soon after my conversion. One month prior, I had encountered God. Ever since then, I was getting more and more serious about my faith. My friends at church encouraged me, "Nan, perhaps it is time you consider baptism. This is the next step to show you are a Christian." This was not a small step, though. It was huge! If I became baptized, I would have to tell my family that I'm a Christian. What would they say?

I wasn't worried about my parents—more about my sister. I had always looked up to my sister. When she got involved in politics, I followed. When she investigated Buddhist philosophy, I followed. With Christianity, though, I was charting my own course. How would she take it? "I'm going to be baptized," I told her. "I believe God is real, and I'm joining the church." "What!" she exclaimed, with a look of shock on her face. "You can't do that. *Farangs* (foreigners) are Christians, not Thais. You will abandon your family, your heritage, and your ethnicity. You will become a *nawk riit."* She was very upset, and then, she started crying. Her words were like daggers piercing my soul. The word she used, *nawk riit*, means "outsider." Thais use it to talk about people who betray their families, their nation, or their tradition. She was telling me, in essence, that I was betraying my family; that I would no longer be part of the group. She was very upset because she thought she would lose me.

When other Thais converted to Christianity, they ended up abandoning their families and friends. They spent more time with foreigners than they did with their own families. I would never do that. This is my family. We may practice different religions and see the world in different ways, but they are still my family. I will never abandon them.

Interpretation

As we have seen, religious alternation entails not only a restructuration of beliefs or a transmutation of ritualistic activity, but also a transfer of social worlds. Post-conversion, individuals inhabit a new intersubjective place-world in which they find plausibility for their altered vision of reality. At the same time, however, they must disaffiliate or segregate, whether physically or mentally, from the co-inhabitants of their former world.[4] This segregation protects converts from the potentially reality-disrupting influence of their former plausibility structure, something which, as Berger and Luckmann highlight, is particularly acute during the early stages of alternation.[5] For Thai Christians, who exist in an allocentric society,[6] group transfer is especially disturbing as it may threaten their place, indeed their very identity, within the collective. They must navigate a lifeworld wherein conversion is perceived as "dis-belonging": abandonment of, deviance from, and disruption to the group. This state of dis-belonging functions as the intersubjective ground for the lived experience of marginalization.

To be marginalized is to be on the outside. In his discussion of lived space, phenomenologist O. F. Bollnow described the outside as a potentially

---

4. Berger and Luckmann, *Social Construction*, 158–59.
5. Berger and Luckmann, *Social Construction*, 159.
6. Allocentrism, or what Markus and Kitayama call "interdependent construals of the self," refers to cultures in which the individual sees oneself "as part of an encompassing social relationship" and recognizes that "one's behavior is determined, contingent on, and, to a large extent, organized by what the actor perceives to be the thoughts, feelings, and actions of *others* in the relationship" (Markus and Kitayama, "Culture and the Self," 227).

Displacement

hostile world, characterized by breadth, strangeness, and distance, that exists beyond the protected realm of trusted relationships, vocation, and home.[7] In a similar vein, Canadian geographer Edward Relph elucidated the disparity between insideness and outsideness. To be inside is to be secure, enclosed, and at ease while, in contrast, to be outside is to feel alienated or separated from place. Outsideness, Relph argued, is the locale of social exclusion, a no-place wherein one is uninvolved and, consequently, does not belong.[8] To be outside is, one might say, to be "left in the dark." The outsider is excluded from the "light" of the inner circle, and, therefore, banished to a dark, disorienting, and foreboding location where ignorance and hopelessness reign.[9] This threat of outsideness or dis-belonging is a preeminent concern among participants. By converting to what is perceived as a foreign religion, participants must then cope with the possibility of being "left in the dark"; that is, of experiencing exclusion from existing in-group memberships. This threat is most prominent in the early stages of alternation, especially during what we may call the "revealing," or the moment when the convert discloses his or her new identity to primary significant others. In the revealing, one comes face-to-face, as it were, with the interwoven texture of social and religious identities within the Thai lifeworld. How may we understand this experience of outsideness arising from religious alternation? We will examine this interpretive theme via a complex and interconnected three-fold structure of dis-belonging: conversion as abandonment, conversion as deviance, and conversion as disruption.

Conversion as Abandonment

Within the collective, the self finds both meaning and belonging. By appropriating the generative sense and commonality of the "us," which is always delimited from the "them," the self becomes a "normal," contributing member of the community and, consequently, feels at home.[10] The "normal" Thai sense of "us," as noted in chapter 5, comprises a commonality that fuses ethnic, religious, and kinship identities. To be a group member within the Thai lifeworld entails not only relational obligation, but also religious

---

7. Bollnow, "Lived-Space," 35.

8. Relph, *Place and Placelessness*, 51–55; Seamon, "Place and Placelessness," 45.

9. The ultimate banishment, according to Jesus, is of the un-redeemed self to the place of "outer darkness" where there is "weeping and gnashing of teeth." This dark place is one of exclusion from "belongingness" with God and the saints. See Luke 13:26–30.

10. Steinbock, *Home and Beyond*, 222–32; Jenkins, *Social Identity*, 80–81.

obligation, and the two are deemed inseparable. In sum, "to be Thai is to be Buddhist." Therefore, should a member decide to disappropriate the religious elements of the group's social identity, the group would interpret such a move as abandonment.

Nan's conversation with her sister exemplifies the threat of conversion to group belonging. Her family in-group was defined, in part, by borders that had been erected between *us*, Thai, ethnic Chinese Buddhists, and *them*, Western Christians. By converting to Christianity, Nan was, in effect, transgressing these boundaries. She was abandoning the tradition of the family in order to "follow people from overseas." As her sister exclaimed, "You will become an outsider. You will not belong to us anymore." For the ethnically Chinese participants, Nan, Kay, and Nid, this abandonment of the "us" exceeds that of existing family relations, extending even to the realm of both predecessors (ancestral worship) and successors (continuance of filial piety among future generations). For other participants, temple attendance and ritual ceremonies were predominantly social affairs. Wit's father was not particularly religious, but the annual temple ceremony provided a means for reuniting with family members, enhancing group cohesion, and demonstrating respect to temple monks. Wit's nonparticipation, therefore, was not perceived as a religious threat as much as a sign of disloyalty and disrespect to the family. From his father's perspective, Wit was severing ties with the family and the family's primary network of relationships by abstaining from ritualistic activity. It was important for Wit, therefore, to demonstrate that he was not going to "leave the pack."

Outside of the family, the convert's membership in community and friendship networks are also threatened by alternation. Within the community, one's sense of belonging is enmeshed with temple attendance. After her conversion, Nid's nonattendance at the temple was met with suspicion and gossip. Only her success as a respected teacher, a high position in the Thai social hierarchy, ameliorated her absence from normal, temple activities. As another Thai convert explains, "When Christians do not go to the temple, they will not be involved with the community."[11] Separation from the temple, therefore, is interpreted as withdrawal from the community. Likewise, friendships suffer due to one's conversion. Kay's best friend throughout high school and roommate in university had observed her increased interest in and involvement with a Christian in-group. The friend interpreted these signs as a "de-friending," as it were, and responded

---

11. Personal conversation with the author, April 20, 2016.

in kind. She moved out of the dorm room, informed all their common friends that Kay was "crazy with religion," and ceased all communication with Kay for one year. From her perspective, Kay had abandoned their friendship in favor a new network of friends that were unified by a form of fanatical religious adherence.

Conversion as Deviance

As Berger and Luckmann remind us, the socially constructed world of a given community is meant to be inhabited in a taken-for-granted attitude. Each member is expected to conform to *our* ways and traditions; that is, to be firmly situated within the community's symbolic universe and objective reality. Deviant versions of the symbolic universe among members, therefore, pose an acute problem. They threaten objective reality itself, thus requiring the community to implement "universe-maintaining conceptual machinery," such as therapy and nihilation, to prevent inhabitants from "emigrating."[12] When these legitimations fail and inhabitants do emigrate, as in conversion, the member then transitions from insider to outsider. They become deviants, strangers to the community's vision of reality and mode of being-in-the-world. In other words, they no longer "fit in."

Several participants allude to the open and accepting nature of Thai people toward difference. "In Thailand, you can be a Christian or a Muslim because we accept people from different cultures and religions," Ploy claims. "Thai people are really open to that." The rural village, Wit asserts, may exert more pressure for conformity, but in the city, and especially in Chiang Mai where the Christian population is largest, religious difference is readily accepted. Similarly, Lek argues that modernization has mitigated the pressure for conformity among the younger generation. His friends are secular, he maintains, and, therefore, "they don't care about different religions." Despite this perspective, however, the lived experience of participants suggests that pressures for social conformity remain strong in Thai society. Within the family, conformity to group norms is a matter of course. Kay's parents had taught her that Christianity is for the *farang*, not for us. "If you convert," they argued, "you will stop respecting your parents." When they did find out about Kay's conversion, they initiated passive-aggressive forms of punishment, kept closer track of Kay's activities and conversations, and even threatened her pastor at gunpoint. For most participants, the father, especially, enacts the role of enforcing conformity.

12. Berger and Luckmann, *Social Construction*, 104–16.

Strangers in a Familiar Land

Nid's father had pressured her to continue performing ancestral worship while Wit's father had expected him to fulfill the family's ritualistic obligations to the temple monks. Lek's friends may be accepting of his new identity, but his father had strongly questioned him when he found out about his son's conversion. Outside of the family, strong social expectations underlie the veneer of acceptance. Lek, Ploy, and Nid all allude to the inscription of their religious identity on ID cards and the occasional looks of derision that it generates. The social pressure for conformity is greatest, however, at community events like funerals where religious performance is expected. Nid explains, "If you are the only Christian joining the Buddhist ceremony like a funeral, it is difficult. If you do not follow what they do (religious performance), they make you feel uncomfortable. They don't know you, and you can't go around telling everyone that you are a Christian." These cases substantiate the claim that social pressure for religious conformity remains strong within the Thai lifeworld. Consequently, converts are commonly considered deviant to accepted ways of being-in-the-world. They are what Nan's sister labelled, "outsiders": "out of our society, and, therefore, different."

Conversion as Disruption

Whereas abandonment refers to disloyalty and deviance to disconformity, we may say that disruption signifies irresponsibility. In disruption, the group perceives conversion as the relinquishment of communal responsibilities and obligations, an act that introduces shame and threatens the harmony of the group. As we noted in chapter 5, religious identity in the Thai lifeworld is understood as inherently communal. One's personal religious activities may convey merit or blessing to the rest of the clan. The community believes together so as to religiously benefit together. The discontinuance of religious activity by one member of the group, therefore, disrupts the harmony of the whole. For example, Ploy's conversion disrupted both her and her mother's provision of food in the afterlife; Wit's nonparticipation disrupted the family's continuing obligation of respect toward the temple monks; and Nid's discontinuance of ancestral worship meant that her father would not be taken care of by his successors.

Even more significant than the disruption of religious benefit, however, is the disrespect that is conveyed through nonparticipation. Within the Thai lifeworld, children are required to *bun khun* their parents. Parents are higher on the social hierarchy and have sacrificially invested in the well-being and future of their children. In response, children are expected to honor them according to an established system of obligation and gratitude.[13] Conversion, which runs contrary to the established beliefs and behaviors of the "we," is consequently considered disrespectful. Out of respect for her mother, Ploy kept her religious identity a secret, performed certain Buddhist rituals on occasion as necessary, and gratefully accepted her mother's religious blessings. However, when asked by her mother to offer food to the monks for her afterlife, Ploy kept quiet. She faced a significant dilemma: she could not say yes because of her religious convictions, but she could not say no out of respect for her mother. Her decision to remain silent, however, was not a good response either. "I chose to remain quiet," she recalls, "but it is even worse because it is ignoring. I felt so bad. Sometimes, I would just say, 'Uh huh.' Not yes, and not no. Just like, 'I understand what you are saying.'" For Kay, disrespect consisted of failing to give the family face by becoming a productive member of the in-group.[14] By choosing to quit her well-paying job as a secretary to join a Christian ministry organization, Kay had embarrassed the rest of the family. "In Thai culture, we always compare. 'My daughter does this, or my son does that.' They expected that after I graduated from university, I would get a good job with a good salary." The shame of the family was so great, in fact, that the family discontinued all communication with Kay, essentially disowning her, for a period of one year.

MISUNDERSTANDING

Tom: The Strange Kid

> In school, I was always considered the strange kid. All my friends were Buddhist, but not me. I was a Christian. My school friends thought I was strange. Christianity was weird to them, not because they had anything against God or Jesus, but just because it was different. They didn't understand it.
>
> The school I had attended was a public school, so we were required by our teachers to go to the temple several times throughout the year. During these visits, all the students would pray to the Buddha, listen to chanting, and, on occasion, even profess our desire to be Buddhist. Really, we had no choice. Our school made us do these things. As an immature Christian, I wasn't sure what to

13. Podhisita, "Buddhism and Thai World View," 46–48.

14. For more on the Asian conception of face and its relation to Christian theology and mission, see Wu, *Saving God's Face*; Flanders, *About Face*.

do. Sometimes I would participate, and other times I would not. It depended on who was there, and how I felt at the time.

On one occasion, I decided not to participate. When everyone *wai*-ed the Buddha, I kept my hands to my side. One of friends looked over at me and said, "Tom, what are you doing? Why aren't you *wai*-ing?" I knew he would notice. "I'm a Christian," I told him. "Remember?" "Oh, yeah," he replied. "I forgot. It's strange that you don't do what everyone else is doing." The teacher heard us talking and came over. Just like my friend, she questioned why I was not participating. "It is disrespectful," she insisted. I explained that as a Christian I can't *wai* the Buddha, but I don't think she understood what I was saying. I was the oddball, the strange kid, the only one who was different. My friends and even my teachers didn't understand me, and, to tell you the truth, I'm not sure I understood myself either. Maybe I was strange.

Nid: The ID Card

Every year, I dread going to the government office to renew my ID card. They always make me feel so uncomfortable. For some reason, the government requires us to declare our religion and have it inscribed on our national ID card. We use that card for everything such as opening a bank account, purchasing a home, boarding domestic flights, or applying for a job. So, every time I show my ID card, which is often, I am also informing people of my religious affiliation. I don't like that.

It was time to renew my card again. I walked into the government office. A man sat behind the desk, and I gave him my card, informing him that it is time for renewal. He took the card in his hands, looked at it carefully, and then it happened. His facial expression became distorted, and then he looked at me as if he was trying to figure out a puzzle. He's afraid to say anything, but I know what he's thinking. "A Christian? Why are you a Christian? You look Thai." I get this a lot. "Just give it some time," I think to myself. "He'll figure it out." Just then, his face changed. The light finally dawned on his perplexed mind. He spoke and asked me to confirm my last name. I'm a Christian, he assumes, because my last name is *farang*. He thinks I converted because of my husband. Of course, that is not true. I became a Christian on my own before I was even married. I searched for God and I found Him, or, rather, He found me. But, it is much easier for me to just smile, remain quiet, and let him think what he wants. I don't want to have to explain why I am different, even though I'm Thai. It's not worth it.

Interpretation

In Thailand, Christians exist as a minority sub-group within a predominantly Buddhist society. They are what sociologist Everett Stonequist called, "cultural hybrids": persons of mixed cultural heritage "who have been pulled out of the old order of things without necessarily becoming a part of the new order."[15] The result, as Stonequist highlighted, is a "break with the tribe, which, though not always severe, will include some social ostracism."[16] For participants, social ostracism may be experienced as either mild or severe, depending on the level of felt dissonance with one's intersubjective lifeworld. Mild marginalization, or what we may term, "misunderstanding," refers to occasions of subtle or blatant presumption and confusion regarding the convert's identity which, when corrected, require a cognitive adjustment on the part of the other. While these forms of marginalization are generally experienced as relatively innocuous, they still contribute to the re-formation of the self into a "marginal man." To comprehend better this interpretive theme, we will divide this section into two forms of misunderstanding: confusion and presumption.

For Heidegger, one's circumspective absorption in the world, or what he had termed the "everyday Being-one's-Self," occurs as one is "dispersed into the 'they.'"[17] The "they" (*das Man*), as we discussed in chapter 2, is an everyday, primordial phenomenon of *Dasein*. It refers to the shared social horizon that determines what is normative for a given society, or the average way one functions as a member of a public environment.[18] When absorbed in the "they," the self acts in the with-world non-thematically "for the sake of the 'they.'"[19] In other words, the self is like everyone else and everyone else is like the self. Consequent to conversion, Thai Christians become, in many ways, extricated from the predominant Thai "they." Their conversion distinguishes them from other members of their with-world, expressed in divergent modes of thinking, acting, and even feeling. Thus, that which is typically experienced non-thematically, i.e., circumspective absorption in the "they," is, for converts, experienced thematically. From this dissonance between the self and the "they" arises experiences of marginalization, most notably confusion and presumption.

15. Stonequist, *Marginal Man*, 54, 61.
16. Stonequist, *Marginal Man*, 61.
17. Heidegger, *Being and Time*, 163–67.
18. Blattner, *Heidegger's Being and Time*, 69–70; Heidegger, *Being and Time*, 164–65.
19. Heidegger, *Being and Time*, 167.

Strangers in a Familiar Land

Among participants, a common and relatively mild form of marginalization arises due to confusion or ignorance regarding Christian ways of being-in-the-world. This confusion is largely generated from the perception in Thai society that Christianity is a foreign religion, leading to misrepresentations of the primary tenets or activities of Christian belief and practice. As a freshman in university, Kay had attended a class on the subject of world religions. During his summation of the Christian faith, the professor claimed that Christianity was about "loving God, loving people, and working hard to get to heaven." When he asked his class of nearly one thousand students whether they agreed, Kay boldly stood up and pronounced, "No, you are wrong! I am a Christian and that is not what Christianity teaches." While Kay's courageous outburst may have been unusual among participants, the perspective of the professor was not. Lek, a philosophy major in university, learned early on that Christianity is the religion of the "Western people," just as Islam is the religion of Middle Eastern people, and Buddhism is the religion of Asians, especially Thais. Other participants allude to similar teachings during their childhood education. However, confusion does not only occur at the academic level. Ploy's mother expressed cognitive dissonance regarding the Christian doctrine of grace, a religious perspective that runs contrary to her karmic worldview. Nid's father assumed that most Thai Christians were "brainwashed," having converted to Christianity for purposes of personal gain, usually in connection with foreigners. Wit's father, by asking Wit to follow both God and Buddha, was confused regarding the exclusive nature of Christian belief and practice, holding instead to a form of religious inclusivism that is common among Thai folk Buddhists.

Besides confusion, another form of mild marginalization common among Christian converts is what we may refer to as "presumption." According to the Oxford dictionary, presumption, as opposed to assumption, carries the strong sense of "supposing" in that something is "supposed to be the case on the basis of probability" rather than supposed "without proof."[20] Given the predominance of Buddhism within the Thai lifeworld, and its fusion with kinship, ethnic, and national identities, the idea that all Thais are Buddhist is a frequently encountered presumption among participants. Presumption occurs when one encounters his fellow-man within a common environment. This encounter activates the culture's sedimented stock of knowledge, a system of recipes which includes typifications for entering

---

20. "'Assume' or 'Presume'?"

a "they-relation."[21] These typifications provide a ready-made apparatus by which one may easily and quickly grasp the other. For Thais, included in this stock of knowledge is the typification that all Thais are Buddhist, a recipe which allows one to presume that the other will think, behave, and relate in ways typical of *us*.

Within their work environments, Nan, Nid, and Ploy often encounter temple representatives whose job it is to solicit funds from local businesses and institutions for purposes of temple construction. Within the Thai lifeworld, this act of generosity is considered a prime opportunity for the accrual of merit, and, therefore, it is presumed that all Thais would desire to contribute. For participants, since they choose to abstain from such merit-making practices, this intermittent interaction with temple representatives requires the repeated correction of presumption and concomitant assertion of one's religious identity. Solicitation will only cease, Ploy and Nan explain, when temple representatives finally remember the religious identity of converts, a mental alteration that may take a considerable amount of time. The significance of "remembering" and "forgetting" also come to the fore when participants attend community events such as funerals. As a highly respected medical doctor, Nan is often called upon to perform rituals at funerals. On one occasion, she was requested by friends to give a yellow robe to a monk, a special honor that is considered meritorious in nature. "They (my friends) forgot that I was a Christian," she recalls. "I said, 'No, no, no. I cannot. I'm sorry.'" Despite her friends' former knowledge of her religious identity, in this instance they had "forgotten," signifying that they had reverted to the common typifications of *us*.

In all these cases of confusion and presumption, participants encounter a lifeworld wherein Christians are perceived as "alien," that is, as transgressing the boundaries of "normality." While once on the inside as members of *our* homeworld, converts now belong to an alienworld, complete with divergent conceptual systems, values, norms, and traditions.[22] Further, as Steinbock argues, homecomrades constitute the alien, not based on a pre-fabricated sense of "alienness" that relies on definitions internal to the alienworld itself, but through liminal co-constitution within their own homeworld. In other words, the generative sense of the alien, how *we* understand *them*, develops through the privilege of the homeworld.[23]

21. Schütz and Luckmann, *Structures 1*, 64–68, 77.
22. Steinbock, *Home and Beyond*, 180–81.
23. Steinbock, *Home and Beyond*, 178–85.

Or, from a social psychological perspective, out-groups are always defined and categorized according to an in-group bias.[24] For Thai converts, this means that their lived experience will often be that of misunderstanding. Thai Buddhists, as representatives of the "normal" in-group or homeworld, will interpret the beliefs and actions of Thai Christians according to their own stereotypical judgments of what constitutes the alien. The result is, as Schütz highlights, the feeling of being misunderstood, a phenomenon potentially "rooted in hostile prejudices or in bad faith."[25]

ANTAGONISM

Kay: Let Me Go

> It was like a war in my house when I had informed my parents that I would be joining a campus ministry full-time. Given my father's abusive actions in the past, there was no telling what he might do when he learned of this decision. As my family was sitting in the living room, I came in and declared, "Mom, Dad, I am quitting my job to join a campus ministry in Chiang Mai." The shock of the statement quieted the room for about one minute. After that, the events unfolded like a scene from an action movie. My sister was the first to speak, or should I say yell, "Are you crazy! Why are you against this family?" My dad got up to get a drink of whiskey from the kitchen. All my family members were screaming at once. My mind was whirling, confused and frightened by what was taking place around me. I had to get out. I called my pastor, "Come quick! I told my parents about serving God, and they are going crazy. I must leave."
>
> For the next month, my life was a living hell. My father, mother, and sister would repeatedly tell me that I was a bad daughter for betraying the family. I kept praying to God, asking him for help. "I am doing this for you," I told him. "Why is this happening to me?" I remembered the story of the Exodus when Moses told Pharaoh, "Let my people go." That's exactly what I felt. I prayed, "Please, God, convince my mother and father to *let me go*!" Finally, I had enough. I called my mentor and asked her to help me escape. I was able to move out, but my parents were furious. For a whole year after that, my family completely ignored me. I would call on the phone, but when they saw my number, they would not answer. One time, my mother did answer the phone. "Hi, mom. This is

---

24. Tajfel and Turner, "Integrated Theory," 38.
25. Schütz, *On Phenomenology and Social Relations*, 85–86.

Kay," I said. "Who?" she replied. "Your daughter, Kay," I repeated. "Who is that? I don't have any daughter named Kay." Then she hung up. That was a hard year for me. For the first time, I felt like I had no family.

Ploy: The Look

During funerals, I always feel different as a Christian. On one occasion, I had to attend the funeral of a friend's husband. As a Christian, I believe it is not appropriate for me to worship the Buddha, so I decided beforehand that I would not *wai* during the monks' chant. I felt so awkward, though; like, "What am I doing? Am I ok?" I was the only person in the audience not performing the *wai*. It was like a battle in my mind. I had to continually convince myself to keep my hands down.

Usually, during this portion of the ceremony, I would not look around. I would keep my head down to avoid eye contact with those around me. I don't want people to notice that I'm not *wai*-ing. This time, though, I happened to glance at the monks. When I did, I immediately noticed that one of them, the oldest monk, was staring right at me. Strangely, he wasn't looking anywhere else, just at me. It was like he was staring right into my soul. What was he thinking? That I'm a bad person? That I don't know what to do? That I'm being disrespectful? I felt so embarrassed, kind of like being naked in public. I could sense the temptation to start *wai*-ing. I just wanted the monk to look somewhere else. Thankfully, though, I summoned the willpower to abstain. "Please, Lord," I prayed, "let this chanting period end." After what seemed like an eternity, it finally passed.

Interpretation

Social marginalization, or the state of finding-oneself-out-of-place due to one's conversion, may be experienced as either mild or severe. Intensity is most often gauged by the level of felt affective and cognitive dissonance produced by a given experience, which varies according to experiencer, circumstances, and relative stage in the alternation process. What may be experienced as severe by one participant may be experienced as mild by another. In this section, we will explore two of the most common forms of severe marginalization, or antagonism, among participants: "the look" and disapproval. Whereas "the look" may be considered an intense variety of disconformity among the "they," disapproval most often arises via disconformity among the "we." In both forms of marginalization, however, the experiencer perceives the effects of such experiences as negatively imposing on one's emotional and psychological well-being. The result of such experiences is the production of the personality type "marginal man," a concept we will investigate further in the final section of this chapter.

Antagonism conveys the meaning of openly expressed struggle or opposition. To be antagonized is not only to reside outside a given community, as in a general state of dis-belonging, but also to be actively opposed by members of that community. While opposition may occur from any group member, the effects are most strongly experienced among significant others, such as family members, friends, mentors, or colleagues. In these cases, one may begin to question one's membership in the in-group, thus threatening his or her social identity and place in the world. During this period, the opposed is often ostracized, disowned, or, minimally, disenfranchised. Resolution, therefore, is essential to the re-integration and well-being of the self, a process that effectively re-situates the self to his or her place within the collective.

Among the forms of antagonism experienced by participants, "the look" is by far the most common, with no less than thirteen discrete occurrences in the interview data arising from all seven participants. "The look," as we will use the term, refers to the experience of being observed or, even better, scrutinized, due to the disconformity of one's behavior. Edith Stein described it this way, "As soon as I'm conscious of a person paying attention to me . . . I act like I'm conscious of being under the eyes of a 'spectator' who comprehends me and my doings (overt and covert), inspects me, and evaluates and judges me in every possible respect."[26] In his book *Being and Nothingness*, Sartre famously and elaborately elucidated the nature of this unique intersubjective experience. He described someone who is peeking through a keyhole, spurred on by jealousy to peer secretly into the private world of another. While immersed in the act, this person is alone and, therefore, "in no way known." He becomes his acts, "caught up in the circuit of selfness." However, suddenly and unexpectedly, another person appears in the hall and begins looking at him. Because the peeper is observed by another, he now observes himself. While, through the keyhole, he was once perceiving an other as object, now he, himself, has become an object for the other.[27] The

---

26. Stein, *Philosophy of Psychology*, 292.
27. Sartre, *Being and Nothingness*, 347–50.

result, Sartre argues, is shame: "the recognition of the fact that I am indeed that object which the Other is looking at and judging."[28]

For participants, the experience of being observed specifically arises from one's prior decision not to conform to the expected, embodied behavior of the "they." Due to their entrenched commitment to religious exclusivism, participants decide in advance to enact an attitude of nonparticipation when it comes to religious gestures and rituals. The *wai*, given its conspicuous nature as a form of embodied religiosity, presents particular difficulties. Abstaining from this physical gesture, especially at funerals, removes the self from the togetherness of the "us." As the community *wais* together, usually during the chanting of the monks, they are effectively affirming their commonality as members of a mutual with-world. Through their bodies, they self-identify with the group and with the group's shared social and religious identity. Failure to participate, then, results in becoming conspicuous; that is, attracting unwanted attention for not conforming, a particularly dreadful situation for individuals within collectivistic societies.

Included in the experience of "the look" is the presumption of the observed regarding the "in-order-to"[29] of the observer. That is to say, participants apperceive in "the look" certain negative motivations, thoughts, and judgments presumed to be taking place in the mind of the looker. It is understood as a stripping bare of the self or as a condemnation dispensed through the eyes of an other. Nid describes the experience this way, "People look and have eyes on you like, 'Why is she doing this? Why does she behave like this? Why is she so rude?' Probably many questions within them. They get you with the eyes." Nid also wonders whether those who are observing her nonparticipation are questioning her cultural identity; as if she, despite her age and social status, is woefully ignorant of traditional Thai customs. While Nid most frequently encounters "the look" at funerals, primarily because she does not *wai*, she has also experienced it while praying before meals and when displaying her ID card.

Other participants allude to similar experiences. At her mother's funeral, Nan was "on stage," as it were, given her prominent position as daughter. Her nonparticipation, therefore, was preeminently conspicuous. To avoid being stripped bare by the gaze of others, she would bow her head, thus avoiding eye contact. "Our family is a big family," she explains, "and many people know our family. So, many people attended the funeral.

28. Sartre, *Being and Nothingness*, 350.
29. Schütz, *On Phenomenology and Social Relations*, 180.

It was like they were all watching me, but I just tried not to show myself." Ploy, in the story narrated above, admits that she was not certain whether the monk was staring at her, or, if he was, whether it was motivated by ill-intent. Despite that, her memory of the event still resurrects the deep-seated emotions she had initially experienced in the scrutiny. "I felt embarrassed," she recalls. "Was the monk thinking that I am a weird person or that something was wrong with me? Am I a bad person?" As an authority figure in Thai society, the monk's stare was especially potent in stripping bare Ploy's sense of self, exposing a feeling of shame for transgressing societal expectations. "The look," therefore, is the preeminent consequence of difference. In a society where conformity is expected, "the look" is reserved for deviants, a nonverbal expression of condemnation for the purpose of shaming, and potentially rehabilitating, social emigrants. As such, participants experience "the look" as one of the more forceful, negative effects of religious alternation.

Another form of antagonism, besides "the look," is what we may term, "disapproval." Disapproval refers to experiences in which one is at the receiving end of direct verbal or nonverbal expressions of disappointment, anger, or opposition due to one's conversion. While "the look" occurs predominantly in the mode of the "they," arising from disconformity to general Thai customs and norms, disapproval occurs in the mode of the "we," arising from perceived acts of dis-belonging within one's primary in-groups. For example, while abstention from the *wai* at a funeral may incur the condemning gaze from a generalized "other," a decision to join a campus ministry, as in Kay's case above, specifically targets kin-group expectations and, as result, produces opposition from primary significant others.

Disapproval is experienced along a continuum of severity. On the extreme end are cases such as death threats or total group exclusion, both of which, as have seen, were experienced by Kay in response to her decision to join a Christian ministry group. However, these extreme cases are relatively rare among participants. More commonly, participants incur the disapproval of family members and friends via passive-aggressive behavior, verbal and nonverbal expressions of disappointment, and questioning. The disapproval that Wit had experienced from his father was primarily nonverbal. He was so attuned to his father's facial expressions and bodily gestures that he could sense the severity of his father's disapproval via his corporeal states. Wit alluded to this ability several times during the interview. When his parents discovered that Wit was attending church, "They did not say much, but nonverbally I could tell that they were not happy. They did not agree with it, but neither did they forbid it." Later, he mentioned that his father had disapproved of his decision to marry in a church. When asked how he knew this, Wit replied, "I could tell by his face." In both cases, Wit described these nonverbal expressions of disappointment as "difficult," making his father's verbal expression of disappointment even more problematic. In requesting that Wit worship both God and Buddha, Wit's father was boldly and vocally asserting his parental authority, a situation that would typically, within the Thai lifeworld, require Wit's unquestioned obedience.

Both Nid and Lek refer to cases of "questioning" that had arisen in response to their conversions. When Nid returned to her hometown, her difference as a Christian had provoked many questions from family and friends in the community. If they were not questioning her directly, she explains, they were gossiping among themselves. In either case, though, Nid experienced the community's disapproval, a situation that made her feel like a "stranger." Likewise, Lek's conversion provoked a litany of questions from his parents. While some of these questions simply arose out of ignorance of Christian belief and practice, others, such as, "Why would you become a Christian?" signified a deeper level of disapproval. While Lek believes that his parents' questions were predominantly non-antagonistic in nature, they did serve to highlight his difference from the family's social identity and, therefore, exposed an underlying tension regarding Lek's conversion. Lek's negotiation tactic hints at the intensity of the situation. "I received many questions from my family," Lek explains, "but I answered them with love. I showed them my love." The responsive demonstration of love, therefore, seems to indicate that the desire for simple answers to honest questions may not have been the primary motivation of his parents' questioning. In all these cases, however, we should again note that antagonism, as well as misunderstanding, occur most strongly during the early stages of alternation, especially at the "revealing." The initial shock of learning of a son's, daughter's, friend's, or sibling's conversion often provokes strong emotional reactions within existing in-groups. Most frequently motivated by fears of group departure, it is these reactions that are internalized by participants, resulting in the development of the lived experience of "strangeness."

STRANGENESS

Kay: Estranged

She was my best friend. Throughout our high school days, we were inseparable. When I was going through hard times at home, she was always there. We were so close, in fact, that upon graduation from high school, we decided to go to the same university and be dorm roommates. Early on, we didn't care about meeting new friends at the university. We had each other, and that was enough. It was during our freshman year, though, that I had first met a group of Christians. These Christians were part of a campus ministry organization, and they helped me grow in my faith. They assigned a mentor to me, I joined their weekly Bible studies, and, over time, I spent more and more of my free time with them. That also meant that I was spending less time with my best friend.

My friend started to notice. She would ask me, "Kay, do you want to go out drinking tonight?" "No, I don't feel like it," I would reply. I didn't want to say it, but the real reason I refused was because I don't feel comfortable doing those things anymore. Ever since I joined this Christian ministry group, I stopped drinking alcohol, and I was working on my swearing habit. I was a different person now, but my friend didn't understand that. Soon, my relationship with my friend grew worse. One day, she yelled at me, "Kay, you are always hanging out with those new friends, but you never do anything with me anymore. You are crazy with religion. I've had enough. I'm moving out." She left that day and never came back. I cried to my mentor, "Why would this happen to me? I chose God, but God took away my friends." My mentor encouraged me to keep praying, trusting, and waiting on God. Perhaps he would resolve the situation. Maybe he would . . . eventually, but all I knew at the time was that being a Christian is not easy. Because of my faith, I had lost my best friend.

Nid: Guilt

My mother was a Thai Buddhist, but my father was Chinese. So, growing up, I had to perform both Buddhist and Chinese rituals. Buddhism is centered at the temple, and it is very community oriented. Chinese religion, however, is centered in the home. In our house, we had an altar where we venerated our ancestors. The Chinese rituals were very somber, and my father would force all of us kids to participate.

As I became older, I slowly moved away from the Chinese traditions of my father and, instead, adopted the Buddhism of my mother. After I became a Christian, I separated myself even more from the Chinese side of my family. One time, I talked to my father about the gospel. I wanted him to believe in Jesus as I did, but he was not open to it. "You are young, you have studied, and so you have your own belief," he told me. "I am from an older generation, and I have my belief. I'm too old to change. But don't worry about me. I am nothing. The Chinese traditions will end with me. Don't bother to bury me when I die, just burn me and spread my ashes in the water."

What he told me brought tears to my eyes. When he passed away, we followed his wishes. We burned him in the manner of the Buddhists, but we should have buried him in the manner of the Chinese. Even now, I feel guilty when it is Chinese New Year or the anniversary of my father's passing. During those times, I should be respecting him, carrying on the traditions at the family altar. But I don't do that anymore. My father spent his life venerating his ancestors, but now he has no one venerating him. That makes me sad.

Interpretation

The moment of displacement consists of both external occurrences of intersubjectivity and the subsequent internalization of those occurrences within the self. As converts face situations of marginalization, such as misunderstanding and antagonism, their perceptions of the self are, to some extent, altered due to their perceived states of social difference, deviance, or disbelonging. Consequently, their comportment in the Thai lifeworld now occurs in the mode of "stranger"; that is, they thematically experience large portions of their world as "conspicuously unfamiliar"[30] or "uncanny."[31] As Alfred Schütz comments, "The stranger . . . becomes essentially the man who has to place in question nearly everything that seems unquestionable to the members of the approached group."[32] That is to say, the stranger perceives themselves as physically, emotionally, and intellectually "out-of-place."

---

30. A reversal of Heidegger's phrase "inconspicuous familiarity," which refers to the non-thematic, everyday character of that which is "ready-to-hand." Heidegger, *Being and Time*, 137.

31. Heidegger, *Being and Time*, 233.

32. Schütz, "Stranger," 502.

Strangers in a Familiar Land

This phenomenological conception of "strangerness" finds its sociological counterpart in Park's and Stonequist's "marginal man" theorization. As discussed in chapter 1, the "marginal man" denotes "one who is poised in psychological uncertainty between two (or more) social worlds, reflecting in his soul the discords and harmonies, repulsions and attractions of these worlds, one of which is often 'dominant' over the other."[33] By straddling two divergent and opposing worlds, the "marginal man" internally harbors the conflict of the divided self.[34] The result is the emergence of a personality type which, according to Stonequist, may include positive traits, such as the ability to mediate between the two worlds, or negative traits, such as mental conflict, ambivalence, and excessive self-consciousness.[35] As Grant and Breese demonstrated in their 1997 work among African-American students, however, there are multiple possible reactions to marginality (they had discovered eight), based more on the construction of meaning attached to marginality than on the state of being marginal itself.[36] This was true among participants as well. While all of them had experienced external situations of marginalization (as outlined above), not all of them internalized these situations in the same manner. In this section, we will examine, from a phenomenological perspective, the four primary reactions of the self to marginalization as disclosed in the interview data: loss, guilt, callousing, and duality.

Loss

To lose something or someone is to experience the absence of that which was formerly present. This is the phenomenon of "disappearance." However, as Todd DuBose argues, loss, especially the loss of a loved one, not only entails "disappearance," but also "dys-appearance," or the alienating and uncanny presence of absence.[37] For example, we may "see" the deceased in his empty shoes, vacant shirt, or unoccupied chair. "During this time of loss," DuBose explains, "one experiences the acuteness of pain and the disorganization of familiarity in one's life-world."[38] While not as strong as in the death of a loved one, this sense of loss as both "disappearance" and

33. Stonequist, *Marginal Man*, 8.
34. Park, "Human Migration," 892–93.
35. Stonequist, *Marginal Man*, 144–56.
36. Grant and Breese, "Marginality Theory."
37. DuBose, "Phenomenology of Bereavement," 372.
38. DuBose, "Phenomenology of Bereavement," 374.

Displacement

"dys-appearance" is commonly experienced by participants as they are excluded, post-conversion, from primary in-group relations. Wit experienced the loss of "home" during his first trip to visit his family after the revealing. Upon his return, the familiarity and comfort of his childhood home had transfigured into a state of uncanniness due to his father's verbal and nonverbal expressions of disapproval. Also, Kay experienced acute pain and lifeworld disorganization due to the loss of her non-Christian friends. "We had good days together in the past, and I wish we could have that feeling again," she admits. "But times changed, positions changed, and many other things changed. Sometimes, when we talk, it is like we are talking in another language. It is so sad to leave it (the friendship)." Prior to her conversion, Kay and her friends had existed in a commonality of "we," delimited by a common discourse and mode of being-in-the-world. However, due to Kay's hierophanic restructuration and emplacement within the sacred community, what was once held in common is now experienced as uncommon. The result, she explains, is the affective response of sadness; that is, the lived experience of her friends' absence.

Guilt

Besides loss, participants often experience guilt for failing to abide by the expectations of significant others. Essential to establishing social harmony within the Thai lifeworld, especially among family members, is the enactment of what is known as *kreng jai*, or the obligation to be considerate, unimposing, and agreeable toward the other.[39] Failure to demonstrate appropriate *kreng jai*, even for reasons of religious conviction, is perceived by others as disrespectful and inconsiderate, the internalization of which may produce feelings of guilt. This guilt is not the result of a legal transgression against an established law as much as a social transgression against the expectations of the collective.[40] Nid admits to feeling guilty for having abandoned the family's ancestral traditions. Initially, she had attempted to absolve this guilt by resigning her position as teacher so that she may provide on-site care for her father in his old age. However, many years after her father's passing, the feeling of guilt remains. "I feel guilty because his culture will end with me," Nid laments. "I'm 50 percent his blood, half Chinese, but it will end

---

39. Komin, *Psychology of the Thai People*, 164.

40. Because of this, we may appropriately designate this phenomenon more as a guilt-experience than as a shame-experience. For more on the difference between guilt and shame experiences, see Flanders, *About Face*, 60–61.

with my generation. I will not carry it on, and I don't know if I will see him again or not." Ploy experienced guilt during the one-year period when she had kept her conversion a secret from her mother. Because of her mother's expectations for Ploy, and, conversely, Ploy's sense of *kreng jai* toward her mother, Ploy believed that keeping her conversion a secret would effectively avoid feelings of disappointment and disrespect within their relationship. However, and somewhat unexpectedly, the keeping of the secret itself became a transgression. "I had to keep it a secret, but I felt it was not right," she explains. "I should be able to tell people freely that I am a Christian, but I couldn't do that." The guilt was only alleviated when her mother eventually discovered Ploy's true religious identity.

Callousing

While the state of being marginal is a given for Thai Christians, the felt experience, or internalization, of that marginality varies among participants. While some may experience significant loss, guilt, or duality as they respond to marginal situations, others seem impervious to the emotional and psychological effects of being an "outsider." We will call this response, "callousing," or the "hardening" of the self to the negative effects of marginalization. Of all the participants, Lek's interview data was most indicative of this phenomenon of callousing. In response to his family's questioning regarding his new identity, Lek was convinced that the experience was a non-issue. When asked whether his parents were against his conversion because of the tradition of Buddhism in the family, Lek responded, "Maybe, but I don't care." As he faced the prospect of baptism, including the public nature of the event, Lek expressed unconcern about what others might think of his conversion. "I don't care what everyone thinks of me," he explains. "I care what God thinks of me. I want love from God more than others." Likewise, Lek was indifferent to the perspective of monks or other Buddhists when he disposed of his old idols in the trashcan, and he is apparently impervious to "the look" that he receives at Buddhist ceremonies such as funerals. For Lek, therefore, the social pressure he faces from the Thai lifeworld is only minimally transformative to the self. It is difficult to ascertain whether Lek's responses would fit Grant and Breese's categories of uninvolved (one that gives little thought to marginalization) or balanced (situated comfortability in a "marginal culture" such that the situation is perceived as normal and stable).[41] It is more likely that Lek's callousing re-

---

41. Grant and Breese, "Marginality Theory," 193.

flects a defiant approach, one that aggressively deflects negativity based on the perceived strength or superiority of the self. At the end of the interview, Lek admitted that he was the lone Christian among his friends, but he does not find this strange. The reason, he explains, is because "sometimes I feel better because I walk in the good way . . . confident." In other words, the quality of being a Christian far outweighs the negative effects of being a member of a marginal sub-group within Thai society.

Duality

By far the most ubiquitous response of participants to situations of marginalization is what we may call "duality." Duality, or what DuBois referred to as "double consciousness,"[42] describes the internal mental conflict that one experiences by existing in two disparate worlds, resulting in attitudes of divided loyalty, ambivalence, or confusion.[43] In cases of duality, one's self is torn, as it were, between divergent expectations of what constitutes "normal" embodied performance within conflicting regional lifeworlds. For participants, the adoption and enactment of a new religious identity introduces a felt tension between two divergent social identities and group loyalties. Wit, for example, when asked by his family to participate in Buddhist ceremonies faced the dilemma of duality. On the one hand, he upheld a strong conviction regarding religious exclusivism, a display of loyalty directed toward God and the sacred community. On the other hand, he was a member of a kin group, enacting the role of "oldest son" with all the privileges and responsibilities that pertain thereunto. His responsibility to his family social identity, therefore, required him to demonstrate respect, loyalty, and obedience appropriately. To manage the duality, Wit avoided confrontation by pursuing non-aggressive means for breaking the horns of the dilemma. Despite that, he still experienced the conflict as "difficult." However, duality is best illustrated in Nid's insistence on assigning percentages to her religious identity. Being 50 percent Christian and 50 percent Buddhist (or, later 80/20), for Nid, entailed balancing her dual social responsibilities and roles within both lifeworlds. She explains, "Surely, being a Christian is not all smooth. There are many difficulties, especially when you live in a very strong Thai community. If you don't go to their ceremonies, it is rude, but if you do go and don't participate, they make you feel uncomfortable." At Buddhist ceremonies, especially, her duality produces

42. DuBois, *Souls of Black Folk*, 8.
43. Stonequist, "Problem of the Marginal Man," 145.

in her a sense of awkwardness since she fails truly to fit in with either world. As she describes it, "I feel like I'm a stranger." As we will explore in the next chapter, this experience of duality as "strangerness" is the phenomenological basis for the moment of negotiation.

CONCLUSION

As we conclude this chapter, it is important to note that the experience of displacement among Thai converts, namely as dis-belonging, misunderstanding, antagonism, and strangerness, closely parallels that of the first-century world. During that time, early Christians had to navigate a society in which ethnic, family, and religious identities were thoroughly fused. Because of their exclusivist religious convictions, Christians had to face ongoing suspicion, misunderstanding, and even ridicule for their apparent anti-social behavior. Commenting on the book of Hebrews, de Silva states,

> Christianity's commitment to the One God and rejection of all other deities led serious Christians to withdraw from participation in the cultic ceremonies which were a part of most political, business, and social enterprises in the Greco-Roman world. As a result, Christianity inherited much of the suspicion and prejudice which had fallen to Judaism in a world where loyalty to the gods was intimately connected with loyalty to ruler, city, authorities, friends, family, and associates. Along with this suspicion came reproach, rumor, and slander, which together made it not only disgraceful but also dangerous to be associated with the name of "Christian."[44]

Christian conversion, therefore, in the first-century Roman world as well as in twenty-first-century Thailand, involves significant social costs due to both the fusion of ethnic and religious identities among Middle Eastern and Asian cultures and the priority of religious exclusivism among converts. Also, as in the first century, Thai Christians respond to these social dilemmas in various ways, ranging from callousing to extreme duality. However, as Hurtado highlights, the benefits of conversion are perceived by converts as far outweighing the social costs. He states, "Those who joined Christian groups must have perceived some sort of 'religious capital' specific to Christianity that relativized radically the social disincentives of identifying themselves as adherents."[45] Included in this capital, he argues, were such

---

44. deSilva, *Despising Shame*, 146.
45. Hurtado, *Why on Earth*, 131.

Displacement

theological incentives as belief in a loving God and eternal life.[46] Whatever the case, the surpassing value of Christian belief and identity requires adherents to develop negotiation tactics for appropriately navigating the lived experience of displacement. We will now turn to this final moment of the phenomenon under investigation: the moment of "negotiation."

---

46. Hurtado, *Why on Earth*, 108–29.

9

Negotiation

INTRODUCTION

IN THEIR BOOK *THE Homeless Mind*, Peter Berger, Brigitte Berger, and Hansfried Kellner write, "Men not only define themselves, but they actualize these definitions in real experience—*they live them*."[1] In other words, humans do not merely conceptualize their identities, they present them, and, indeed, become them, via their everyday, embodied performance within an intersubjective place-world.[2] To put it succinctly, "Men are what they do."[3] Up to this point in our investigation, we have noted that Thai Christian identity formation, as both a religious and social phenomenon, is grounded in hierophanic encounters with the Sacred and molded through immersive participation in the sacred community. While finding emplacement in a new religious homeworld, however, converts concurrently experience displacement from pre-existing social groups and identities. They re-enter the Thai lifeworld in the mode of stranger, thus requiring the successful negotiation of their new religious identities within the context of social marginalization. It is in this moment of negotiation, the final moment of the phenomenon of in-marginality, where we find the quotidian lived performance of Thai Christian identity. Stated differently,

---

1. Berger et al., *Homeless Mind*.
2. For more on identity as performance, see Jenkins, *Social Identity*, 124–25.
3. Geertz, *Interpretation of Cultures*, 385. Heidegger makes a similar assertion, claiming that the "subject character" of one's self and that of others is to be defined existentially. He claims, "In that with which we concern ourselves environmentally, the Others are encountered as what they are; they *are* what they do" (Heidegger, *Being and Time*, 163).

Negotiation

as Thai Christians negotiate marginality, there we find the intersection of "Thainess" and "Christianness."

In this final chapter, we will explore the moment of negotiation as occurring among Thai Christians. Negotiation includes the strategies for navigating marginality, the motivations for these strategies, and the contexts in which these strategies are enacted. This chapter will be structured via the strategies for negotiation as disclosed in the interview data, highlighting motivations and contexts as appropriate. The interpretive theme of (1) *risk* refers to strategies that either expose or protect the self to the potential undesirable consequences of marginalization. Included in this theme are the data analysis categories of "assertion of religious identity," "risk-taking," "confrontation with previous world," "revealing of new identity," and "Christian identity as secret." (2) *Presence and absence* refers to the attempt of converts to balance religious and social identities so as to maintain religious exclusivism on the one hand and in-group membership on the other. Categories include "avoidance as coping strategy," "performance of non-Christian ritual," "maintenance of primary group identity," and "locality as tied to social identities." Finally, (3) *testimony* will explore strategies of the self, beginning with a revised self-conception, to successfully influence significant others toward accepting or perhaps even converting to a Christian identity. This theme covers the categories of "alternation as benefitting significant others," "testimony of Christian identity," "argument in favor of Christian identity," "family adjustment to new identity," "mitigation of effects of marginalization," and "significant others as recognizing new identity."

RISK

Ploy: The Secret

> Throughout my childhood, I had attended a Christian school. Many Buddhists went to this school because it had a good reputation for academics. However, my mother would often tell me, "Don't become a Christian because it is against our beliefs. If you do, then you will not go to the temple anymore, and, when you die, you will have nothing to eat in the afterlife." At the time, of course, I had no intention of converting. When I did become a Christian as an adult, though, this conversation kept running through my mind. What would my mother say if I told her I am a Christian? Would she be upset? I was very close to my mother, and I did not

want to disrespect her in any way. That's why I decided to keep my new faith a secret from her.

I didn't want to keep my conversion a secret from my mother. I felt very guilty about it, but I wanted her to be happy. I am everything to her. I was always a good girl, beyond her expectations. I earned a PhD and am now a university professor. She is very proud of me. The one thing she had requested from me was to remain Buddhist; not to convert to Christianity. But that is exactly what I did. How could I tell her? How could I face her disappointment? I would often pray to God, "Please open my mother's mind. Help her understand that I am a Christian." I kept waiting for God to do something without me having to confront my mother. When she was diagnosed with cancer, I went to her bedside in the hospital, held her hand, and told her that I and my entire church were praying for her. When she recovered, I overheard her telling her friends, "Ploy's church prayed for me!" From that point on, she knew I was a Christian, and she stopped asking me to perform Buddhist rituals. But, I have never talked to her about my conversion. God worked it out in his way and in his time.

Wit: I am a Christian

As a psychiatrist, I am often placed in positions of honor at ceremonies like funerals or weddings. The hosts will have me sit in the front and will ask me to perform certain rituals throughout the ceremony, such as placing flowers at the altar or giving gifts to the monks. The problem, of course, is that as a Christian, I cannot do those things. So, I have a strategy. As soon as I arrive at the ceremony, I will go straight to the hosts and inform them that I am a Christian. I don't hesitate . . . I just say it.

The first time I tried this strategy was soon after I had moved to Chiang Mai. I was new to the hospital where I was working. The mother of one of my colleagues had died, so I had to attend the funeral. I was a bit nervous about attending, as it is always awkward not to *wai* when everyone else is *wai*-ing. What I wasn't expecting was that my colleague would ask me to perform a ritual in front of everyone. I wasn't sure what to do. Finally, I decided that I just had to say it, "Sorry, but I am a Christian. I cannot do those things." They just smiled, said they understood, and then found someone else to do the activity. That went well, so I decided to be up front about my identity at every funeral that I attend. I am confident to do that now.

Interpretation

As members of a marginalized sub-group, Thai Christians face potential social hazards for manifesting their authentic Being-one's-Self.[4] These potential hazards place converts in positions of risk due to the conflict between underlying expectations among group members for religious conformity and the conviction among converts regarding religious exclusivism. The closer the proximity of kinship or friendship relations, therefore, the greater the risk of revealing or performing one's religious identity. In anticipation of these hazards, converts enact various negotiation strategies for navigating their religious identity in ways that will either avert or confront the undesirable consequences of marginalization on the self. These strategies, which are often interconnected and multifaceted, include what we will call assertion, the secret, and reliance.

Risk begins by anticipating via imagination potentially undesirable occurrences and outcomes based on one's stock of knowledge of other occurrences of the same type.[5] For participants, these anticipated occurrences are the revealing and enactment of one's liminal, religious identity within the Thai Buddhist lifeworld. What is at risk is one's placement in and relational interconnectedness with the collective. They have heard stories among the sacred community or have had past experiences, often negative in nature, that form the content of the typification. With this typified content, they then, through imagination, not only anticipate their own performance of the occurrence, but also, to some extent, fear it. They enter a mode of anxiety regarding potential outcomes, thus requiring courage as well as projected strategies for facing that which is perceived as inevitable. As that which was anticipated becomes actualized in lived experience, participants find their anticipations either fulfilled or "exploded,"[6] thereby contributing to the modification of the type among the sacred community. To understand this theme further, we will now explore the specific risk strategies utilized by participants.

Assertion

When confronting potential situations of marginalization, perhaps the riskiest negotiation strategy utilized by participants is that of an outright assertion

---

4. Heidegger, *Being and Time*, 168.
5. Schütz, *On Phenomenology and Social Relations*, 137–45.
6. Schütz, *On Phenomenology and Social Relations*, 138.

of religious identity. Like the martyrs of the early church, the declaration, *Christiana sum* ("I am a Christian") constitutes for participants, through repeated and almost ritualistic use, the primary social identity of the speaker in the face of social marginalization.[7] The voicing of this self-designation not only informs the other of one's unique, and perhaps unanticipated, identity, but also reminds the self of one's primary social categorization. In social psychological terms, we may say that this statement expresses the categorization salience of one's religious identity. Because of the predominantly Buddhist social context of participants, the salience of one's social identity, "Christian," is guided by an unusually high level of "fit." In other words, participants regularly encounter situations wherein they must maximize intergroup differences and minimize intragroup differences in order to avoid Buddhist ritual or to justify "abnormal" behavior. As a result, the repeated and frequent assertion of one's religious identity serves to solidify not only one's self-perception as an in-group member but also one's differentiation from out-group behavior and norms.[8]

Participants assert their identity within numerous social contexts, three of which stand out as being most significant: the revealing, ceremony, and the everyday lifeworld. The revealing of one's identity to primary in-group members, usually within the family, is perceived by participants as representing the greatest possibility for untoward consequences, and therefore the greatest risk. These significant others carry the potential of either bolstering or nullifying the self through their responses of acceptance or unacceptance. Narratives within the sacred community substantiate this risk, often describing extreme cases of ostracism, abuse, or rejection, thus contributing to the self's state of anxiety.[9] This anxiety often motivates participants to avoid a direct assertion of their identity, instead favoring "the secret" or other more passive strategies. In fact, of the seven participants, only two directly and explicitly asserted their new religious identity in the revealing. In Nan's case, her sister had reacted with anger and fear, labelling Nan an "outsider" for betraying the family. Lek, on the other hand, reports an amenable response from his parents, involving only

---

7. Lieu, *Neither Jew nor Greek?*, 225–27; Boyarin, *Dying for God*, 95.

8. Ellemers et al., "Self and Social Identity," 165; Hornsey, "Social Identity Theory," 208; Brewer and Gardner, "Who Is This 'We'?," 91–92.

9. At the same time, however, these narratives comfort and encourage converts as they suggest that one is not alone when facing marginalization.

some generalized questions about the motivations for conversion and the nature of Christian belief and practice.[10]

Community ceremonies, such as funerals, represent another, and much more common, context for assertion. The presumption that all Thais are Buddhist necessitates the convert's verbal self-identification in order to explain religious nonparticipation. Wit's story illustrates the strategy of some participants to "clear the air" in advance of a pending ceremony to avoid potentially awkward situations during the ceremony itself. Nid explains the motivation for such a strategy, "I just tell them that I'm a Christian to make sure they do not feel like I am offending their religion when I do not participate." Context is important to this strategy, however. In some cases, such as ceremonies involving close relatives or those in which there are few Christians in attendance, participants prefer a more passive approach such as avoidance or conformity.

Besides the revealing and ceremonies, a third context for the assertion of one's identity is in general lifeworld situations. In this setting, the assertion as strategy is more readily utilized due to the relative anonymity of these intersubjective encounters. The occasional visit by temple representatives, for example, requires Wit, Nan, Ploy, and Nid to assert their religious identity to explain their nonparticipation. Kay had declared her identity in front of nearly one thousand students during a university lecture, while Nan occasionally informs her medical patients about her religious identity in order to initiate witnessing conversations. The inscription of one's religious affiliation on his or her ID card is an interesting case of assertion. In a sense, each time a participant presents his or her ID card, a relatively frequent occurrence in the Thai lifeworld, the act itself becomes a passive assertion of one's religious identity. While passive, in that it does not require a verbalization, it is also performed with cognizance, resulting in feelings of anxiety and a sense of risk. Overall, therefore, the assertion of one's religious identity is perceived as an effective, but high-risk, strategy for negotiating marginality. However, as Nid explains, "You cannot explain to everybody all the time that you are a Christian." Consequently, she and other participants must enact, at times, alternative strategies for negotiating a variety of marginal situations.

---

10. As we argued in chapter 8, however, it is likely that many of these questions were antagonistic in motivation.

Strangers in a Familiar Land

The Secret

Participants appropriate "the secret" as a possible low-risk strategy for avoiding negative social effects within primary group relations. However, in the end, this strategy is often deemed ineffective in that it frequently serves to strain relationships rather than maintain them. Keeping a secret, Max van Manen suggests, is a fundamentally relational experience. However, while grounded in certain relational norms and expectations, secrets do not actually unite relations but separate them (secret comes from the Latin root, *secretus*, meaning "to separate"). In keeping a secret, one removes or hides a portion of one's self from the other. He or she "wears a mask," as it were, thereby withholding a certain level of intimacy within the relationship. We may say that one lives in two worlds: an inner world of privacy and hidden knowledge, and an outer world of play-acting and avoidance. Consequently, the secret-holder may perceive oneself as being deceptive or as having transgressed proper relational boundaries, a self-perception that often results in feelings of guilt.[11]

Ploy's case above illustrates the nature of secret as separation. Founded on a prior knowledge of her mother's religious expectations, combined with her perceived family role as a "good girl," Ploy believed that her conversion posed a threat to the existing intimacy of their mother-daughter relationship. Ploy anticipated that, should she reveal her identity, her mother would likely interpret her conversion as sign of disrespect and, therefore, would respond with disappointment and possibly anger. These anticipated unpleasant consequences had prompted Ploy to conceal her identity within the self so as to maintain relationship-as-normal with her mother. However, as Ploy explains, over time the secret had morphed into an almost object-like state, becoming increasingly thematic due to her mother's religiosity. Each request by her mother for Ploy to perform some Buddhist activity only served to intensify the secret, thus, further separating Ploy from her mother. Therefore, while the secret was initially perceived as a strategy for maintaining relational intimacy, it ended up further straining, or even severing, that intimacy. When asked what it was like to keep a secret from her mother, Ploy immediately responded, "I felt guilty. I have kept secrets from her before, but this one was a big deal. I should be able to tell her that I am a Christian, but I could not do it."

Other participants also enacted "the secret" to avoid potential negative responses from significant others. Despite the public nature of baptism, Wit

---

11. Manen, *Phenomenology of Practice*, 303–5.

did not inform his parents about the event. "It was a difficult issue to discuss (with them)," he recalls. "I thought they would not agree with it and would argue with me." Kay had kept her conversion a secret from her parents for nearly a year. Since she was still living at home and had experienced verbal and physical abuse from her father in the past, she was afraid to inform them of her new identity. She explains, "I didn't know how they would respond (to my conversion), so I just kept quiet. I was not ready to be kicked out and live on my own." To maintain the secret, Kay occasionally lied to her parents regarding her activities and pretended to perform altar rituals in the home. Like Ploy, she experienced feelings of guilt, but not as much toward her parents as toward God. "I felt guilty because I know that being a Christian, I should not lie. I knew what was right, but I could not do it. It was hard. God knows, right? I didn't want to lie, but I can't say that I was lying for Jesus. So, I felt guilty." The secret, for Kay, entailed protecting a portion of her self from the scrutiny of the other. While a form of relational separation, the secret, in itself, was not perceived as dangerous or morally wrong. However, her act of lying had escalated the secret into the arena of blatant transgression, not just before others but also before God. Specifically, Kay's secret had metamorphosed into occasions for explicit falsehood. Her guilt, therefore, was more the result of lying than of keeping the secret.

RELIANCE

In the face of risk, converts perceive the self in the mode of impotence and the revealing in the mode of inevitability. As we noted in chapter 6, hierophanies exert an almost inexorable pull on participants, drawing them into an intuitive and direct encounter with the Sacred. Through this encounter, converts enter a new world, as it were, firmly emplaced in a new intersubjective community and decidedly re-oriented in their self-understandings. Post-conversion, however, they must come to terms with the social implications of such an event. Participants recognize that their internal transformation must necessarily be externalized through the performance of their new religious identity among family and friends. This performance, however, introduces the risk of straining, or perhaps even losing, primary in-group relations. Consequently, a tension arises within the self between the necessary externalization of one's new religious identity and the desirable avoidance of untoward social consequences. In other words, one faces the inevitability of religious performance on the one hand, and the impotence of the self to control the circumstances or the outcomes on the other. Participants negotiate this tension via reliance. Since God is perceived as preeminently loving, potent, and present, that is, the God-who-is-there-for-me, the convert may, therefore, passively "wait" or rely on Him to resolve the situation.

Within her family and friendship networks, Kay had encountered numerous social obstacles in the performance of her Christian identity. Whether it was navigating the required religious rituals at home, informing her parents of her conversion and desire to serve in a campus ministry, or dealing with the loss of friends, Kay perceived each obstacle as insurmountable and herself as "not strong enough" to endure or overcome it. Consequently, she appropriated a strategy of reliance that typically followed a five-act plot line: struggle, prayer, waiting, resolution, and growth. First, an obstacle presents itself in the form of struggle, bearing either the potentiality or reality of negative social consequences and, thus, resulting in states of anxiety. Second, due to the impotence of the self either to resolve or even to endure the obstacle, Kay is driven toward the Transcendent, seeking, through prayer, God's powerful intervention to "miraculously" resolve the situation. Third, Kay enters a period of anxious expectation, unsure regarding the outcome but confident that her God is actively listening, working, and guiding in the situation. Fourth, resolution occurs, often in unexpected and seemingly impossible ways and decidedly outside of Kay's control. Finally, Kay interprets the resolution as the direct intervention of God, and, thus, as an answer to her prayers, resulting in the growth of her identity and strengthening of her ability to face future obstacles. As she explains, "Many times, God showed that I can pass through difficulties, struggles, problems, and anything else. So, (in this difficult situation), I have hope that one day, I don't know when, God will help me again." Significantly, throughout all these stages, Kay experiences God not only as guide and intervener, but also as friend. "Every time I prayed, God answered," she recalls. "When I felt sad, depressed, or lonely, he comforted me. There were not many Christians around me, but, then, I would remember that I could talk to Him when I was in trouble. I didn't have friends, but Jesus was with me."

While reliance may be understood as a negotiation strategy in itself, more often it is enacted in conjunction with other strategies. For Ploy, keeping her conversion a secret from her mother represented a period of intense anxiety, guilt, and frustration. She perceived her strategy as less-than-adequate and her self as impotent to resolve the situation. Ploy's solution, therefore, was to maintain the secret while, at the same time, relying

Negotiation

on God to overcome her inadequacies and resolve the dilemma on his own. The word she used to describe this existential state of reliance was "wait," conveying the sense that God would intervene but that it might take some time. Inherent in her world transfer, therefore, existed a legitimating apparatus for coping with marginalization. The God who was present, powerful, and relational in enacting her conversion process was perceived as the same God who can be called upon to intervene and resolve her daily problems, especially those related to marginalization.

PRESENCE AND ABSENCE

Ploy: Ritual as Duty

> Living in a Buddhist society is sometimes difficult. As a Christian, I am always in the minority and, therefore, I often feel out of place. At funerals or other Buddhist ceremonies, I am usually the only one who is not *wai*-ing or offering gifts to the monks. Instead, I sit in the back and try to avoid everyone's attention. However, sometimes, depending on the circumstances, I have no choice but to *wai* or perform a ritual. If I am the only Christian there, for instance, I feel very awkward being different. To fit in or not offend, I may decide to *wai* along with everyone else, but I don't do it in a Buddhist way.
>
> On one occasion, I had attended a funeral where I was the only representative from my family. So, on behalf of my family, I had to present an offering to the monk. I don't have a problem with that, though, because it is like a duty. I am fulfilling my role as daughter, and I can't escape that responsibility just because I am a Christian. My church would probably not agree with my strategy, and I would prefer to avoid the rituals altogether. However, I still live in society, and I believe that God knows what I am thinking when I do these things. I'm sure He understands.

Nid: Two Worlds

> The funeral setting is very familiar. I have been to cremations before, and this is a typical one: the chairs are arranged in neat rows facing the cremation furnace; the monks are up front, wearing orange robes and sitting in lotus position; and the ornate casket, complete with a picture of the deceased, takes center stage. As the mourners enter the cremation site, they choose their seats near family and friends while the most significant individuals, family members and people of high social status, sit in the front. Despite

my respected status as a teacher, I purposefully choose a seat in the back. I prefer not to be noticed.

As the service starts, my anxiety heightens. The monks begin their chanting, and, all around, everyone knows what to do. Each observer presses his hands together at nose level, with a slight bow of the head, and holds that position for several minutes. Everyone, that is, except me. I keep my hands and head down, all the while attempting to avoid eye contact with those around me. This is why I decided to sit in the back: to avoid being noticed as I purposefully abstain from *wai*-ing.

However, I can't shake the feeling that I am being observed. I know many of the people here; they are from my home community. Many are personal friends of the family. However, I sense that they are giving me "a look": like, why is she doing this? Why does she behave like this? The look makes me feel like I don't belong. Don't they know that I am a Christian and that's why I abstain? Despite my efforts to blend in, I am, instead, sticking out. I feel uncomfortable and wish I hadn't come. Of course, I knew I had to. I am still Thai, still a member of my family, and still a part of the community, and that is what makes these ceremonies so difficult. It is like I live in two different worlds. I feel like a stranger.

Interpretation

As we observed in the last chapter, the fusion of ethnic, religious and kinship identities within the Thai lifeworld poses an acute problematic for Thai converts. Because of their transfer of exclusive allegiance to the Christian God, which required their "de-conversion" from Buddhist belief and practice, converts are often accused by significant others of abandoning, disrupting, or deviating from the group. Their nonparticipation in Buddhist ritual is interpreted as a sign of disloyalty and disrespect, a form of dis-belonging, as it were, thus potentially threatening their place in the collective. The result of this displacement is the lived experience of duality, or the internal mental conflict that arises within the self from straddling two disparate worlds. To navigate this tension, namely their adherence to religious exclusivism on the one hand and their membership in existing social groups on the other, converts must negotiate both presence and absence. Presence entails one's being-there; that is, the convert's continued, embodied participation with and commitment to the "we." Absence, conversely, refers to one's not-being-there, or the convert's deliberate pursuit of the transparency of the self as it relates to non-Christian

Negotiation

religious practice and identity. Stated another way, presence and absence seeks to separate that which is deemed inseparable within Thai society; namely, religious adherence and in-group social identity. We will explore this interpretive theme of presence and absence per two primary negotiation strategies: conformity and avoidance.

According to Robert Sokolowski, the philosophical exploration of presence and absence has been one of the most original and productive themes of phenomenology.[12] For him, the concept adequately elucidates Husserl's famous distinction between empty and filled intentions. As intentionality is always a consciousness "of" something, empty intentions may be understood as an intention of something that is not there or absent, while filled intentions target that which is there or present to the one who intends.[13] The two are intimately interconnected. Sokowlowski comments, "When we appreciate the presence of a thing, we appreciate it precisely as not absent: the horizon of its being possibly absent must be there if we are to be aware of the presence."[14] For Heidegger, presence, as understood spatially, but, even more, temporally, is at the heart of his fundamental ontology. He states, "Entities are grasped in their Being as 'presence'; this means that they are understood with regard to a definite mode of time—the '*Present*.'"[15] This concept of Being as presence is implicit in his choice of terminology for describing the human subject: *Dasein,* or "Being-there." For our purposes, the theme of presence and absence will be explored primarily within the horizon of intersubjectivity; that is, as the embodied and cognitive "thereness" or "not-thereness" of the self within a determinate, social environment.

Participants appropriate two primary strategies for navigating presence and absence: conformity, which prioritizes one's presence among and commonality with the community, and avoidance, which prioritizes one's absence from Buddhist practice and identity. Both strategies are founded on the prior commitment of participants to maintain one's in-group memberships while, at the same time, adhering to accepted standards of Christian religious exclusivism. The strategy of conformity is most often utilized to mitigate the potential social hazards implicit in marginal situations. It

12. Sokolowski, *Introduction*, 22.
13. Husserl, *Logical Investigations*, 191–93; Sokolowski, *Introduction*, 33–41. See also Sokolowski, *Presence and Absence*.
14. Sokolowski, *Introduction*, 37.
15. Heidegger, *Being and Time*, 47.

involves the participant's external performance of Buddhist ritual such that one appears to be conforming to the commonality of the "we" while, internally, one maintains a level of cognitive absence from a Buddhist motivational structure. One performs the ritual, which we may understand as play-acting, but intentionally withdraws from the "in-order-to" of the ritual's generative sense. In this way, the participant seeks to maintain both one's place in the collective and one's religious identity.

Ploy's narrative above illustrates this strategy of conformity. First, we notice that her performance of certain Buddhist rituals, such as releasing fish or *wai*-ing at religious ceremonies, is motivated by a desire either to assimilate into the group or to gratify significant others. Depending on context, such as cases in which she is alone or those which involve her mother, Ploy may decide to prioritize a perspective of appeasement so as to preserve harmony, avoid disruption, and maintain her place in the collective. In her words, "If I am around people I know, I would try to blend." This motivation, in a sense, permeates Ploy's being-in-the-world as evidenced in her pre-baptismal conversation with her brother. During that conversation, Ploy had informed her brother of her conversion and impending baptism but mitigated his potential negative response by reaffirming her continuing loyalty to the family. However, while Ploy's motivation for conformity may appear to compromise her commitment to religious exclusivism, we must note, second, that her actual performance of the activity entails a revised intentionality which prioritizes cognitive absence. In other words, she enacts a dual self: an outer self that performs the Buddhist activity in the mode play-acting, and an inner self that essentially restructures, and, thus, nullifies, the religious motivation of the act. So, while, on the one hand, she may be physically *wai*-ing, on the other, she is engaging in an innocuous mental conversation with God, the deceased, or even a fish. To accomplish this, she may perceive herself as enacting a role-based identity (daughter, family member, esteemed teacher, etc.), or she may choose to de-sacralize the activity ("just" giving a gift or "just" body language). In consequence, she preserves her religious allegiance while, at the same time, fitting in or pleasing those around her. Finally, Ploy copes with her performance of conformity by assuring herself that, while her church may not agree with her strategy, God understands the purity of her motivations. "I am still in a society where people do this, and I have to survive in this society," Ploy explains. "Who is to say it is wrong?

Who draws the line? I know I am not worshipping something that is not God. So, I believe God understands."[16]

Other participants have also utilized the strategy of conformity. The day after Kay's conversion experience, she was required by her father to perform the normal, daily rituals at the family altar. However, "inside her heart" she intuitively "knew," prior to any contact with the sacred community, that respecting idols was contrary to her new religious identity. Her solution to the dilemma was to play-act the rituals before the audience of her father while, internally, praying to God in the mode of reliance. She recalls, "I prayed to God, 'Help me. I don't want to do this, but he (her father) is here. I don't want to be punished. I don't want him to hit me or kick me out of the house. Show him that I am a Christian now.'" Similarly, Nan, despite her belief that performing any Buddhist ritual is an act of "hiding" and "lying to yourself," admits that she did utilize the strategy of conformity on at least one occasion. While attending a village funeral, she was asked to place the yellow cloth on top of the coffin, an act that is considered merit-making in nature. As she perceived that there were no other attendees to accept this responsibility and in order to save face for the family, she reluctantly performed the ritual. While she describes her emotional and mental state at the time as feeling "awkward," she did not experience guilt as there appeared to her to be no other choice.[17] All these cases of conformity, therefore, highlight one further element to the strategy's structure; namely, it's inherent inferiority. Ploy, Kay, and Nan all allude to the strategy as a last resort and the least preferred. Ploy explains, "I feel like I should not do it, but sometimes, I have no choice. If I have a choice, though, I will choose not to do it." In fact, if there are other Christians present, Ploy feels very comfortable abstaining from Buddhist ritual. For Kay and Nan, the implementation of conformity ought to be understood genetically. Early in their Christian identity, due to their self-perceived "laziness" or "weakness,"

---

16. Relevant to this concept of conformity are the discussions among missiologists regarding what is known as "insider movements." For a compendium of the various arguments related to this phenomenon, see Talman and Travis, *Understanding Insider Movements*.

17. Participants' experiences of conformity, namely its occasional necessity but inherent inferiority, seems to align, at least in part, with that of the biblical story of Naaman who had pleaded with Elisha, "May the Lord forgive your servant for this one thing: When my master enters the temple of Rimmon to bow down and he is leaning on my arm and I have to bow there also—when I bow down in the temple of Rimmon, may the Lord forgive your servant for this." Elisha's response was, "Go in peace" (2 Kgs 5:18–19, NIV).

conformity was considered a necessary strategy for averting social risk. However, post-revealing, they now prefer alternative strategies that prioritize their absence. As Nan asserts, "When you go public, you can't hide anymore. If you give (gifts) to the monk, you will feel bad. It's lying to yourself. I think, no, I can't do that."

While conformity is a strategy of presence, we may say that avoidance is predominantly a strategy of absence. In avoidance, one's absence is thoroughly corporeal in nature; that is, it entails not only one's mental absence from non-Christian, religious motivation, but also one's physical abstention from Buddhist gestures, acts, prayers, and ceremonies. At the extreme end of avoidance is the complete separation of the self from certain events and people within the Thai lifeworld.[18] In discussing the difficulties inherent in attending funerals, Lek, for instance, admits that he prefers to avoid them altogether. Instead of attending a funeral and, thus, placing himself in an awkward position of presence and absence, he may, instead, phone the family to convey his condolences. "It is best not to go," he explains, "but sometimes I have to." Similarly, since her conversion, Kay has gradually removed herself from her former friendship networks so as to avoid reentering their perceived immoral habitus. In addition, she avoids participation in Buddhist holidays and festivals, believing that, if she were to participate, she would be compromising her religious allegiance. In all these cases, therefore, complete absence is believed to be the best means for preserving one's religious identity, even if it may entail compromising one's presence.

For most participants, however, avoidance requires the delicate negotiation of presence and absence such that one remains "there," but evades participation in Buddhist activity. The convert's "thereness" is founded on an allocentric perspective of one's personal identity, namely the belief that the self is necessarily interdependent with the thoughts, feelings, and actions of significant others within a group context. This interdependence instills in the convert a sense of obligation to the in-group such that one's continuing presence and loyalty is considered essential to maintaining his or her social identity. In other words, complete separation from the group, no matter one's religious convictions, would not only introduce relational conflict, but would also threaten the self's

---

18. For more on extreme cases of separation of Thai Christians from the Thai lifeworld, see Chinawong and Swanson, "Religion and the Community."

psychological well-being.[19] Consequently, Wit, Nan, and Lek all allude to the importance of attending their families' annual, religious rituals at the temple. "I attend every time," Nan explains. "It is like a family gathering. I would like to show them love, but they know I will not participate. They are happy to have me there, though, and, afterward, we will have lunch together." Similarly, participants prioritize their attendance at community events, such as funerals, in order to demonstrate their unabating loyalty to existing kinship and friendship relations. After discussing the gossip and other difficulties that she often faces at community events, Nid concludes, "But, I am there!" Her "thereness" represents the purposeful visibility of the self within a determinate social environment, a presence that effectively maintains her in-group memberships.

Presence, however, requires participants to devise numerous avoidance strategies that will effectively maintain their in-group memberships while, at the same time, not compromise their religious convictions. These strategies pursue the transparency or "not-thereness" of the self during periods of Buddhist ritual. One such strategy is the physical removal of the self from the specific locale of religious activity. During a family, religious ceremony, for instance, Wit's prior awareness of the order of service allowed him to time his bathroom visit perfectly so as to avoid his portion of the ritual. Likewise, while his family is performing Buddhist rituals, Lek often volunteers to babysit the younger children in a separate room, or he prepares food in the kitchen for the meal after the service. As Kay highlights, this strategy often requires the formulation of an excuse that will successfully remove the self while, at the same time, appease the family. If removal is not an option, however, one may decide to then pursue a form of "embodied transparency" by which one attempts to recede or become inconspicuous during the ritual period. Most participants attempt this form of absence by sitting on the periphery. Nid's story above highlights the nature of this strategy in that, while her status as a teacher would require her to sit in the front, she purposefully chose a seat in the back. Wit explains that sitting in the back allows him to avoid "the look" while he abstains from participating in the *wai*. "I do not *wai*, so I sit in the back so no one observes me," he states. The back, therefore, is a place of anonymity and, therefore, comfort; the boundary of "thereness"

---

19. Another motivation for presence and absence, which we will explore later in this chapter, is the desire of converts to function as testimony; that is, their demonstration and verbalization of divine realities for purposes of witness.

and "not-thereness" wherein one may freely exhibit one's authentic Being-one's-Self. Another form of embodied transparency is exhibited in the bowing of the head or the averting of eye contact. During her mother's funeral, Nan was required to sit in front due to her role as daughter, but she bowed her head to avoid being observed by others. "I tried not to show myself," she explains, a strategy founded on the belief that if she did not visually notice others, they would not notice her. As Nid highlights, though, embodied transparency is often ineffective, resulting, instead and somewhat ironically, in a form of conspicuous absence. "People look and have eyes on you like, 'Why is she doing this? Why does she behave like this? Why is she so rude?" Her nonparticipation, therefore, resulted in her becoming the center of attention, both through observation and, after the service, by becoming the subject of gossip.

As we conclude this section, we should note that presence and absence strategies are not entirely individual in origination and enactment, but often encompass the entire sacred community. Mentors, pastors, and fellow church members may advise converts as to what they ought and ought not to do during festivals, ceremonies, or other Buddhist events. Kay's mentor had advised her regarding her performance of rituals at home, and now, as a mentor herself, she advises her "disciples" regarding what they can or can't do during religious festivals and ceremonies. However, at times, the strategies enforced by the sacred community may be deemed ineffective or, even worse, patently erroneous. Ploy's church had advised her regarding accepted negotiation strategies, which mainly prioritized absence, but Ploy finds these strategies impracticable in real-life marginal situations. From her perspective, the church enforces uniformity without a clear authority or objective standard. Not only is strategy enforcement communal in nature, but so also is the actual enactment of those strategies. For participants immersed in marginal situations, strategies of absence are both preferred and easier to perform when one is with other Christians. For Ploy, this co-presence serves both to enforce conformity to accepted Christian norms (i.e., social pressure to "do what is right") and to mitigate deviance by making the experience less embarrassing. In these situations, therefore, the sacred community performs, in unison, a distinct social identity that, while prioritizing absence, remains present to the Thai lifeworld in the mode of testimony. To this topic of testimony, we now turn.

TESTIMONY

Lek: A Better Way

When I told my parents about my new faith, they were not surprised. My wife was a Christian, so I suppose they just expected that, eventually, I would become a Christian as well. However, they did ask me many questions. "Why did you become a Christian?"; "All of our ancestors are Buddhist. Why would you leave Buddhism?"; "Are Christians allowed to eat pork?"; "Can you still go to the temple?" With each question, I just responded in love. I had become a Christian because I wanted God's love, so I figured the best thing I could do was to show that love to my parents. Thank God, my parents did not argue with me. Not only that, they eventually started to appreciate the new Lek.

Rather than arguing with my parents, my plan has always been to show them love and proper Christian behavior. I changed my speech habits, I help my parents around the house, and I provide for them with the money I earn at work. I truly believe that if I show the love of Jesus, it is good for my family. They will benefit. One time, my mother came up to me and said, "Lek, I can tell your life has changed so much. You seem better; more responsible." I told her that it was because of Jesus. She is not a Christian, but she is starting to accept the fact that I am. She sees the benefit of Christianity in my life, and I think she is appreciating it more and more. I hope that one day, my parents will become Christians, too.

Kay: Change in Attitude

One of the most difficult changes in my life after I had become a Christian related to my attitude toward my parents. I always believed that I had the worst parents. They were so bad, in fact, that I had attempted suicide to rid my life of them. After I became a Christian though, I sensed that God was saying to me, "You have to respect your parents." I told him, "Don't ask that! I can do anything else that you command, but I can't do that." I was so angry. I sought advice from my mentor, but she told me what I knew already: I have to do this, but God will help. Rather than trying to change my parents, though, I realized that what I needed to change first was my own attitude. I remember vividly the day that change happened. In our family, we never hug or say, "I love you." Instead, to show that we care, we often say the opposite. One time, I was sick, and my dad said to me, "Take some pills. If you don't, you will die. It's your choice." Usually, when he said things like that to me, I would get angry. This time, though, it suddenly dawned on me: my father does care for me. This is just his way of showing it.

That change of attitude was what I needed to start influencing my parents toward Christianity. Rather than being angry with them, I started to pity them. They don't know the truth. They don't know the love of Jesus. What I wanted most, though, was for my parents to become Christians. When my father was in the hospital with cancer, very close to death, I was with him the whole time. He had a lot of pain, so I would encourage him to pray to God for help. He never did it while I was there, but one time, as I glanced into his room, I saw him praying with closed fists. I knew he was praying to God. I read him a book about how to become a Christian, and he asked many questions. He asked me, "How will God help? How can you believe you will go to heaven?" He didn't pray to receive Jesus then, but, who knows, maybe my father is in heaven right now.

Interpretation

As we have noted time and again throughout this research, Christian conversion and identity formation, while founded on a vertical encounter between God and the believing soul,[20] is deeply saturated with sociality. Successful alternation requires not only the availability of a plausibility structure to mediate the new reality, but also the appropriate performance of one's altered identity on the "stage" of his or her regional lifeworld. This performance necessarily encompasses the delicate presentation of the self so as to persuade significant others to accept, or possibly even embrace, one's new religious identity. Should this persuasion prove successful, the convert will not only retain his or her place in the collective, but also possibly and ideally accomplish a reintegration of the collective's social identity with a new and "superior" religious identity; that of Christianity. It is this theme of persuasion, or what we will call, "testimony," therefore, that forms the heart of the convert's identity negotiation within contexts of marginality. In fact, as we will see, testimony, while engendering strategies of its own, is often the primary motivation for the convert's management of both risk and presence and absence. We will explore this interpretive theme per the three-fold structure of legitimation, exhibition, and invitation.

Testimony, as a judicial metaphor, refers to the act of a witness in relating what one has seen or heard so as to prove an opinion or a truth. Within

---

20. For more on the term "believing soul," see Ricoeur, *Symbolism of Evil*, 10–19.

the context of a trial, an audience listens to the testimony, makes a judgment regarding its veracity and relevance (usually based on the perceived reliability of the witness), then uses it as a proof in producing a judicial decision. As Paul Ricoeur highlights, however, testimony entails not only what a witness says, but also the character of the witness themselves; namely, whether they are a false or faithful witness.[21] Therefore, testimony is not just an action of speech, but is the action itself in that "it attests outside of himself, to the interior man, to his conviction, to his faith."[22] For the convert, testimony is of the absolute: originating from the Divine, historically embodied in the "facts and gestures" of Jesus of Nazareth, recorded in Scripture, and interpreted and internalized within the self as the self "lets go" of its own sovereign consciousness.[23] Further, by internalizing the testimony of the biblical witnesses, the believing soul then becomes a testimony themselves; seized by the absolute to be living "proof and persuasion"[24] of the reality of God and his life-changing irruption in the world of the profane. For participants, it is this understanding of testimony that encompasses their lived experience of negotiation, allowing them to understand themselves as living "proof and persuasion" of divine realities.

LEGITIMATION

Testimony first requires a revised conception of the self, namely, the perspective of self-as-witness, which occurs by means of legitimation. Legitimation refers to the ways something can be explained and justified. It ascribes "cognitive validity" to objectivated meanings such that, by becoming subjectively plausible, one may effectively make sense of reality and one's individual biography.[25] While these explanations may arise from within the individual, more often they are communal in nature, firmly entrenched in the sedimented tradition and ethos of a given community. Either way, legitimations are essential to perceiving one's self and one's world in the mode of testimony. In a sense, they represent the internal conversations that take place within the convert or the sacred community regarding one's proper being-in-the-world. The result, as we will see, is the perception of the self as inhabiting a "special" social identity and symbolic universe that, while often

21. Ricoeur and Mudge, *Essays*, 84.
22. Ricoeur and Mudge, *Essays*, 85.
23. Ricoeur and Mudge, *Essays*, 74, 85–93.
24. Ricoeur and Mudge, *Essays*, 83.
25. Berger and Luckmann, *Social Construction*, 92–94.

misunderstood and even rejected by "outsiders," is inherently superior to that which is predominant in the Thai lifeworld.

One such legitimation consists of the act of social comparison whereby one's self-esteem is enhanced through achieving and maintaining a positive distinctiveness between one's own group and relevant out-groups. This entails the depersonalization or stereotyping of both in-group and out-group members such that one may properly distinguish *our* beliefs and behavior from *theirs*.[26] Low-status groups may then appropriate these comparisons in ways that make them appear more flattering; such as focusing only on dimensions of the group that look relatively good or devaluing the dimensions that reflect on them poorly.[27] Participants appropriate strategies of social comparison not only to diminish their marginal status but also to attract outsiders. Ploy, for example, frequently compares Buddhism and Christianity, most often to highlight their ethical similarities. "The only difference," she maintains, "is that Christians believe in one God." Her motivation for this comparison is two-fold. First, the perceived similarity of the two great faith traditions mitigates the deviance of her own conversion. That is, since she upholds essentially the same system of morality post-conversion as she did pre-conversion, her family members should accept her conversion as feasible. Second, the similarity of the two faiths presents Christianity as not only feasible, but possibly even attractive. Through comparison, family members will realize that Christian identity is in line with traditional Thai morality, thus reducing the "foreignness" of Christianity and potentially prompting their own conversion.

Several participants take social comparison even further by not only demonstrating Christianity's acceptability, but also its patent superiority.[28] Nan, for instance, states, "I never said Buddhism is not good. It's just not real. It is not true." Since Buddhism prioritizes law while Christianity prioritizes grace, she argues, "It (Christianity) is more fit to human beings." Further, Kay and Lek both argue that Christians are not merely similar to Buddhists, but are, in fact, religiously and morally superior. While Buddhists are required to attend the temple on a weekly basis, Kay explains, very few of them actually do. Christians, on the other hand, by attending

---

26. Hogg et al., "Tale of Two Theories," 261; Turner et al., "Self and Collective," 457.

27. Hornsey, "Social Identity Theory," 207.

28. This legitimation regarding Christianity's inherent superiority is reminiscent of the ethnoracial or "third race" discourse predominant in pre-Constantinian martyrological literature. See chapter 3 for further discussion.

church every Sunday, are exemplifying a better and truer religiosity.[29] Similarly, Lek describes himself as "feeling better" than Buddhists because he is "walking in a good way." For example, he does not "waste" his money purchasing lottery tickets as do many Buddhists. Other Thai converts mention the avoidance of improper language or the abstention from alcohol and tobacco as setting them apart from their Buddhist neighbors. All three of these moral prohibitions, interestingly, align with the "five commandments" of Buddhist morality. The underlying legitimation appears to be that, when comparing Buddhism and Christianity, Christians are, ironically, better Buddhists than the Buddhists. In other words, they more properly follow accepted Thai standards of religiosity and morality than those who self-designate as Buddhist; therefore, they are, in fact, more Thai.

This conception of Christianity as "more Thai" introduces the second legitimation strategy, that of social creativity. Social creativity refers to the altering or redefining of the elements of the comparative situation in order to enhance the positive distinctiveness of the in-group. This strategy, as David Horrell argues, was commonly utilized among the early Christ-followers. The adoption of the outsider designation, *Christianus*, for example, was the result of a creative alteration that effectively transfigured what was originally a label of shame into an accepted designation of honor.[30] By doing so, these early Christians had shaped a new understanding of themselves, i.e., those who belong to Christ, as well as the world around them, i.e., those who do not.

In a similar manner, many participants utilize self-designations or perspectives that allow them to embrace positively their marginal status while, at the same time, legitimating the persistent unbelief of significant others. For example, Kay periodically refers to herself using the biblical metaphors of pilgrim and alien. Like the great heroes of the faith, she understands herself as a "stranger and exile on the earth" who "desires a better country, that is, a heavenly one" (Heb 11:13, 16). When asked how she had coped with willfully disobeying her parents to join a campus ministry, Kay explains:

---

29. This idea that many Buddhists are not "strong" in their religious adherence is a common argument among Christian converts. Wit states, "Most Thai people are not very Buddhist. They worship many things, and they might not go to the temple. They may not do what Buddha teaches." Missionary Alan Johnson suggests that this is a common perception among Thai Christians. See Johnson, "Context-Sensitive Evangelism," 65.

30. Horrell, *Becoming Christian*, 207–9.

> I felt like it was because they don't know God. That's why they understand another way. I believed that I was doing what God wanted me to do. It was right before God. So, I understood them and didn't feel guilty, but I just felt like I wanted them to understand more. They didn't know what they were doing. That was why they told me that it was not that good. But I knew that life right now will be no longer. Our home is not here; it's in heaven. I believe that, but they didn't. So, I just feel sad that they don't know the truth.

In addition, when discussing her displacement from former friendships, Kay expounds that she has no desire to re-enter her friends' shallow and immoral habitus. However, she recognizes that her absence and alternative moral standards mean that her friends now perceive her as strange. "My friends think I am different because I am! The Bible says I am. I'm not surprised, and I don't care what they think of me." In a similar vein, Lek repeatedly affirms his lack of concern regarding the negative opinions or ridicule of outsiders. "I believe I have a good thing," he avers, "so, I don't care if they don't like it. I only care about what God thinks." Kay and Lek, therefore, both embrace certain self-designations or perspectives that allow them to redefine the elements of the social situation. Since they know that they are on the right path and, thus, have adopted a superior identity, they also know that outsiders, out of ignorance, will often misunderstand and ridicule them. Marginalization, therefore, is to be expected and perhaps even embraced since Christian identity is necessarily out of step with that of the dominant society. However, despite the shame that society may seek to bring upon them, participants, like the early Christ-followers, are assured of their honor as members of God's chosen people.[31]

A final strategy of social creativity arises as participants reinterpret "Thainess" to align better with "Christianness." As we noted in chapter 5, within the Thai lifeworld, Buddhist religious adherence is thoroughly intermeshed with predominant perceptions of what constitutes Thainess, thus engendering the common belief that Christianity is inherently foreign. Moreover, the displacement that converts experience among existing social groups fundamentally arises out of this deep fusion of social and religious identities, thus requiring numerous negotiation strategies that will effectively separate the two without compromising one's ethnic identity or group memberships. The necessary starting point for these strategies, however, is the

---

31. Horrell, *Becoming Christian*, 162.

construction of legitimations which argue that, far from being discordant with traditional Thai identity, Christianity is, in point of fact, the fulfillment of true Thainess. As we noted above, one such argument is the perception that Christian morality and religiosity are inherently superior to that of Buddhism, thus making Christians "more Thai" than Buddhists. In a similar vein, Nan argues that not only are Christians better at morality, but they are also better citizens. "In terms of love of country, I think Christians, because of God's teachings, have a greater sense of responsibility to the country," she claims. "Even when political leaders are dishonest, Christians still believe that God is doing his work through them. So, that makes me love the country even more." Since this is the case, Nan believes that should more Thais become Christian, the country would significantly improve.

In addition to demonstrating the inherent superiority of fusing Christianness with Thainess, participants must, conversely, legitimate the fundamentally non-foreign nature of Christianity. When asked whether they perceive themselves as more foreign because of their conversion, participants unequivocally and uniformly respond in the negative. For Ploy and Kay, the very fact that there exist many Thai Christians, in itself, demonstrates its non-foreign nature. Nan, on the other hand, argues that since Christianity is not a religion but a relationship with God based on personal choice, it has nothing to do with ethnic identity. It is just a "different way of thinking" than Buddhism. Lek takes this legitimation a step further by first admitting that, yes, Christianity did originate outside of Thailand, but then again, so did Buddhism. Therefore, the issue is not as much whether a religion is foreign as which religion is better. Since Lek has personally experienced a significantly improved quality of life as a Christian, there is no doubt in his mind that Christianity is not only superior to Buddhism, but also more appropriate for Thai people in general. Overall, therefore, despite the common perception that to be Thai is to be Buddhist, participants do not experience their ethnic identities as having been diminished in any way due to their conversion. As Nid succinctly avers, "No, I'm still Thai. Just a special one. Not a Buddhist."

Exhibition

Armed with legitimations that "prove" the patent superiority of Christian identity and its inherent Thainess, participants then seek to persuade others to accept or possibly even embrace this identity via exhibition. Exhibition refers to a mode of testimony whereby converts display an alternate and attractive being-in-the-world through their everyday, embodied performance such that one's actions and behavior become, in themselves, testimony of divine realities. As Ricoeur reminds us, "Testimony is oriented toward proclamation, divulging, propagation . . . [but] this profession implies a total engagement not only of words but of acts and, in the extreme, in the sacrifice of a life."[32] For participants, exhibition entails, first, an embodied presence or "being-there," and, second, the enactment of an alternate lifestyle and ethic rooted in love.

As we observed above, participants must necessarily balance both presence and absence as they negotiate their new religious identities within contexts of marginalization. One motivation for remaining present, that is, for deciding not to separate entirely from pre-existing social relations, is to preserve one's place in the collective, and, thus, maintain a sense of emotional and psychological well-being. However, another motivation, or quite possibly the premier motivation, for remaining present is for purposes of testimony. For participants, one's embodied "being-there" is a necessary precondition for positively influencing significant others toward accepting, or perhaps even adopting, a Christian identity. Therefore, Nan prioritizes her attendance at her family's annual temple gathering so that she might "show them love." Her presence demonstrates that, contrary to her sister's initial fears, Nan remains loyal to the family; but, even more, it provides an opportunity for her to enact her alternate identity before the audience of her family. A similar strategy underlies participants' attendance at funerals, family and friend gatherings, and community events. In a sense, therefore, these determinate social events form the necessary platial and intersubjective contexture or "stage" for the embodied performance of one's self-as-witness.

How do participants exhibit their alternate identity for purposes of testimony? Based on the interview data, we may adumbrate the modes of exhibition under four primary categories: improved character, improved behavior, improved ethic, and improved community. First, participants seek to demonstrate to significant others that their character and quality of life has been significantly enriched since their conversion. Wit states that Christians appear "more happy" as exemplified in their facial expressions, while Lek and Tom claim to be "better sons" due to a greater level of obedience, responsibility, and hard work. Nan is known for her wisdom, with family members often approaching her for advice, while Nid's success as

---

32. Ricoeur and Mudge, *Essays*, 86.

a teacher demonstrates to her family the superiority of her new identity. In fact, Nid's success has brought so much honor to the family that, she claims, "I can say I'm anything, and they would have no criticism about that." Second, participants desire to exhibit improved behavior, rooted in attitudes of love and acceptance, toward significant others. Example behaviors include preparing and serving food at family or community events, responding to questions or arguments with patience and kindness, being present and available during significant life events such as sicknesses or funerals, performing gestures of physical affection, and providing financial and material resources for those in need.

Third, as we have already observed, participants actively pursue an alternate ethic so as to exhibit the superiority of their Christian identity. By avoiding sin, being trustworthy, or abstaining from alcohol, tobacco, and gambling, participants communicate that being Christian effectively makes one a better Thai. As Ploy explains, "We are different from other people in the way we live our lives. We live our lives in a good way." Significantly, even one's absence from Buddhist ritual may be understood as modeling an alternate and improved ethic. By abstaining from Buddhist gestures and activities, participants perceive themselves as enacting a testimony of monotheism which, they believe, represents an inherently superior mode of religious adherence. Finally, participants allude to the unity, care, and love exhibited within the sacred community as testimony of God's love and presence. For Kay, the egalitarian and loving environment within the liminal community highlights the attractive nature of Christian religious adherence. Nid describes it this way: "We hold on to each other.... We have to go to church. We cannot be a Christian and just stay home. So, this shows Christian character: that we do things together; help one another. We show (love) in action."

Overall, we may say that these four modes of exhibition perform two primary functions for the sacred self. First, they provide a non-confrontational means for displaying the benefits of Christian conversion such that significant others may gradually and positively adjust to the convert's new identity. This means that, while friends and family members may initially react negatively to news of one's conversion, over time, they will observe its superior benefits, learn that conversion does not, in itself, threaten group membership, and eventually come to appreciate and accept the convert's new mode of being-in-the-world.[33] Second, exhibition not only

---

33. In this way, displacement and negotiation must be understood genetically. Over

Strangers in a Familiar Land

makes one's religious identity feasible, but also preeminently attractive, allowing participants to transition from *showing* Christian identity to *inviting* others to join that identity. This aspect of testimony as invitation will be explored next.

Invitation

Like the early, pre-Constantinian church, Thai Christians view themselves according to both fixity and fluidity.[34] As fixed, converts perceive Christianity as the fulfillment of true morality and religiosity, the exemplar of genuine Thainess founded on a fundamental relationship with the Creator God. Therefore, Christians represent a circumscribed in-group of "pilgrims" and "aliens" who exist as distinct from "the world" while *en route* to a heavenly country. As fluid, the boundaries of this circumscribed group always remain porous, persistently open and welcoming to new members who have "tasted the kindness of the Lord" (1 Pet 2:3). Therefore, while, on the one hand, fixity legitimates one's "superior" religiosity or morality, fluidity, on the other, forms the basis of one's testimony; namely, the unremitting invitation for the "other" to become "one of us." For participants, fluidity fundamentally founds strategies of legitimation and exhibition. The goal of testimony is the eventual embracement of Christian identity by family and friends, resulting in the re-integration of social and religious identities among primary in-group members. The accomplishment of this goal requires strategies of invitation whereby one is a verbal or otherwise direct witness to divine realities. However, while invitation is believed to be a necessary means for achieving this goal, it is also perceived as a high-risk strategy, possibly resulting in rejection or ridicule.

The goal of invitation is, for the convert, to achieve acceptance and integration within primary in-groups. Having worked hard to demonstrate the divisibility of social and religious identities within the Thai lifeworld, participants then seek to reintegrate these two identities with a distinctly Christian mode of being-in-the-world. Specifically, participants do not desire to secularize the Thai lifeworld by removing the interconnection of social and religious identities, but, instead, seek to replace the Buddhist components of in-group social identities with those of Christianity.

---

time, Thai converts typically experience both the diminution of marginality and the intensification of acceptance among in-group members.

34. For more on perspectives of fixity and fluidity in the early church, see Buell, *Why This New Race*; "Race and Universalism."

Should this strategy prove successful, this reintegration would effectively reestablish their place in the collective and ensure the group's commonality both in this life and the next (i.e., family members will now join the convert in heaven). A positive step in this direction is the embracement of the convert among family and friends, resulting in the convert's elevation within the in-group. For example, Nan's family members now come to her for advice, indicating that, due to her new faith, she has surpassed her older siblings in wisdom and knowledge. Likewise, Nid's success as a teacher has elevated her not only within the family, but also among the entire community. Because of her success, she explains, many members of her home community have become interested in Christianity. However, while this form of embracement as elevation is a welcomed benefit for the convert, it is perceived as only a step toward the ultimate goal; namely, the conversion of significant others.

The desired conversion of significant others is firmly entrenched in the social imaginary of the sacred community. Narratives are conveyed that highlight both successes and failures, seminars are conducted that train converts in evangelism techniques, and numerous materials are produced to assist converts in the invitation process. Because of this, the convert's everyday "being-with" is often, if not always, conducted in the mode of testimony. In other words, when converts interact with others, especially family members and friends, they do so with a persistent, underlying motivation both to exhibit and to invite. They are always looking for opportunities to present their new identity, testify to the importance of their faith, verbalize the theological "how to's" of conversion, and invite significant others to join the sacred community.

While the early steps of exhibiting and testifying are on-going, everyday activities, the latter steps of verbalizing and inviting are, in fact, rare occurrences. Kay had an opportunity to verbalize the gospel with her father, but only during the final moments before his death. For the rest of the participants, however, the opportunity for a formal "gospel presentation" to family members has not yet materialized. While most of them have already been embraced by the family and have had opportunities to answer questions about their faith, very few report specific and focused incidents of invitation. The reason for this appears to be the inherent riskiness of the strategy, namely, the possibility of rejection and conflict. As one convert describes it, "New Christians would like to share the gospel with the family first. But I never knew that it would be so difficult. The most difficult thing is to share the gospel to our own family. They will never believe, they will resist, and they will be angry with us. It is very difficult in Thailand."[35]

However, several participants relate stories of invitation that had occurred among colleagues, patients, or anonymous strangers. Nan frequently shares with her medical patients about the nature of God's control and power over seemingly impossible life circumstances. Wit has invited several people to consider conversion, but these invitations have always been met with rejection due to their deeply ingrained sense of religious inclusivism. "Thai people think that everything is okay," he explains. "Believe in Buddha . . . okay; believe in Jesus . . . okay. They don't want to choose." In the end, though, participants see invitation as most effective when enacted in conjunction with exhibition. Kay explains, "When I used to share with non-Christians, I was very direct. Like, 'I know this, so accept this.' I was not sensitive with people. Now I use another way to share with them like showing them how I value my work. . . . I want to live my life to show people that God lives inside me."

CONCLUSION

As we have seen, the negotiation of Thai Christian identity requires the self's delicate performance on the stage of the Thai lifeworld and before the audience of significant others. This performance entails the formation and enactment of strategies of risk, presence and absence, and testimony, which, if successful, will justify one's conversion, maintain one's place in existing social groups, preserve one's sense of religious exclusivism, and potentially even lead to the conversion of friends and family members.

However, as we conclude this final chapter in our analysis of the phenomenon of in-marginality among Thai Christians, it is appropriate to summarize our findings with the following question: "In the face of social marginalization, why on earth would any Thai become and remain a Christian?"[36] As Thai Christians face the significant social costs of displacement, and allocate a considerable amount of available "lifepower" to negotiate that displacement, what, from their perspective, motivates them to endure such costs? To answer this question, we must return, once again, to the moment of verticality. For participants, the perceived cost benefits of being loved, accepted, guided, and forgiven by the singular Creator of the

---

35. Personal conversation with the author, April 21, 2016.

36. Adapted from the title of Hurtado's book, *Why on Earth Did Anyone Become a Christian?*

universe and, thus, finding a new and improved identity as a member of God's household, far outweighs the costs of social marginalization. While each participant consistently and summarily attests to the veracity of this "cost benefit analysis," perhaps Kay's description is most fitting. When asked why she had boldly decided to stand up in front of 1000 students to defend her faith publicly, Kay unreservedly declared, "When you fall in love with someone, you want to protect them. I am in love with Jesus. I am in love with Christianity. So, I stood up." Indeed, it is this same love-motivation that allowed Nan to endure being called an "outsider" by her sister, that gave Tom the boldness to inform his parents about his new faith, that encouraged Nid to carry on despite her frustrations with the church, that instills in Lek a sense of "I don't care" when facing marginalization, that provided the support Wit needed to cope with an autistic daughter, and that delivered so much "more value" in Ploy's life that she was willing to face the potentiality of her mother's disapproval. For all the participants, therefore, to love God and be loved by Him is considered to be the supreme motivating factor for facing marginalization and, indeed, for life itself.

As Kay entered the waters for her impending baptism, a moment she likened to a marriage between her and God, a song was sung by those in attendance. It is a song that adequately summarizes a personal biography that was, at minimum, complicated, and at most, arduous, but, in the end, resulted in the bestowal of a new and precious identity. This song succinctly encapsulates not only Kay's journey of transformation, but that of the rest of the participants as well. The song is entitled, "Your Beloved."

> Lord it was you who created the heavens;
> Lord it was your hand that put the stars in their place;
> Lord it was your voice that commands the morning;
> Even oceans and their waves bow at your feet.
> Lord who am I compared to your glory?
> Lord who am I compared to your majesty?
> I am your beloved, your creation, and you love me as I am.
> You have called me chosen for your kingdom,
> Unashamed to call me your own.
> I am your beloved.[37]

---

37. Helming, "Your Beloved."

Conclusion: Retrospect and Prospect

OUR INVESTIGATION OF THE Thai Christian experience of in-marginality as arising from religious alternation has taken us on an expansive journey through a varied and, at times, surprising landscape of meanings, perspectives, and horizons. After our review of the literature pertaining to identity formation and marginality within the fields of sociology, cultural anthropology, social psychology, philosophical phenomenology, biblical studies, and Christian identity studies, we imaginatively and empathically re-entered the lived experiences of the seven participants of this study. As we have observed, the phenomenon of in-marginality is primordially constituted of four essential moments: verticality, emplacement, displacement, and negotiation.

First, through a direct, intuitive, and personal encounter with the Holy, participants powerfully experience the fulfillment of their deepest yearnings and the transformation of their religious identities. This vertical experience initiates a process whereby one increasingly "becomes Christian," effectively reorienting the believing soul within a new sacred lifeworld that is imbued by the singular and loving presence of the God-who-is-there-for-me. Second, the emplacement of participants under a new sacred canopy also situates them, concomitantly, in an altered intersubjective reality; an egalitarian and kin-like community of saints who, through their relations, discourse, and behavior, embody the very presence and love of God. In community, participants are molded by the generative sense implicit in the sacred myths, rituals, and liturgies, immersed in the community's everyday mode of being-with, and, consequently, re-formed and trans-formed in

Conclusion: Retrospect and Prospect

both their self-understandings and perspective of the world. Third, arising from their encounter with the Holy and their immersion in the sacred community is the lived experience of displacement, or the marginalization of the convert from pre-existing relationships within the Thai Buddhist lifeworld. Perceived as a form of dis-belonging due to the "foreign" nature of Christian belief and practice, conversion prompts numerous forms of misunderstanding and antagonism among family, friends, and consociates, resulting in the lived experience of strangerness. Finally, to navigate this new and strange world of marginalization, participants must then negotiate their religious and social identities in such a way as to preserve their place in the collective as well as their commitment to religious exclusivism. To do this, participants implement numerous strategies that manage both risk and presence and absence, while, at the same time, allowing them to act as testimonies of divine realities, demonstrating that Christianity is not only amenable with Thainess, but also an attractive option for the reintegration of the in-group's social and religious identities.

RETROSPECT AND PROSPECT

To conclude this study, it is necessary for us to be reminded, once again, of the unique nature of phenomenological research. Max van Manen, who has proven to be an able guide throughout this study, states concerning the final appraisal of a phenomenological text: "A high-quality phenomenological text cannot be summarized. It does not need to contain a list of findings—rather, one must evaluate it by meeting with it, going through it, encountering it, suffering it, consuming it, and, as well, being consumed by it."[1] What Manen is underscoring, I believe, is that the "findings" of phenomenological research reside neither in the production of new theorizations nor in the generalizability of results, but in the descriptions and interpretations themselves as existentially encountered by the reader. Does the text induce a sense of contemplative wonder? Does it awaken pre-reflective or primal experience? Are readers taken on a journey that moves them beyond the taken-for-granted understandings of everyday life?[2] Whether this text is successful in that regard, I leave to the reader to decide, but I anticipate that at least for Christians whose daily existence is that of marginalization, the material presented in this study will evoke a significant resonation. Having said that, it is apposite, and perhaps necessary, for me to present some

1. Manen, *Phenomenology of Practice*, 355.
2. Manen, *Phenomenology of Practice*, 355–56.

thematic conclusions, not as a summary or list of "findings," but simply as a form of retrospect and prospect pertaining to the phenomenon of in-marginality, broadly speaking.

1. Religious identity formation within contexts of marginalization is fundamentally and necessarily complex, processual, and performance-driven

Navigating marginality is an inherently dynamic process. Contexts, situations, attitudes, motivations, and self-understandings are perpetually in flux, requiring not only the procurement of immediate solutions to resolve new and unexpected crises, but also, and at the same time, demanding and, indeed, effecting the continual formation and re-formation of the self. Identity, therefore, is never static or once-for-all, but is, instead, complex, processual, and performance-driven. As marginalization ebbs and flows, so, too, does one's self-understanding. In the face of life circumstances, one will experience periods of growth and reversion, confidence and timidity, singular and hybrid religious perspectives, and the increased or decreased salience of religious and social identities. To meet a convert at one point in time, therefore, is always a mere snapshot or, in Husserlian terms, a profile of that person's genetic and generative journey of identity (trans-)formation.[3] Thus, it would be profoundly mistaken, not to mention unfair, to pass judgment as to the "maturity" of one's Christian identity or the "appropriateness" of one's course of action based simply on a single snapshot or even a series of snapshots. Christian identity is much more complex than that. What I am arguing, in essence, is that Christian identity is not constituted primarily by the inward search for the "true me" or the endless pursuit of becoming the "ideal Christian," but is, instead, performed and negotiated in actual, quotidian, lived experience. Christian identity is formed "out there," so to speak, or, as Heidegger repeatedly affirmed, the basic state of *Dasein* is *being-in-the-world*.[4]

Admittedly, this notion of identity formation as a dynamic, performance-driven process, is neither original nor unexpected. As we observed in our literature review, recent theoretical and qualitative studies dealing with the topic of identity have consistently presented a similar assessment. However, despite the proliferation of this perspective across numerous

---

3. Husserl, *Ideas*, 124–28.
4. Heidegger, *Being and Time*, 78–90.

Conclusion: Retrospect and Prospect

disciplines, it seems there remains a deep-seated penchant among evangelical missiologists to understand Christian identity formation in cross-cultural contexts in categorically essentialist terms. The utilization of comparative religion or worldview theory, especially, have been instrumental in presenting a static perspective of the religious self, thus leading to oversimplified and hasty judgments concerning syncretism, faulty beliefs, or an "un-Christian" motivational structure.[5] Besides being a-contextual and cognitivistic, these methodologies essentially flatten that which is inherently complex and staticize that which is inherently dynamic. A better approach is one that carefully considers the processual nature of conversion and identity transformation, understands the reality and necessity of "orthodox hybridities"[6] in "becoming Christian," reveals the complex motivational-structure underlying contextual performance, and allows for a variance in expression of authentic Christian identity within a multitude of contexts.

2. Religious identity formation within contexts of marginalization is a profoundly socio-religious phenomenon

Within the field of religious conversion, several recent, qualitative studies have bemoaned the tendency of contemporary scholarship to prioritize the social, political, or cultural dimensions of conversion over, and often to the neglect of, the spiritual or religious dimension.[7] The value of phenomenology, for these authors, has been its ability to reveal the complexities inherent in religious experience without reducing the phenomenon to what may be understood via the prevailing theories of the social sciences. The same may be said regarding the phenomenon of in-marginality. How religious identity is formed within contexts of marginalization is, as we noted above, deeply complex. To highlight only the social dimension, as is the tendency in the social sciences, or only the religious dimension, as is the tendency in theological and ministerial studies, is to sever that which is inherently inseparable and, therefore, to miss the "manifold of aspects"[8] appertaining to the phenomenon.

---

5. For examples of this oversimplification in the Thai context, see Dahlfred, "Animism"; Taylor, "Gaps in Beliefs"; Hughes, "Christianity and Buddhism."

6. Zehner, "Orthodox Hybridities."

7. See, for example, Iyadurai, *Transformative Religious Experience*, 2–3; Radford, *Religious Identity and Social Change*, 1–5.

8. Husserl, *Logical Investigations*, 155–57.

On the one hand, religious identity is always and already a social identity. Being Christian or being Buddhist is primordially a shared mode of being-in-the-world. As a result, issues of obligation, respect, honor and shame, tradition, belonging, testimony, kinship, etc. are essential to the phenomenon, and, consequently, require the appropriate use of the social sciences to elucidate understanding. On the other hand, religious experience, whether in the form of hierophanies or religious understandings, form the ground and motivation for identity transformation within contexts of marginalization. As we have seen, to love and be loved by God and to encounter Him mystically in vertical experience not only initiates religious alternation, but also provides the primary mechanisms by which converts may then cope with the lived experience of displacement. Therefore, we may say that the phenomenon of in-marginality resides at the point of intersection between the social and religious components of alternation as occurring, at least, within allocentric, cultural contexts. That is, marginalization arises from and personal identity is formed amid the ongoing dialectic of separating and re-integrating social and religious identities.

3. Theological and ministerial solutions for the successful negotiation of Christian identity within contexts of marginalization must remain particularly attuned to concrete, lived experience

Following from points one and two, we may now affirm the integral value of phenomenological inquiry for theological and ministerial studies as it relates especially to Christian identity formation within contexts of marginalization. As noted above, there resides a tendency in evangelical missiology to reduce Christian identity to static snapshots of an individual's worldview or stated religious beliefs. Besides reducing the complexity inherent in religious identity, this approach concomitantly de-situates the believing soul from concrete, embodied, lived experience, re-situating him or her within an a-contextual and disembodied realm of ideas to be cognitively evaluated by an "objective," and usually Western, Cartesian observer. Sadly, a similar methodology is often true of evangelical theology which, while properly focused on the text of Scripture, tends to produce formulations of the ideal type, "Christian," without any consideration of how that identity is performed in actual, lifeworld experience. These methodologies beg the question, what is Christian identity outside of the embodied, lived performance of those who profess to be Christian? Has evangelical missiology and theology, in their laudable efforts to be

Conclusion: Retrospect and Prospect

gospel-centered, instead produced a docetic Christianity, dangerously divorced from created, embodied realities?[9]

By saying this, I am certainly not decrying the proper place of a Bible and gospel-centered missiology and theology, nor am I advocating for a quasi-relativistic theological outlook that assumes what is, is what ought to be. Instead, I am appealing for the fundamental and thorough re-integration of Scripture and life, gospel and experience. If all theological formulations are contextual, then lived experience must at least have a place in the conversation, even if relegated to the "back seat," in order to ensure that theological and ministerial formulations are successful in generating consistent and appropriate religious transformation. Without a doubt, Christian identity is not one-size-fits-all. Not only may we observe genetic variability in the relative growth of Christian identity in individuals, we may also observe, along with many majority world theologians, that, to put it succinctly, context matters. If it is indeed the case that religious identity is complex and processual, that it exhibits thoroughgoing and inseparable socio-religious components, and that it varies, to some extent, based on circumstances and setting, then phenomenology, by attuning the scholar to concrete experience as lived, is an essential element to the production of effective theological and ministerial solutions to in-marginality.

SIGNIFICANCE AND LIMITATIONS

In light of this retrospect and prospect, I would like to present briefly what I believe to be the significance and limitations of this research for Thai ministry contexts. Regarding significance, as we have noted throughout this book, issues of social identity form the primary hindrances to the formation and maintenance of Christian identity in Thailand. The common belief that "to be Thai is to be Buddhist" has produced strong social pressures toward religious conformity, effectively discouraging conversion and presenting the possibility for reversion or the loss of faith. By providing a phenomenological interpretation of how actual Thai Christians are navigating their social identities within contexts of marginalization, I have not only identified the points of tension between social and religious identities in Thailand, but I have also highlighted workable solutions that are currently being performed by Thai converts. I would suggest, therefore, that the Thai church may appropriately

---

9. Of course, I am not the first to express concern regarding the a-contextual, cognitivistic nature of much of Christian theology and missiology. For a more thorough discussion, see Smith, *Desiring the Kingdom*.

enhance its evangelism and discipleship methods, that is, make them more contextually relevant, by closely orienting them to these findings. Revised methods must pursue the elaboration of a genuine Thai Christian identity, not simply by constructing a list of "do's" and "don'ts," but by tapping into the processual and performance-driven nature of identity formation in general. This should include the understanding that identity formation is a lengthy process whereby converts are not only increasingly immersed in the mythos, narratives, habitus, and "thinking as usual" of the sacred community, but also increasingly equipped to harmonize their altered self-understandings with their ongoing ethnic, community, and kinship social identities. By remaining keenly attuned to real, lifeworld contexts, then, practitioners may better guide Thai converts in the fluid navigation of both authentic Thainess and authentic Christianness.

While the significance of this work for enhancing ministerial practice in Thailand is manifold, I do recognize the limitations inherent in a phenomenological study of this nature. First, I have not been able to provide a historical perspective on the formation of Christian identity in Thailand, especially the considerable role of foreign missionaries, which may contribute greatly to our understanding of how and why Thai Christians navigate their marginalized identities in the ways they do. Second, while touching on biblical literature, my purpose has not been to produce a "biblical theology of Christian identity" for the Thai context, something which is certainly needed. Third, my research has solely focused on Thai Christian identity in Chiang Mai, a city known for containing the highest concentration of Christians in Thailand. More work is required to understand variances in displacement experiences and negotiation strategies among Thai Christians from other regions of the country, both rural and urban. Finally, as with all phenomenological studies, this book is, by nature, more descriptive than prescriptive. However, given the urgency for enhancing conversion and discipleship efforts in Thailand, formulating a properly Thai Christian identity, and assisting converts with performing that identity, prescription is necessary. While it has not been my purpose to prescribe, I strongly encourage Thai theologians, pastors, and missionaries working in Thailand to utilize this research when formulating practicable and biblical solutions for the successful negotiation of Christian identity in Thailand. Indeed, I would suggest that issues of religious and social identity, grounded in careful phenomenological analysis, ought to form the backbone for the production and enactment of ministry strategies throughout Thailand.

Conclusion: Retrospect and Prospect

RECOMMENDATIONS FOR FURTHER RESEARCH

Finally, to promote the furthering of scholarship in this fecund and critical field of Christian identity formation within contexts of marginalization, I would like to briefly present a few recommendations for further research.

1. This research has focused on the lived experience of Thai Christians who have converted from Buddhism to Christianity as adults within the Thai lifeworld. While the meanings implicit in their pre-reflective narratives may align, in many ways, with that of Christians in other parts of the world, we would expect that there exist significant variances from marginalization narratives within Islamic, Hindu, or atheistic contexts. Therefore, I perceive a need to conduct phenomenological research on identity formation in other contexts of marginalization, allowing for the possibility of comparison analysis by theologians and practitioners.

2. In the field of theological anthropology, I would suggest that the phenomenological interpretations presented in this study may contribute to ongoing discussions concerning the nature of the image of God and the essence of Christian identity. How does identity negotiation as complex, processual, performance-driven, and contextual align with theological theorizations of what constitutes Christianness? How may we understand image of God and Christian conversion in light of preexisting social identities and modes of being-in-the-world? How may concrete, lived experience assist in the production of local anthropologies?

3. In the fields of missiology and pastoral theology, the material of this book may aid in the production of context-appropriate solutions for evangelism and discipleship that avoids a one-size-fits-all approach. This may, perhaps, be the most pressing need for further scholarship as it appears that many missionaries and church leaders working in contexts of marginalization may be dangerously out of touch with the everyday, lived experience of their parishioners, and, as a result, may be producing solutions that are impracticable for real-life performance.

4. Finally, as the West faces the increasing reality of the church's marginalized existence in a post-Christian, post-secular environment, how might Western Christians navigate their identities in this new and strange world of marginalization? Further, in what ways may Western

Christians learn from the lived experience of their Asian brothers and sisters who have, for centuries, performed their subordinate, religious identities in ways that effectively maintain a sense of religious exclusivism on the one hand, and preexisting social identities and group memberships on the other? Answers to these questions are of urgent concern for the Western church, and, therefore, represent a significant arena for further study.

In this book, we have explored the deep meanings implicit in the pre-reflective, lived experience of Thai Christians as they face a marginalized existence. It has been my intent throughout this research to re-attune both myself and the reader to the "thing itself" by moving us beyond the taken-for-granted understandings of everyday life so that we may, once again, recognize that Christian identity is, first and foremost, lived by real people in real lifeworld contexts. Indeed, it is only in lived experience that we truly understand the depth of Paul's profound and timeless statement regarding the essential nature of religious identity transformation: "If anyone is in Christ, he is a new creature; the old things passed away; behold, new things have come" (2 Cor 5:17).

Appendix on Interview Questions

INTERVIEW QUESTIONS WERE CHOSEN with three priorities in mind. First, I selected questions that would reveal the narrative structure of the participants' conversion and marginalization experiences, thus aligning with the original experiences as lived and allowing for a base comparison analysis between the participants' pre-conversion "home" and their post-conversion displacement. Consequently, questions followed a loose, three-fold temporal structure of pre-conversion, conversion, and post-conversion. Second, I selected questions that prioritized the procurement of lived experience descriptions in narratival form rather than opinions, personal views, or interpretations. Interpretations or opinions, however, were included toward the end of the interviews so to reveal not only the experiences as lived but also the participants' understanding of the meanings inherent in those experiences. Finally, while seeking a diachronic, biographical orientation to participant narratives, I also organized the questions per a synchronic, thematic structure to adequately disclose the multiple lifeworld perspectives appertaining to the phenomenon. Therefore, the interviews oscillated between a thematic and temporal flow, a process that was navigated both by the interview guide and by the participants themselves. See chapter 4 for a description of how the data was processed and analyzed.

The interview questions were as follows:

1. *Conversion*
    a. In as much detail as possible, tell me about how you became a Christian?

Appendix on Interview Questions

    b. Did you find Christianity strange at first?

    c. Tell me about your baptism.

    d. Was it hard to leave Buddhism?

2. *Family*

    a. What did your family think of Christians when you were growing up?

    b. What happened when your parents first heard about your conversion?

    c. (If married) What happened when your spouse heard about your decision?

    d. How has your family treated you since your conversion? Example.

    e. What is it like when you go home now?

3. *Village*

    a. Do people in your village know you are a Christian? How did they react? Example.

    b. When you go back to your village, do you believe your faith has changed the way you fit into that community? Example.

    c. Do you feel separate from Thai people or alone at times? Left out?

4. *Friendships*

    a. How have your friendships changed since you became a Christian? Example.

    b. Tell me a story of a friend who helped you during this time.

    c. Tell me a story of a friend who did not help or abandoned you.

5. *Festivals and Ceremonies*

    a. Do you ever go to the Buddhist temple with family/friends?

    b. How do you feel during a Buddhist funeral or wedding? Example.

    c. Do you participate in Buddhist holidays like Loi Kratong? Example.

    d. How do family members and friends view your participation or non-participation in Buddhist festivals and ceremonies? Example.

Appendix on Interview Questions

   e. Are Christian holidays like Easter or Christmas important to you?

   f. Reconstruct an experience of a Christian holiday that was particularly meaningful to you as a Christian.

6. *Work*

   a. How has your work changed since you became a Christian? Example.

7. *Church*

   a. How has your church helped you in adjusting to your new life as a Christian?

   b. How often are you with church members each week? What do you do with them?

   c. What do you appreciate the most about church services and activities?

   d. Has the pastor or church leadership been important in your growth?

   e. What teaching of the Bible has helped you most in your life?

   f. What makes Jesus so attractive to you?

8. *Spirituality*

   a. Has there ever been a time when you acted like a Buddhist after you became a Christian?

   b. Do you ever hide your faith from friends, colleagues, or family?

   c. Have you ever thought about going back to Buddhism or your former life?

   d. How would you compare your spiritual life in Buddhism and Christianity?

   e. What are some of the changes in your life after conversion?

   f. How would you describe God in light of your experience?

   g. How has God helped you since you became a Christian?

   h. How does God speak to you and guide you? Do you feel Him with you?

Appendix on Interview Questions

    i. In 1 Peter, Christians are called "aliens and strangers." What do you think this means? Have you ever felt like an alien or stranger?

    j. Favorite verse, favorite song?

9. *Nation and Culture*

    a. What is it that makes you different from other Thais?

    b. Has there been a time when being a Christian meant doing something differently than what Thais would normally do?

    c. Have you ever felt ashamed of being a Christian?

    d. Have you ever experienced what you would call persecution?

    e. What do you think of the phrase, "To be Thai is to be Buddhist"?

    f. By becoming a Christian, do you feel in any way less "Thai"? Example.

    g. Some say Christianity is a foreign religion. Has anyone told you that? Have you ever felt like a foreigner here in Thailand because of your faith?

    h. Is it hard to be a Christian in Thailand?

Bibliography

Amara, Pongsapich. *Traditional and Changing Thai World View*. Bangkok: Chulalongkorn University Press, 1998.
The Ante-Nicene Fathers. Edited by Alexander Roberts and James Donaldson. 10 vols. 1885–1887. Reprint, Peabody, MA: Hendrickson, 1994.
Applebaum, Marc H. "Intentionality and Narrativity in Phenomenology Psychological Research: Reflections on Husserl and Ricoeur." *The Indo-Pacific Journal of Phenomenology* 14.2 (2014) 1–19.
Aspers, Patrik. "Empirical Phenomenology: A Qualitative Research Approach (the Cologne Seminars)." *The Indo-Pacific Journal of Phenomenology* 9.2 (2009) 1–12.
"'Assume' or 'Presume'?" *Lexico* (blog), 2019. Online. https://www.lexico.com/grammar/assume-or-presume.
Baker, Christopher John, and Phongpaichit Pasuk. *A History of Thailand*. 3rd ed. Port Melbourne, Australia: Cambridge University Press, 2014.
Bandhumedha, Navavan. "Thai Views of Man as a Social Being." In *Traditional and Changing Thai World View*, edited by Pongsapich Amara, 86–109. Bangkok: Chulalongkorn University Press, 1998.
Barbour, John D. *Versions of Deconversion: Autobiography and the Loss of Faith*. Studies in Religion and Culture. Charlottesville: University Press of Virginia, 1994.
Bartholomew, Craig G. *Where Mortals Dwell: A Christian View of Place for Today*. Grand Rapids: Baker Academic, 2011.
Barua, Archana. "Husserl, Heidegger, and the Transcendental Dimension of Phenomenology." *The Indo-Pacific Journal of Phenomenology* 7.1 (2007) 1–10.
———. *Phenomenology of Religion*. Lanham, MD: Lexington, 2009.
Bechtler, Steven Richard. *Following in His Steps: Suffering, Community, and Christology in 1 Peter*. Dissertation Series/Society of Biblical Literature 162. Atlanta: Scholars, 1998.
Bediako, Kwame. *Theology and Identity: The Impact of Culture Upon Christian Thought in the Second Century and in Modern Africa*. Eugene, OR: Wipf and Stock, 1999.
Beech, Nic. "Liminality and the Practices of Identity Reconstruction." *Human Relations* 64.2 (2011) 285–302.

Bibliography

Behnke, Elizabeth A. "Body." In *Encyclopedia of Phenomenology*, edited by Lester E. Embree, 66–71. Contributions to Phenomenology 18. Dordrecht: Kluwer Academic, 1997.

Bengtsson, Jan. "With the Lifeworld as Ground: A Research Approach for Empirical Research in Education—The Gothenburg Tradition." Special Edition of *The Indo-Pacific Journal of Phenomenology* 13 (2013) 1–12.

Berg, Jan Hendrik van den. *A Different Existence: Principles of Phenomenological Psychopathology*. Pittsburgh: Duquesne University Press, 1972.

Berger, Peter L. *The Heretical Imperative: Contemporary Possibilities of Religious Affirmation*. Garden City, NY: Anchor, 1979.

———. *The Sacred Canopy: Elements of a Sociological Theory of Religion*. New York: Anchor, 1990.

Berger, Peter L., et al. *The Homeless Mind: Modernization and Consciousness*. New York: Vintage, 1974.

Berger, Peter L., and Thomas Luckmann. *The Social Construction of Reality: A Treatise in the Sociology of Knowledge*. New York: Anchor, 1990.

Bevans, Stephen B. *Models of Contextual Theology*. Faith and Cultures Series. Maryknoll, NY: Orbis, 1992.

Blattner, William D. *Heidegger's Being and Time: A Reader's Guide*. Continuum Reader's Guides. New York: Continuum, 2006.

Bollnow, O. F. "Lived-Space." *Philosophy Today* 5.1 (1961) 31–39.

Bolt, John, et al., eds. *The J. H. Bavinck Reader*. Grand Rapids: Eerdmans, 2013.

Bouma-Prediger, Steven, and Brian J. Walsh. *Beyond Homelessness: Christian Faith in a Culture of Displacement*. Grand Rapids: Eerdmans, 2008.

Bourdieu, Pierre. *The Logic of Practice*. Stanford, CA: Stanford University Press, 1990.

Boyarin, Daniel. *Border Lines: The Partition of Judaeo-Christianity*. Divinations. Philadelphia, PA: University of Pennsylvania Press, 2004.

———. *Dying for God: Martyrdom and the Making of Christianity and Judaism*. Figurae. Stanford, CA: Stanford University Press, 1999.

Bradfield, Bruce. "Examining the Lived World: The Place of Phenomenology in Psychiatry and Clinical Psychology." *The Indo-Pacific Journal of Phenomenology* 7.1 (2007) 1–8.

Brewer, Marilynn B., and Wendi Gardner. "Who Is This 'We'? Levels of Collective Identity and Self Representations." *Journal of Personality and Social Psychology* 71.1 (1996) 83–93.

Bruijne, Jurjen de. "Conversion: Discovering the Conversion of Thai Buddhists Towards Christianity." BA thesis, Christelijke Hogeschool Ede, 2010.

Buckley, R. Philip. "Edmund Husserl." In *Encyclopedia of Phenomenology*, edited by Lester E. Embree, 326–32. Contributions to Phenomenology 18. Dordrecht: Kluwer Academic, 1997.

Buell, Denise Kimber. "Race and Universalism in Early Christianity." *Journal of Early Christian Studies* 10.4 (2002) 429–68.

———. *Why This New Race: Ethnic Reasoning in Early Christianity*. Gender, Theory, and Religion. New York: Columbia University Press, 2005.

Bureau of Democracy, Human Rights, and Labor (BDHRL). "International Religious Freedom Report, Thailand (2005)." *US Department of State*, 2005. Online. https://2009-2017.state.gov/j/drl/rls/irf/2005/51531.htm.

Bushur, James G. "Ignatius of Antioch's Letter to the Romans: The Passionate Confession of Christian Identity." *Logia* 24.2 (2015) 13–18.

Bibliography

Butler-Kisber, Lynn. *Qualitative Inquiry: Thematic, Narrative, and Arts-Informed Perspectives*. Los Angeles: Sage, 2010.

Campbell, William S. "Gentile Identity and Transformation in Christ According to Paul." In *The Making of Christianity: Conflicts, Contacts, and Constructions; Essays in Honor of Bengt Holmberg*, edited by Bengt Holmberg, et al., 23–56. Coniectanea Biblica New Testament Series 47. Winona Lake, IN: Eisenbrauns, 2012.

Carlisle, Steven. "Creative Sincerity: Thai Buddhist Karma Narratives and the Grounding of Truths." *Ethos* 40.3 (2012) 317–40.

Casey, Edward S. *Getting Back into Place: Toward a Renewed Understanding of the Place-World*. Studies in Continental Thought. Bloomington: Indiana University Press, 1993.

Cassaniti, Julia. "Agency and the Other: The Role of Agency for the Importance of Belief in Buddhist and Christian Traditions." *Ethos* 40.3 (2012) 297–316.

Cassaniti, Julia, and Tanya Marie Luhrmann. "Encountering the Supernatural: A Phenomenological Account of Mind." *Religion and Society: Advances in Research* 2.1 (2011) 37–53.

Castelli, Elizabeth A. *Martyrdom and Memory: Early Christian Culture Making*. Gender, Theory, and Religion. New York: Columbia University Press, 2004.

Chadwick, Henry. *The Early Church*. Vol. 1 of *The Pelican History of the Church*. Harmondsworth, UK: Penguin, 1967.

Chan, Simon. *Grassroots Asian Theology: Thinking the Faith from the Ground Up*. Downers Grove, IL: InterVarsity, 2014.

Chidester, David. "The Poetics and Politics of Sacred Space: Towards a Critical Phenomenology of Religion." In *From the Sacred to the Divine: A New Phenomenological Approach*, edited by Anna-Teresa Tymieniecka, 211–31. Analecta Husserliana 43. Dordrecht: Kluwer Academic, 1994.

Chinawong, Kummool, and Herbert R. Swanson. "Religion and the Community Formation in Northern Thailand: The Case of Christianity in Nan Province." Paper presented at the Fifth International Conference on Thai Studies, 1993. *HeRB: Herb's Research Bulletin* 4 (2002) 5–30.

Christofferson, Ethan J. *Negotiating Identity: Exploring Tensions between Being Hakka and Being Christian in Northwestern Taiwan*. American Society of Missiology Monograph Series 13. Kindle ed. Eugene, OR: Pickwick, 2012.

Churchill, Scott D. "Considerations for Teaching a Phenomenological Approach to Psychological Research." *Journal of Phenomenological Psychology* 21.1 (1990) 46–67.

Coats, Karen. "Identity." In *Keywords for Children's Literature*, edited by Philip Nel and Lissa Paul, 109–12. New York: New York University Press, 2011.

Cohen, Erik. "Christianity and Buddhism in Thailand: The 'Battle of the Axes' and the 'Contest of Power.'" *Social Compass* 38.2 (1991) 115–40.

Colona, Jacklyn, and Guillermo J. Grenier. "Structuring Liminality: Theorizing the Creation and Maintenance of the Cuban Exile Identity." *Ethnic Studies Review* 33.2 (2010) 43–61.

Costelloe, Martin J. "Acts of the Martyrs." In *New Catholic Encyclopedia*, edited by Catholic University of America, 90–94. Detroit: Gale, 2003.

Cox, James L. *An Introduction to the Phenomenology of Religion*. New York: Continuum, 2010.

Bibliography

Crook, Zeba. "Agents of Apostasy, Delegates of Disafilliation." In *Conversion and Initiation in Antiquity: Shifting Identities, Creating Change*, edited by Birgitte Bøgh, 119–34. Early Christianity in the Context of Antiquity 16. New York: Peter Lang, 2014.

Csordas, Thomas J. "Embodiment and Cultural Phenomenology." In *Perspectives on Embodiment: The Intersections of Nature and Culture*, edited by Gail Weiss and Honi Fern Haber, 143–62. New York: Routledge, 1999.

———. *The Sacred Self: A Cultural Phenomenology of Charismatic Healing*. Berkeley: University of California Press, 1994.

Dahlberg, Karin. "The Essence of Essences: The Search for Meaning Structures in Phenomenological Analysis of Lifeworld Phenomena." *International Journal of Qualitative Studies on Health and Well-being* 1.1 (2006) 11–19.

Dahlberg, Karin, et al. *Reflective Lifeworld Research*. Lund: Studentlitteratur, 2008.

Dahlfred, Karl. "Animism, Syncretism, and Christianity in Thailand." Unpublished paper, 2011. Online. http://2sowers.com/Assets/Animism.pdf.

Davis, John. "Poles Apart? Contextualizing the Gospel." Unpublished paper, 1993. Online. http://www.thaicrc.com/collect/MIS/index/assoc/D5672.dir/5672.pdf.

Denzin, Norman K., and Yvonna S. Lincoln. *The Sage Handbook of Qualitative Research*. 4th ed. Thousand Oaks, CA: Sage, 2011.

deSilva, David Arthur. "Despising Shame: A Cultural-Anthropological Investigation of the Epistle to the Hebrews." *Journal of Biblical Literature* 113.3 (1994) 439–61.

———. *Despising Shame: Honor Discourse and Community Maintenance in the Epistle to the Hebrews*. Dissertation Series/Society of Biblical Literature 152. Atlanta: Scholars, 1995.

———. *Honor, Patronage, Kinship, and Purity: Unlocking New Testament Culture*. Downers Grove, IL: InterVarsity, 2000.

Devenish, Stuart. "An Applied Method for Undertaking Phenomonological Explication of Interview Transcripts." *The Indo-Pacific Journal of Phenomenology* 2.1 (2002) 1–20.

———. "The Dancing Sharma: A Review of 'to the Things Themselves.'" *The Indo-Pacific Journal of Phenomenology* 2.2 (2002) 1–5.

———. *Knowing Otherwise: The Phenomenology of Meaning Change in Christian Conversion*. Riga: Lambert Academic, 2011.

———. *Ordinary Saints: Lessons in the Art of Giving Away Your Life*. Eugene, OR: Cascade, 2017.

———. *Seeing and Believing: The Eye of Faith in a Visual Culture*. Eugene, OR: Wipf and Stock, 2012.

"Dharma." In *The Princeton Dictionary of Buddhism*, edited by Robert E. J. Buswell and Donald S. J. Lopez. Princeton, NJ: Princeton University Press, 2013. Online. http://0-search.credoreference.com.eaglelink.cornerstone.edu/content/entry/prdb/dharma/0?institutionId=6459.

Dinkins, Larry. "Towards Contextualized Creeds: A Perspective from Buddhist Thailand." *International Journal of Frontier Missiology* 27.1 (2010) 5–9.

Dreyfus, Hubert L. "Overcoming the Myth of the Mental." *Topoi* 25.1–2 (2006) 43–49.

Du Bois, W. E. B. *The Souls of Black Folk*. Edited by Brent Hayes Edwards. Oxford World's Classics. Oxford: Oxford University Press, 2007.

DuBose, J. Todd. "The Phenomenology of Bereavement, Grief, and Mourning." *Journal of Religion and Health* 36.4 (1997) 367–74.

Duling, Denis C. "Matthew and Marginality." *HTS Teologiese Studies/Theological Studies* 51.2 (1995) 358–87.

Duméry, Henry, and Louis K. Dupre. *Faith and Reflection*. New York: Herder and Herder, 1968.

Dunn, James D. G. *Neither Jew nor Greek: A Contested Identity*. Christianity in the Making 3. Grand Rapids: Eerdmans, 2015.

Dupré, Louis K. *A Dubious Heritage: Studies in the Philosophy of Religion after Kant*. New York: Paulist, 1977.

———. *Religious Mystery and Rational Reflection: Excursions in the Phenomemology and Philosophy of Religion*. Grand Rapids: Eerdmans, 1998.

Duranti, Alessandro. "Husserl, Intersubjectivity, and Anthropology." *Anthropological Theory* 10.1–2 (2010) 16–35.

Eliade, Mircea. *The Sacred and the Profane: The Nature of Religion*. New York: Harcourt, 1959.

———. "The World, the City, the House." In *Experience of the Sacred: Readings in the Phenomenology of Religion*, edited by Sumner B. Twiss and Walter H. Conser, 189–99. Hanover, NH: University Press of New England, 1992.

Ellemers, Naomi, et al. "Self and Social Identity." *Annual Review of Psychology* 53 (2002) 161–86.

Elliott, John Hall. *A Home for the Homeless: A Social-Scientific Criticism of 1 Peter, Its Situation and Strategy*. Minneapolis, MN: Fortress, 1990.

Embree, Lester. "The Continuation of Phenomenology: A Fifth Period?" *The Indo-Pacific Journal of Phenomenology* 1.1 (2001) 1–7.

Esler, Philip Francis. *Conflict and Identity in Romans: The Social Setting of Paul's Letter*. Minneapolis, MN: Fortress, 2003.

———. "Family Imagery and Christian Identity in Gal 5:13 to 6:10." In *Constructing Early Christian Families: Family as Social Reality and Metaphor*, edited by Halvor Moxnes, 121–49. New York: Routledge, 1997.

Falque, Emmanuel, and Reuben Shank. *Crossing the Rubicon: The Borderlands of Philosophy and Theology*. Perspectives in Continental Philosophy. Kindle ed. New York: Fordham University Press, 2016.

Farley, Edward. *Ecclesial Man: A Social Phenomenology of Faith and Reality*. Philadelphia: Fortress, 1975.

Fiddes, Paul S. "Ecclesiology and Ethnography: Two Disciplines, Two Worlds?" In *Perspectives on Ecclesiology and Ethnography*, edited by Pete Ward, 13–35. Studies in Ecclesiology and Ethnography. Grand Rapids: Eerdmans, 2012.

Fine, Michelle, and Selcuk R. Sirin. "Theorizing Hyphenated Selves: Researching Youth Development in and across Contentious Political Contexts." *Social and Personality Psychology Compass* 1.1 (2007) 16–38.

Finlay, Linda. "A Dance between the Reduction and Reflexivity: Explicating the 'Phenomenological Psychological Attitude.'" *Journal of Phenomenological Psychology* 39.1 (2008) 1–32.

Flanders, Christopher L. *About Face: Rethinking Face for Twenty-First-Century Mission*. American Society of Missiology Monograph Series 9. Eugene, OR: Pickwick, 2011.

Flinn, Frank K. "Conversion: The Pentecostal and Charismatic Experience." In *Religious Conversion: Contemporary Practices and Controversies*, edited by Christopher Lamb and M. Darrol Bryant, 51–74. Issues in Contemporary Religion. New York: Cassell, 1999.

Fordham, Graham S. "Ancestors and Christians in Rural Northern Thailand." *The Journal of the Siam Society* 81.1 (1993) 117–29.

Bibliography

Freeman, Melissa, and Mark D. Vagle. "Grafting the Intentional Relation of Hermeneutics and Phenomenology in Linguisticality." *Qualitative Inquiry* 19.9 (2013) 725–35.
Gadamer, Hans-Georg. *Philosophical Hermeneutics*. Berkeley: University of California Press, 1976.
Geertz, Clifford. *The Interpretation of Cultures: Selected Essays*. New York: Basic, 1973.
———. *Local Knowledge: Further Essays in Interpretive Anthropology*. New York: Basic, 1983.
Gennep, Arnold van. *The Rites of Passage*. Chicago: University of Chicago Press, 1960.
Giorgi, Amedeo. "Difficulties Encountered in the Application of the Phenomenological Method in the Social Sciences." *The Indo-Pacific Journal of Phenomenology* 8.1 (2008) 1–9.
———. "The Theory, Practice, and Evaluation of the Phenomenological Method as a Qualitative Research Procedure." *Journal of Phenomenological Psychology* 28.2 (1997) 235–60.
Giroux, Henry A. *Border Crossings: Cultural Workers and the Politics of Education*. 2nd ed. New York: Routledge, 2005.
Given, Lisa M. *The Sage Encyclopedia of Qualitative Research Methods*. 2 vols. Los Angeles: Sage, 2008.
Goldberg, Chad Alan. "Robert Park's Marginal Man: The Career of a Concept in American Sociology." *Laboratorium* 4.2 (2012) 199–217.
Gonzalez, Justo L. *The Story of Christianity*. 2nd ed. Peabody, MA: Prince, 2010.
Goodman, Nelson. *Ways of Worldmaking*. Indianapolis, IN: Hackett, 1978.
Grant, G. Kathleen, and Jeffrey R. Breese. "Marginality Theory and the African American Student." *Sociology of Education* 70.3 (1997) 192–205.
Groark, Kevin P. "Toward a Cultural Phenomenology of Intersubjectivity: The Extended Relational Field of the Tzotzil Maya of Highland Chiapas, Mexico." *Language and Communication* 33.3 (2013) 278–91.
Gushiken, Kevin M. "Is a Christian Identity Compatible with an Ethnic Identity? An Exploration of Ethnic Identity Negotiation Influences and Implications for Multiethnic Congregations." *Christian Education Journal* 11.1 (2014) 33–51.
Gustafson, James W. "Syncretistic Thai Religion and Church Growth." Unpublished paper, 1971. Online. http://www.thaicrc.com/collect/MIS/index/assoc/D1743.dir/1743.pdf.
Haney, Kathleen M. *Intersubjectivity Revisited: Phenomenology and the Other*. Series in Continental Thought 20. Athens, OH: Ohio University Press, 1994.
Hart, Addison Hodges. *Strangers and Pilgrims Once More: Being Disciples of Jesus in a Post-Christendom World*. Grand Rapids: Eerdmans, 2014.
Hart, James G. *The Person and the Common Life: Studies in a Husserlian Social Ethics*. Phaenomenologica 126. Dordrecht: Kluwer Academic, 1992.
Haug, Kari S., and Knut Holter. "No Graven Image? Reading the Second Commandment in a Thai Context." *Asia Journal of Theology* 14.1 (2000) 20–36.
Hegedus, Tim. "Naming Christians in Antiquity." *Studies in Religion/Sciences Religieuses* 33.2 (2004) 173–90.
Heidegger, Martin. *Being and Time*. Translated by John Macquarrie and Edward Robinson. New York: Harper and Row, 1962.
———. "Building, Dwelling, Thinking." Translated by Albert Hofstadter. In *Poetry, Language, Thought*, 141–60. New York: Harper and Row, 1971.

Bibliography

Held, Klaus. "The Finitude of the World: Phenomenology in Transition from Husserl to Heidegger." In *Ethics and Danger: Essays on Heidegger and Continental Thought*, edited by Arleen B. Dallery, et al., 187–98. Selected Studies in Phenomenology and Existential Philosophy 17. Albany: State University of New York Press, 1992.

———. "World, Emptiness, Nothingness: A Phenomenological Approach to the Religious Tradition of Japan." *Human Studies* 20.2 (1997) 153–67.

Helming, Brent. "Your Beloved." Lyrics. Mercy/Vineyard, 1996. Online. https://vineyardsongs.com/songs/your-beloved.

Hogg, Michael A. "Social Identity Theory." In *Encyclopedia of Identity*, edited by Ronald L. Jackson, 749–53. Los Angeles: Sage, 2010.

Hogg, Michael A., and Dominic Abrams. *Social Identifications: A Social Psychology of Intergroup Relations and Group Processes*. London: Routledge, 1998.

Hogg, Michael A., et al. "A Tale of Two Theories: A Critical Comparison of Identity Theory with Social Identity Theory." *Social Psychology Quarterly* 58.4 (1995) 255–69.

Holmes, Urban Tigner, III. "Liminality and Liturgy." *Worship* 47.7 (1973) 386–97.

Holroyd, Ann E. McManus. "Interpretive Hermeneutic Phenomenology: Clarifying Understanding." *The Indo-Pacific Journal of Phenomenology* 7.2 (2007) 1–12.

Hornsey, Matthew J. "Social Identity Theory and Self-Categorization Theory: A Historical Review." *Social and Personality Psychology Compass* 2.1 (2008) 204–22.

Horrell, David G. *Becoming Christian: Essays on 1 Peter and the Making of Christian Identity*. Early Christianity in Context 394. New York: Bloomsbury, 2013.

Hourigan, Ryan M. "The Invisible Student: Understanding Social Identity Construction within Performing Ensembles." *Music Educators Journal* 95.4 (2009) 34–38.

Hovemyr, Anders. "Towards a Theology of the Incarnation in the Thai Context." *East Asia Journal of Theology* 1.2 (1983) 79–84.

Howat, Holly. "Marginality." In *Encyclopedia of Social Deviance*, edited by Craig J. Forsyth and Heith Copes, 412–13. Thousand Oaks, CA: Sage, 2014.

Huebner, Chris K. "Between Victory and Victimhood: Reflections on Culture and Martyrdom." *Direction* 34.2 (2005) 228–40.

Hughes, Philip J. "Christianity and Buddhism in Thailand." *Journal of the Siam Society* 73 (1985) 23–41.

———. "Theology and Culture: Implications for Methodology of a Case Study in Northern Thailand." *Colloquium* 18.1 (1985) 43–53.

Hurtado, Larry W. *Why on Earth Did Anyone Become a Christian in the First Three Centuries?* Milwaukee, WI: Marquette University Press, 2016.

Husserl, Edmund. *Cartesian Meditations*. The Hague: M. Nijhoff, 1965.

———. *The Crisis of European Sciences and Transcendental Phenomenology: An Introduction to Phenomenological Philosophy*. Northwestern University Studies in Phenomenology and Existential Philosophy. Evanston, IL: Northwestern University Press, 1970.

———. *Ideas: General Introduction to Pure Phenomenology*. Muirhead Library of Philosophy. New York: Allen and Unwin, 1969.

———. *Logical Investigations*. Edited by Dermot Moran. International Library of Philosophy. New York: Routledge, 2001.

———. *The Phenomenology of Internal Time-Consciousness*. Bloomington: Indiana University Press, 1964.

Iyadurai, Joshua. *Transformative Religious Experience: A Phenomenological Understanding of Religious Conversion*. Eugene, OR: Pickwick, 2015.

Bibliography

Jacobsen, Anders-Christian. "Identity Formation through Catechetical Teaching in Early Christianity." In *Conversion and Initiation in Antiquity: Shifting Identities, Creating Change*, edited by Birgitte Bøgh, 203–24. Early Christianity in the Context of Antiquity 16. New York: Peter Lang, 2014.

James, William. *The Varieties of Religious Experience: A Study in Human Nature*. New York: Simon and Schuster, 2004.

Jenkins, Richard. *Rethinking Ethnicity*. 2nd ed. Thousand Oaks, CA: Sage, 2008.

———. *Social Identity*. Key Ideas. New York: Routledge, 1996.

Jensen, Michael P. *Martyrdom and Identity: The Self on Trial*. T&T Clark Theology. New York: T&T Clark, 2010.

Jobes, Karen H. *1 Peter*. Baker Exegetical Commentary on the New Testament. Grand Rapids: Baker Academic, 2005.

Johnson, Alan. "Context-Sensitive Evangelism in the Thai Setting: Building Capacity to Share Good News." In *Becoming the People of God*, edited by Paul de Neui, 63–92. Seanet 11. Pasadena, CA: William Carey, 2015.

———. "A Contextualized Presentation of the Gospel in Thai Society." In *Sharing Jesus Holistically with the Buddhist World*, edited by David Lim and Steve Spaulding, 179–216. Seanet 2. Pasadena, CA: William Carey, 2005.

———. "Exploring Social Barriers to Conversion among the Thai." In *Communicating Christ in the Buddhist World*, edited by Paul de Neui and David Lim, 133–48. Seanet 4. Pasadena, CA: William Carey, 2006.

Johnson, Luke Timothy. *Religious Experience in Earliest Christianity: A Missing Dimension in New Testament Studies*. Kindle ed. Minneapolis, MN: Fortress, 1998.

Johnson, Mark. *The Meaning of the Body: Aesthetics of Human Understanding*. Chicago: University of Chicago Press, 2007.

Kern, Iso. "Intersubjectivity." In *Encyclopedia of Phenomenology*, edited by Lester E. Embree, 355–59. Contributions to Phenomenology 18. Dordrecht: Kluwer Academic, 1997.

Kersten, Fred. "Alfred Schütz." In *Encyclopedia of Phenomenology*, edited by Lester E. Embree, 636–40. Contributions to Phenomenology 18. Dordrecht: Kluwer Academic, 1997.

Keyes, Charles F. "Millennialism, Theravada Buddhism, and Thai Society." *The Journal of Asian Studies* 36.2 (1977) 283–302.

———. "Why the Thai Are Not Christians: Buddhist and Christian Conversion in Thailand." In *Conversion to Christianity: Historical and Anthropological Perspectives on a Great Transformation*, edited by Robert W. Hefner, 259–83. Berkeley: University of California Press, 1993.

Kirsch, A. Thomas. "Complexity in the Thai Religious System: An Interpretation." *The Journal of Asian Studies* 36.2 (1977) 241–66.

Kisiel, Theodore J. "Husserl and Heidegger." In *Encyclopedia of Phenomenology*, edited by Lester E. Embree, 333–39. Contributions to Phenomenology 18. Dordrecht: Kluwer Academic, 1997.

Knapp, Stan J. "The Ethical Phenomenology of Emmanuel Levinas: Drawing on Phenomenology to Explore the Central Features of Family Life." *Journal of Family Theory and Review* 7.3 (2015) 225–41.

Komin, Suntaree. *Psychology of the Thai People: Values and Behavioral Patterns*. Bangkok: Research Center, National Institute of Development Administration, 1990.

———. *Social Dimensions of Industrialization in Thailand*. Bangkok: Research Center, National Institute of Development Administration, 1989.
Kovacs, George. *The Question of God in Heidegger's Phenomenology*. Northwestern University Studies in Phenomenology and Existential Philosophy. Evanston, IL: Northwestern University Press, 1990.
Koyama, Kosuke. *Waterbuffalo Theology*. London: SCM, 1974.
Kreider, Alan. "Worship and Evangelism in Pre-Christendom (The Laing Lecture 1994)." *Vox Evangelica* 24 (1994) 7–38.
Kreider, Alan, and Eleanor Kreider. *Worship and Mission after Christendom*. After Christendom. Scottdale, PA: Herald, 2011.
Kuhn, Thomas S. *The Structure of Scientific Revolutions*. 3rd ed. Chicago, IL: University of Chicago Press, 1996.
Kvale, Steinar. *Interviews: An Introduction to Qualitative Research Interviewing*. Thousand Oaks, CA: Sage, 1996.
Landgrebe, Ludwig. "The World as a Phenomenological Problem." *Philosophy and Phenomenological Research* 1.1 (1940) 38–58.
Laverty, Susann M. "Hermeneutic Phenomenology and Phenomenology: A Comparison of Historical and Methodological Considerations." *International Journal of Qualitative Methods* 2.3 (2003) 1–29.
Laycock, Steven William. *Mind as Mirror and the Mirroring of Mind: Buddhist Reflections on Western Phenomenology*. Albany: State University of New York Press, 1994.
Leemans, Johan. "The Martyrdom of Sabas the Goth: History, Hagiography, and Identity." In *Christian Martyrdom in Late Antiquity (300–450 AD): History and Discourse, Tradition and Religious Identity*, edited by Peter Gemeinhardt and Johan Leemans, 201–23. Berlin: de Gruyter, 2012.
Leeuw, Gerard van der. *Religion in Essence and Manifestation*. 2 vols. New York: Harper and Row, 1963.
Levinas, Emmanuel. *Totality and Infinity: An Essay on Exteriority*. Duquesne Studies Philosophical Series 24. Pittsburgh: Duquesne University Press, 1969.
Lieu, Judith. *Christian Identity in the Jewish and Graeco-Roman World*. Oxford: Oxford University Press, 2004.
———. *Neither Jew nor Greek? Constructing Early Christianity*. Studies of the New Testament and Its World. 2nd ed. New York: T&T Clark, 2016.
Loder, James E. *The Transforming Moment: Understanding Convictional Experiences*. San Francisco: Harper and Row, 1981.
Lubac, Henri de. *The Discovery of God*. Ressourcement. Grand Rapids: Eerdmans, 1996.
Luckmann, Thomas. "Preface." In *The Structures of the Life-World*, edited by Alfred Schütz and Thomas Luckmann, xvii–xxvi. Evanston, IL: Northwestern University Press, 1973.
Lusthaus, Dan. *Buddhist Phenomenology: A Philosophical Investigation of Yogacara Buddhism and the Ch' eng Wei-Shih Lun*. Curzon Critical Studies in Buddhism Series. New York: RoutledgeCurzon, 2003.
Malpas, Jeff. *Heidegger and the Thinking of Place: Explorations in the Topology of Being*. Cambridge, MA: MIT Press, 2012.
———. *Place and Experience: A Philosophical Topography*. Cambridge: Cambridge University Press, 1999.

Bibliography

———. "Thinking Topographically: Place, Space, and Geography." *Il Cannocchiale: Rivista di studi filosofici* 42.1–2 (2017) 25–53. Online. https://jeffmalpas.com/wp-content/uploads/Thinking-Topographically-Place-Space-and-Geogr.pdf.

Manen, Max van. *Phenomenology of Practice: Meaning-Giving Methods in Phenomenological Research and Writing*. Developing Qualitative Inquiry 13. Walnut Creek, CA: Left Coast, 2014.

———. *Researching Lived Experience: Human Science for an Action Sensitive Pedagogy*. SUNY Series in the Philosophy of Education. Albany: State University of New York Press, 1990.

Markus, Hazel Rose, and Shinobu Kitayama. "Culture and the Self: Implications for Cognition, Emotion, and Motivation." *Psychological Review* 98.2 (1991) 224–53.

Marohl, Matthew J. *Faithfulness and the Purpose of Hebrews: A Social Identity Approach*. Cambridge: James Clarke, 2010.

Matthews, Shelly. *Perfect Martyr: The Stoning of Stephen and the Construction of Christian Identity*. Oxford: Oxford University Press, 2010.

McGrath, Alister E. "The Cultivation of Theological Vision: Theological Attentiveness and the Practice of Ministry." In *Perspectives on Ecclesiology and Ethnography*, edited by Pete Ward, 107–23. Studies in Ecclesiology and Ethnography. Grand Rapids: Eerdmans, 2012.

McLemore, S. Dale. "Simmel's 'Stranger': A Critique of the Concept." *The Pacific Sociological Review* 13.2 (1970) 86–94.

Mejudhon, Nantachai. "Meekness: A New Approach to Christian Witness to the Thai People." DMiss diss., Asbury Theological Seminary, 1997.

———. "Meekness: A New Approach to Christian Witness to the Thai People." In *Sharing Jesus Effectively in the Buddhist World*, edited by David Lim, et al., 147–86. Seanet 3. Pasadena, CA: William Carey, 2005.

Mejudhon, Ubolwan. "Evangelism in the New Millenium: An Integrated Model of Evangelism to Buddhists Using Theology, Anthropology, and Religious Studies." In *Sharing Jesus in the Buddhist World*, edited by David Lim and Steve Spaulding, 95–120. Seanet 1. Pasadena, CA: William Carey, 2003.

———. "The Ritual of Reconciliation in Thai Culture: Discipling New Converts." *Global Missiology* 4.2 (2005) 1–19.

———. "The Ritual of Reconciliation in Thai Culture: Discipling New Converts." In *Family and Faith in Asia: The Missional Impact of Social Networks*, edited by Paul de Neui, 101–30. Seanet 7. Pasadena, CA: William Carey, 2010.

Merleau-Ponty, Maurice. *Phenomenology of Perception*. New York: Routledge, 1962.

———. *The Structure of Behavior*. Boston: Beacon, 1963.

Mesa, Jose M. de. "Inculturation as Pilgrimage." In *Mission and Culture: The Louis J Luzbetak Lectures*, edited by Stephen B. Bevans, 5–34. The American Society of Missiology Series 48. Maryknoll, NY: Orbis, 2012.

Middleton, Paul. "Enemies of the (Church and) State: Martyrdom as a Problem for Early Christianity." *Annali di Storia Dell'esegesi* 29.2 (2012) 161–81.

Mohanty, J. N. *Transcendental Phenomenology: An Analytic Account*. Oxford: Basil Blackwell, 1989.

Moran, Dermot. *Introduction to Phenomenology*. New York: Routledge, 2000.

Moss, Candida R. "On the Dating of Polycarp: Rethinking the Place of the Martyrdom of Polycarp in the History of Christianity." *Early Christianity* 1.4 (2010) 539–74.

Bibliography

Moustakas, Clark E. *Phenomenological Research Methods.* Thousand Oaks, CA: Sage, 1994.

Muck, Terry C. "Three Reasons Why Christian Witness to Buddhists Has Failed." In *Communicating Christ through Story and Song,* edited by Paul de Neui, 108–26. Seanet 5. Pasadena, CA: William Carey, 2008.

Muehlhoff, Tim. *Winsome Persuasion: Christian Influence in a Post-Christian World.* Downers Grove, IL: InterVarsity, 2017.

Mulder, Niels. *Inside Thai Society: An Interpretation of Everyday Life.* 3rd ed. Bangkok: Editions Duang Kamol, 1990.

Murray, Stuart. *Church after Christendom.* After Christendom. Bletchley, UK: Paternoster, 2004.

Nagel, Joane. "Constructing Ethnicity: Creating and Recreating Ethnic Identity and Culture." *Social Problems* 41.1 (1994) 152–76.

Natanson, Maurice. "Alfred Schütz: Philosopher and Social Scientist." *Human Studies* 21.1 (1998) 1–12.

Nenon, Thomas. "Martin Heidegger." In *Encyclopedia of Phenomenology,* edited by Lester E. Embree, 298–304. Contributions to Phenomenology 18. Dordrecht: Kluwer Academic, 1997.

Neui, Paul de. "Contextualizing with Thai Folk Buddhists." In *Sharing Jesus in the Buddhist World,* edited by David Lim and Steve Spaulding, 121–46. Seanet 1. Pasadena, CA: William Carey, 2003.

Neumann, Iver B. "Introduction to the Forum on Liminality." *Review of International Studies* 38.2 (2012) 473–79.

Nichols, Stephen J. *A Time for Confidence: Trusting God in a Post-Christian Society.* Orlando: Reformation Trust, 2016.

Nisbett, Richard E. *The Geography of Thought: How Asians and Westerners Think Differently—and Why.* New York: Free Press, 2003.

Oliveira, Nythamar de. "Husserl, Heidegger, and the Task of a Phenomenology of Justice." *Veritas* 53.1 (2008) 123–44.

Onorato, Rina S., and John C. Turner. "Fluidity in the Self-Concept: The Shift from Personal to Social Identity." *European Journal of Social Psychology* 34.3 (2004) 257–78.

Otto, Rudolf. *The Idea of the Holy: An Inquiry into the Non-Rational Factor in the Idea of the Divine and Its Relation to the Rational.* New York: Oxford University Press, 1958.

Otubanjo, Olutayo. "Embedding Theory in Corporate Identity through the Social Construction Lens." *International Journal of Business and Management* 7.22 (2012) 62–75.

Park, Jin Y., and Gereon Kopf. *Merleau-Ponty and Buddhism.* Lanham: Lexington, 2009.

Park, Robert E. "Human Migration and the Marginal Man." *American Journal of Sociology* 33.6 (1928) 881–93.

———. "Introduction." In *The Marginal Man: A Study in Personality and Culture Conflict,* edited by Everett V. Stonequist, xiii–xviii. New York: Russell and Russell, 1961.

Pavlović, Srdja. "Literature, Social Poetics, and Identity Construction in Montenegro." *International Journal of Politics, Culture, and Society* 17.1 (2003) 131–65.

Pearl, J. Leavitt. "World Restructuring: Toward a Phenomenology of Parable." MST thesis, Boston University, 2012.

Bibliography

Pentikainen, Juha. "Liminality." In *Folklore: An Encyclopedia of Beliefs, Customs, Tales, Music, and Art*, edited by Kim Kennedy White and Charlie T. McCormick, 790–93. Santa Barbara, CA: ABC-CLIO, 2011.

Petchsongkram, Wan. *Talk in the Shade of the Bo Tree*. Bangkok: Thai Gospel, 1975.

Petrus, Theodore S., and David L. Bogopa. "Natural and Supernatural: Intersections between the Spiritual and Natural Worlds in African Witchcraft and Healing with Reference to Southern Africa." *The Indo-Pacific Journal of Phenomenology* 7.1 (2007) 1–10.

Platz, Roland. "Buddhism and Christianity in Competition? Religious and Ethnic Identity in Karen Communities of Northern Thailand." *Journal of Southeast Asian Studies* 34.3 (2003) 473–90.

Pliny the Younger. *Letters of Pliny*. Translated by J. B. Firth. 1900. Online. http://www.attalus.org/info/pliny.html.

Podhisita, Chai. "Buddhism and Thai World View." In *Traditional and Changing Thai World View*, edited by Pongsapich Amara, 25–53. Bangkok: Chulalongkorn University Press, 1998.

Polkinghorne, Donald. *Methodology for the Human Sciences: Systems of Inquiry*. SUNY Series in Transpersonal and Humanistic Psychology. Albany: State University of New York Press, 1983.

Radford, David. *Religious Identity and Social Change: Explaining Christian Conversion in a Muslim World*. Routledge Advances in Sociology. Kindle ed. London: Routledge, 2015.

Rebillard, Eric. "Becoming Christian in Carthage in the Age of Tertullian." In *Conversion and Initiation in Antiquity: Shifting Identities, Creating Change*, edited by Birgitte Bøgh, 47–58. Early Christianity in the Context of Antiquity 16. New York: Peter Lang, 2014.

Relph, Edward C. *Place and Placelessness*. Research in Planning and Design 1. London: Pion, 1976.

———. "Place in Geography." In *International Encyclopedia of the Social and Behavioral Sciences*, edited by Paul B. Baltes and Neil J. Smelser, 11448–51. Amsterdam: Elsevier, 2001.

Ricoeur, Paul. *Oneself as Another*. Chicago: University of Chicago Press, 1992.

———. "Phenomenology and Hermeneutics." *Nous* 9.1 (1975) 85–102.

———. *The Symbolism of Evil*. Religious Perspectives 17. New York: Harper and Row, 1967.

Ricoeur, Paul, and Lewis Seymour Mudge. *Essays on Biblical Interpretation*. Philadelphia: Fortress, 1980.

Roxburgh, Alan J. *The Missionary Congregation, Leadership and Liminality*. Christian Mission and Modern Culture. Harrisburg, PA: Trinity, 1997.

Rumelili, Bahar. "Liminal Identities and Processes of Domestication and Subversion in International Relations." *Review of International Studies* 38.2 (2012) 495–508.

Ryba, Thomas. "The Idea of the Sacred in Twentieth-Century Thought: Four Views (Otto, Scheler, Nygren, Tymieniecka)." In *From the Sacred to the Divine: A New Phenomenological Approach*, edited by Anna-Teresa Tymieniecka, 21–42. Analecta Husserliana 43. Dordrecht: Kluwer Academic, 1994.

Sandnes, Karl Olav. *A New Family: Conversion and Ecclesiology in the Early Church with Cross-Cultural Comparisons*. Studien Zur Interkulturellen Geschichte Des Christentums 91. Bern: Peter Lang, 1994.

Sartre, Jean Paul. *Being and Nothingness: A Phenomenological Essay on Ontology.* Translated by Hazel Estella Barnes. New York: Washington Square, 1992.
Sattayanurak, Saichol. "The Construction of Mainstream Thought on 'Thainess' and the 'Truth' Constructed by 'Thainess.'" Unpublished paper. Online. https://www.semanticscholar.org/paper/The-Construction-of-Mainstream-Thought-on-%E2%80%9C-%E2%80%9D-and-%E2%80%9C-Sattayanurak/9a105c84daaca1b2d41b93aaa5885acd18de7b28.
Schaff, Philip. *History of the Christian Church.* Vol. 2. 5th ed. Peabody, MA: Hendrickson, 1996.
Schaff, Philip, and Henry Wace, eds. *A Select Library of Nicene and Post-Nicene Fathers of the Christian Church.* First Series. 28 vols. 1886–1889. Reprint, Peabody, MA: Hendrickson, 1994.
Scharen, Christian. "Ecclesiology 'from the Body': Ethnographic Notes toward a Carnal Theology." In *Perspectives on Ecclesiology and Ethnography,* edited by Pete Ward, 50–70. Studies in Ecclesiology and Ethnography. Grand Rapids: Eerdmans, 2012.
Schreiter, Robert J. *Constructing Local Theologies.* Maryknoll, NY: Orbis, 1985.
Schütz, Alfred. *On Phenomenology and Social Relations: Selected Writings.* Heritage of Sociology. Chicago: University of Chicago Press, 1970.
———. "The Stranger: An Essay in Social Psychology." *American Journal of Sociology* 49.6 (1944) 499–507.
Schütz, Alfred, et al. *Philosophers in Exile: The Correspondence of Alfred Schütz and Aron Gurwitsch, 1939–1959.* Studies in Phenomenology and Existential Philosophy. Bloomington: Indiana University Press, 1989.
Schütz, Alfred, and Thomas Luckmann. *The Structures of the Life-World.* Northwestern University Studies in Phenomenology and Existential Philosophy. Vol. 1. Evanston, IL: Northwestern University Press, 1973.
Seamon, David. "Place and Placelessness (1976): Edward Relph." In *Key Texts in Human Geography: A Reader Guide,* edited by Phil Hubbard, et al., 43–51. London: Sage, 2008.
———. "Place, Place Identity, and Phenomenology: A Triadic Interpretation Based on J. G. Bennett's Systematics." In *The Role of Place Identity in the Perception, Understanding, and Design of Built Environments,* edited by Hernan Casakin and Fatima Bernardo, 3–21. Oak Park, IL: Bentham, 2012.
Seidman, Irving. *Interviewing as Qualitative Research: A Guide for Researchers in Education and the Social Sciences.* 3rd ed. New York: Teachers College Press, 2006.
Seland, Torrey. "Proselyte Characterizations in 1 Peter?" *Bulletin for Biblical Research* 11.2 (2001) 239–68.
———. "Resident Aliens in Mission: Missional Practices in the Emerging Church of 1 Peter." *Bulletin for Biblical Research* 19.4 (2009) 565–89.
"Simmel, Georg." In *The Penguin Dictionary of Sociology,* edited by Nicholas Abercrombie, et al. London: Penguin, 2006. Online. http://0-search.credoreference.com.eaglelink.cornerstone.edu/content/entry/penguinsoc/simmel_georg/0?institutionId=6459.
Simmel, Georg. "The Stranger." In *The Sociology of Georg Simmel,* edited by Kurt H. Wolff, 402–8. Glencoe, IL: Free Press, 1950.
Smart, Ninian. *Buddhism and Christianity: Rivals and Allies.* Honolulu: University of Hawaii Press, 1993.
———. *The Phenomenon of Religion.* Philosophy of Religion Series. London: Macmillan, 1973.

Bibliography

———. *The Science of Religion and the Sociology of Knowledge: Some Methodological Questions*. Virginia and Richard Stewart Memorial Lectures 1971. Princeton, NJ: Princeton University Press, 1973.

———. *Worldviews: Crosscultural Explorations of Human Beliefs*. 3rd ed. Upper Saddle River, NJ: Prentice Hall, 2000.

Smith, Alex G. *Siamese Gold: A History of Church Growth in Thailand: An Interpretive Analysis 1816–1982*. Bangkok: Kanok Bannasan (OMF), 1982.

Smith, James K. A. *Desiring the Kingdom: Worship, Worldview, and Cultural Formation*. Cultural Liturgies 1. Grand Rapids: Baker Academic, 2009.

Smith, John E. "The Experience of the Holy and the Idea of God." In *Experience of the Sacred: Readings in the Phenomenology of Religion*, edited by Sumner B. Twiss and Walter H. Conser, 189–99. Hanover, NH: University Press of New England, 1992.

Smith, Jonathan A., et al. *Interpretative Phenomenological Analysis: Theory, Method, and Research*. Los Angeles; London: Sage, 2009.

Sokolowski, Robert. *Introduction to Phenomenology*. Cambridge: Cambridge University Press, 2000.

———. "Phenomenology of Friendship." *The Review of Metaphysics* 55.3 (2002) 451–70.

———. *Presence and Absence: A Philosophical Investigation of Language and Being*. Studies in Phenomenology and Existential Philosophy. Bloomington: Indiana University Press, 1978.

Sorajjakool, Siroj. "Religion in Thailand: Pastoral Theological Reflection from the Perspective of Thai Buddhist Monks." In *Pastoral Bearings: Lived Religion and Pastoral Theology*, edited by Jane Frances Maynard, et al., 261–82. Lanham, MD: Lexington, 2010.

Staveren, Karsten van. "Christian Theology in a Country of Temples." PhD diss., McGilvary College of Divinity, 2011.

Stein, Edith. *Philosophy of Psychology and the Humanities*. Edited by Marianne Sawicki. The Collected Works of Edith Stein, Sister Teresa Benedicta of the Cross, Discalced Carmelite (1891–1942) 7. Washington, DC: Institute of Carmelite Studies, 2000.

Steinbock, Anthony J. *Home and Beyond: Generative Phenomenology after Husserl*. Northwestern University Studies in Phenomenology and Existential Philosophy. Evanston, IL: Northwestern University Press, 1995.

———. "Homeworld/Alienworld: Toward a Generative Phenomenology of Intersubjectivity." In *Phenomenology, Interpretation, and Community*, edited by Lenore Langsdorf, et al., 65–81. Selected Studies in Phenomenology and Existential Philosophy 19. Albany: State University of New York Press, 1996.

———. "Husserl's Static and Genetic Phenomenology. Essay 1: Static and Genetic Phenomenological Method." *Continental Philosophy Review* 31.2 (1998) 135–42.

———. *Phenomenology and Mysticism: The Verticality of Religious Experience*. Indiana Series in the Philosophy of Religion. Bloomington: Indiana University Press, 2007.

Stonequist, Everett V. *The Marginal Man: A Study in Personality and Culture Conflict*. New York: Russell and Russell, 1961.

———. "The Problem of the Marginal Man." *American Journal of Sociology* 41.1 (1935) 1–12.

Swanson, Herbert R. "Dancing to the Temple, Dancing to the Church: Reflections on Thai Theology." *Journal of Theologies and Cultures in Asia* 1 (2002) 59–78.

———. "Hughes I: Barriers to Christian Faith in Thailand." *Herb's Research Diary (HeRD)* 312 (1997). Online. https://234b5469-2e3f-4556-8daa-7cea13ecbee3.filesusr.com/ugd/4cfa9b_56e3cc2de9c34873b4bb3fbc0407b6b7.pdf.

Swinton, John. "'Where Is Your Church?' Moving toward a Hospitable and Sanctified Ethnography." In *Perspectives on Ecclesiology and Ethnography*, edited by Pete Ward, 71–94. Studies in Ecclesiology and Ethnography. Grand Rapids: Eerdmans, 2012.

Tafarodi, Romin W. "Toward a Cultural Phenomenology of Personal Identity." In *Self-Continuity: Individual and Collective Perspectives*, edited by Fabio Sani, 27–40. New York: Psychology, 2008.

Tajfel, Henri, and John C. Turner. "An Integrated Theory of Intergroup Conflict." In *The Social Psychology of Intergroup Relations*, edited by William G. Austin and Stephen Worchel, 33–47. Monterey, CA: Brooks/Cole, 1979.

Talman, Harley, and John Jay Travis. *Understanding Insider Movements: Disciples of Jesus within Diverse Religious Communities*. Kindle ed. Pasadena, CA: William Carey, 2015.

Tambiah, Stanley Jeyaraja. *Buddhism and the Spirit Cults in North-East Thailand*. Cambridge Studies in Social Anthropology 2. Cambridge: Cambridge University Press, 1970.

———. *World Conqueror and World Renouncer: A Study of Buddhism and Polity in Thailand against a Historical Background*. Cambridge Studies in Social Anthropology 15. Cambridge: Cambridge University Press, 1976.

Tanner, Kathryn. *Theories of Culture: A New Agenda for Theology*. Guides to Theological Inquiry. Minneapolis, MN: Fortress, 1997.

Taylor, Charles. *Modern Social Imaginaries*. Durham: Duke University Press, 2004.

Taylor, Steve. "Gaps in Beliefs of Thai Christians." *EMQ* 37.1 (2001) 72–81.

———. "A Prolegomena for the Thai Context: A Starting Point for Thai Theology." *Evangelical Review of Theology* 29.1 (2005) 32–51.

Terwiel, Barend Jan. "Thai Buddhism: Some Indigenous Perspectives." *Buddhismus in Geschichte und Gegenwart* 1 (1998) 125–34. Online. https://www.academia.edu/30856756/Thai_Buddhism_Some_Indigenous_Perspectives_1998.

Theissen, Gerd. "The Letter to the Romans and Paul's Plural Identity: A Dialogical Self in Dialogue with Judaism and Christianity." In *The Making of Christianity: Conflicts, Contacts, and Constructions; Essays in Honor of Bengt Holmberg*, edited by Bengt Holmberg, et al., 301–24. Coniectanea Biblica New Testament Series 47. Winona Lake, IN: Eisenbrauns, 2012.

Tobias, Stephen F. "Buddhism, Belonging and Detachment: Some Paradoxes of Chinese Ethnicity in Thailand." *The Journal of Asian Studies* 36.2 (1977) 303–26.

Tongprateep, Tassanee. "The Essential Elements of Spirituality among Rural Thai Elders." *Journal of Advanced Nursing* 31.1 (2000) 197–203.

Trebilco, Paul R. *Self-Designations and Group Identity in the New Testament*. Cambridge: Cambridge University Press, 2012.

Turner, John C. "Foreword." In *Social Identifications: A Social Psychology of Intergroup Relations and Group Processes*, edited by Michael A. Hogg and Dominic Abrams, viii–ix. London: Routledge, 1998.

———. "Social Identity." In *Encyclopedia of Psychology*, edited by Alan E. Kazdin, 341–43. New York: Oxford University Press, 2000.

Turner, John C., et al. "Self and Collective: Cognition and Social Context." *Personality and Social Psychology Bulletin* 20.5 (1994) 454–63.

Bibliography

Turner, Victor W. "Betwixt and Between: The Liminal Period in *Rites De Passage*." In *Magic, Witchcraft, and Religion: An Anthropological Study of the Supernatural*, edited by Arthur C. Lehmann and James E. Myers, 46–55. Mountain View, CA: Mayfield, 2001.

———. *Dramas, Fields, and Metaphors: Symbolic Action in Human Society*. Symbol, Myth, and Ritual Series. Ithaca, NY: Cornell University Press, 1974.

———. *The Ritual Process: Structure and Anti-Structure*. Symbol, Myth, and Ritual Series. Ithaca, NY: Cornell University Press, 1977.

———. "Variations on a Theme of Liminality." In *Secular Ritual*, edited by Sally Falk Moore and Barbara G. Myerhoff, 36–52. Assen: Van Gorcum, 1977.

Vagle, Mark D. *Crafting Phenomenological Research*. Walnut Creek, CA: Left Coast, 2014.

Vagle, Mark D., et al. "Remaining Skeptical: Bridling for and with One Another." *Field Methods* 21.4 (2009) 347–67.

Varma, Chandra B. *Buddhist Phenomenology: A Theravada Perspective*. Delhi: Eastern Book Linkers, 1993.

Wagner, Helmut R. "Introduction." In *On Phenomenology and Social Relations: Selected Writings*, edited by Alfred Schütz, 1–50. Chicago: University of Chicago Press, 1970.

Waldenfels, Bernhard. "The Boundaries of Orders." *Philosophica* 73 (2004) 71–86.

Ward, Pete. *Perspectives on Ecclesiology and Ethnography*. Studies in Ecclesiology and Ethnography. Grand Rapids: Eerdmans, 2012.

Watkins, Clare. "Practical Ecclesiology: What Counts as Theology in Studying the Church?" In *Perspectives on Ecclesiology and Ethnography*, edited by Pete Ward, 167–81. Studies in Ecclesiology and Ethnography. Grand Rapids: Eerdmans, 2012.

Wood, Margaret Mary. *The Stranger: A Study in Social Relationships*. Studies in History, Economics and Public Law 399. New York: Columbia University Press, 1934.

Wright, David F. "The Baptismal Community." *Bibliotheca Sacra* 160.637 (2003) 3–12.

———. "The Testimony of Blood: The Charisma of Martyrdom." *Bibliotheca Sacra* 160.640 (2003) 387–97.

Wu, Jackson. *Saving God's Face: A Chinese Contextualization of Salvation through Honor and Shame*. EMS Dissertation Series. Pasadena, CA: William Carey, 2012.

Yanow, Dvora, and Peregrine Schwartz-Shea. *Interpretation and Method: Empirical Research Methods and the Interpretive Turn*. 2nd ed. Armonk, NY: ME Sharp, 2014.

Ybema, Sierk, et al. "Articulating Identities." *Human Relations* 62.3 (2009) 299–322.

Yung, Hwa. *Mangoes or Bananas? The Quest for an Authentic Asian Christian Theology*. Regnum Studies in Mission. Oxford: Regnum, 1997.

Zehner, Edwin. "Beyond Anti-Syncretism: Gospel, Context, and Authority in the New Testament and in Thai Conversions to Christianity." In *Power and Identity in the Global Church: Six Contemporary Cases*, edited by Brian M. Howell and Edwin Zehner, 155–83. Pasadena, CA: William Carey, 2009.

———. "Orthodox Hybridities: Anti-Syncretism and Localization in the Evangelical Christianity of Thailand." *Anthropological Quarterly* 78.3 (2005) 585–616.

www.ingramcontent.com/pod-product-compliance
Lightning Source LLC
Chambersburg PA
CBHW071246230426
43668CB00011B/1613